California English Language Development Standards

Kindergarten Through Grade 12

Adopted by the California State Board of Education
November 2012

Publishing Information

When the *California English Language Development Standards: Kindergarten Through Grade 12* was adopted by the California State Board of Education (SBE) in November 2012, the members of the SBE were the following: Michael W. Kirst, President; Trish Williams, Vice President; Carl Cohn; Bruce Holaday; Aida Molina; James C. Ramos; Patricia A. Rucker, Ilene W. Straus; and Josephine Kao, Student Member.

The *California English Language Development Standards: Kindergarten Through Grade 12* was prepared under the direction of the English Learner Support Division, California Department of Education (CDE). It was edited by Faye Ong and John McLean, working in cooperation with Gustavo Gonzalez, Education Programs Consultant, English Learner Support Division. It was designed and prepared for printing by the staff of CDE Press, with the cover and interior design created and prepared by Tuyet Truong. The document was published by the Department of Education, 1430 N Street, Sacramento, California 95814. It was distributed under the provisions of the Library Distribution Act and *Government Code* Section 11096.

ISBN 978-0-8011-1738-1

Ordering Information

Copies of this publication are available for purchase from the California Department of Education. For pricing and ordering information, please visit http://www.cde.ca.gov/re/pn/rc/ or call the CDE Press sales office at 1-800-995-4099. Prices on all publications are subject to change.

Notice

The guidance in the *California English Language Development Standards: Kindergarten Through Grade 12* is not binding on local educational agencies or other entities. Except for the statutes, regulations, and court decisions that are referenced herein, the document is exemplary, and compliance with it is not mandatory. (See *Education Code* Section 33308.5.)

Contents

A Message from the State Board of Education and the State Superintendent of Public Instruction

In California, home to more than one million English learner students, English language development has always been a top priority. Last year's adoption of the California English Language Development Standards (CA ELD Standards) maintains California's commitment to providing English learner students with a high-quality program that will enable them to attain proficiency in English—developing the skills and confidence in listening, speaking, reading, and writing that are at the core of achievement inside and outside the classroom.

These CA ELD Standards are unique in that they correspond with the rigorous *California Common Core State Standards: English Language Arts and Literacy in History/Social Studies, Science, and Technical Subjects.* The CA ELD Standards define the progression of language acquisition through three stages of proficiency and recognize that the student's native language plays an important role in learning English. Teachers can use the CA ELD Standards document as a tool to inform their practice, making clear relationships between the English language and the student's other language(s).

This document was a collaborative effort between the California Department of Education and the California Comprehensive Assistance Center at WestEd, with counsel and input provided by experts, researchers, educators, and key stakeholder groups with expertise and a passion for educating English learners. We appreciate their comprehensive and exhaustive work to provide our students with the very best thinking and the most current practices.

Now all of us—teachers, administrators, librarians, parents, students, educators, and other stakeholders—must implement these standards for English learner students. We look forward to working together with you to ensure that all our English learner students meet the goals embodied in these standards. The potential is endless.

Michael W. Kirst

MICHAEL W. KIRST, President
California State Board of Education

Tom Torlakson

TOM TORLAKSON
State Superintendent of Public Instruction

Acknowledgments

Assembly Bill 124, signed into law on October 8, 2011, required the State Superintendent of Public Instruction (SSPI), in consultation with the State Board of Education (SBE), to update, revise, and align the state's current English language development (ELD) standards by grade level with the state's English language arts (ELA) standards by November 2012.

The development of the ELD standards was made possible under the leadership and direction of Tom Torlakson, State Superintendent of Public Instruction; Richard Zeiger, Chief Deputy Superintendent; and Lupita Cortez Alcalá, Deputy Superintendent of the Instruction and Learning Support Branch at the California Department of Education (CDE). Karen Cadiero-Kaplan, Director of the CDE's English Learner Support Division, led the internal efforts in collaboration with leadership and staff across four CDE divisions and the State Board of Education. The following CDE and SBE staff members provided leadership, administrative support, input, and technical assistance during the development and publication process of the ELD standards:

Executive Office

Tom Torlakson, State Superintendent of Public Instruction

Richard Zeiger, Chief Deputy Superintendent

Lupita Cortez Alcalá, Deputy Superintendent, Instruction and Learning Support Branch

English Learner Support Division—Language Policy and Leadership Office

Karen Cadiero-Kaplan, Director

Elena Fajardo, Education Administrator

Carlos Rivera, (Former) Education Administrator

Dianna Gutierrez, Education Programs Consultant

Michele Anberg-Espinosa, Education Programs Consultant

Deborah Busch, Education Programs Consultant

Lilia Sanchez, Bilingual/Migrant Education Consultant

James Shields, Education Programs Consultant

Sandra Covarrubias, Education Programs Consultant

Gustavo Gonzalez, Education Programs Consultant

Will Lee, Associate Governmental Program Analyst

Barbara Garcia, Office Technician

Juan Marmolejo, Office Assistant

Curriculum Frameworks and Instructional Resources Division

Thomas Adams, Director

Kristen Cruz Allen, Education Administrator

Lillian Perez, Education Programs Consultant

Assessment Development and Administration Division

Patrick Traynor, Director

Lily Roberts, Education Research and Evaluation Administrator

Gaye Lauritzen, Education Programs Consultant

Professional Learning Support Division

Carrie Roberts, Director

Phil Lafontaine, (former) Director

Erin Koepke, Education Programs Consultant

State Board of Education

Aida Molina, Member

Ilene Straus, Member

Patricia de Cos, Deputy Executive Director

To accomplish this important work in the required time frame, the CDE requested the assistance of the California Comprehensive Assistance Center at WestEd. Specifically, WestEd's California Comprehensive Center, in partnership with the Assessment and Standards Development Services Program at WestEd, worked in concert with the CDE to analyze current ELD standards relative to the new California ELA standards; review information on other states' and organizations' ELD standards revision and alignment efforts; analyze statewide public and expert input on revision parameters; draft the proposed ELD standards; and revise the standards as needed, based on stakeholder review and feedback.

Under the CDE's direction, the following WestEd staff members led the critical process of developing the new California ELD standards, including co-facilitating weekly meetings with CDE staff, working in tandem with the English Learner Support Division to draft the new CA ELD Standards, and writing the content of the supporting chapters and glossary.

California Comprehensive Center at WestEd

Rachel Lagunoff

Pamela Spycher

Robert Linquanti

Christopher Camacho

Edynn Sato

In addition, the following WestEd staff members contributed to drafting the new standards: Karin Cordell, Kevin Jepson, John Thorpe, and Nicole Waltermire.

Assembly Bill 124 also directed the SSPI to convene a group of experts to provide input and guidance in revising and aligning the updated California ELD Standards. The CDE acknowledges the contributions this group made to informing drafts of the standards and related documents, as well as their model of collaboration.

Name	Affiliation
Cristina Alfaro	San Diego State University
Leticia Bhatia	Sonoma Valley Unified School District
Constance Cervera	Oxnard High School
Lizette Diaz	Ontario–Montclair School District
Silvia Dorta-Duque de Reyes	San Diego County Office of Education
Richard Duran	University of California, Santa Barbara
Ludmila Elliott	Yuba City Unified School District
Marta Escobar	Kern County Office of Education
Elizabeth Fralicks	Fresno Unified School District
Ana García	San Francisco Unified School District
Laura Gonzalez	Tulare County Office of Education
Kenji Hakuta	Stanford University
Magaly Lavadenz	Loyola Marymount University
Barbara Merino	University of California, Davis
Gisela O'Brien	Los Angeles Unified School District
Keila Rodriguez	Imperial County Office of Education
Maritza Rodriguez	Riverside County Office of Education
Magdalena Ruz Gonzalez	Los Angeles County Office of Education
Maria Santos	Oakland Unified School District
Socorro Shiels	Morgan Hill Unified School District
Emily Tsai	Monterey Peninsula Unified School District

Note: The names, titles, and affiliations of the persons listed in these acknowledgments were current at the time this publication was developed.

Introduction

Introduction

In 2010, the California State Board of Education (SBE) adopted the California Common Core State Standards for English Language Arts and Literacy in History/Social Studies, Science, and Technical Subjects (CA CCSS for ELA/Literacy), which describe the knowledge, skills, and abilities in reading, writing, speaking and listening, conventions, knowledge of language, and vocabulary that all students need for college and career readiness across key academic content areas. Those standards, along with the Common Core State Standards for Mathematics and the Next Generation Science Standards, were adopted by California to ensure K–12 (kindergarten through grade 12) students gain the necessary literacy/language arts, science, and mathematics understanding and practices required for twenty-first-century higher-education and workplace participation. The sponsors of the Common Core State Standards Initiative specify that these new standards are intended to apply to all students, including English learners (ELs):

> The National Governors Association Center for Best Practices and the Council of Chief State School Officers strongly believe that all students should be held to the same high expectations outlined in the Common Core State Standards. This includes students who are English language learners . . . However, these students may require additional time, appropriate instructional support, and aligned assessments as they acquire both English language proficiency and content area knowledge.[1]

California's ELs need instructional support in developing proficiency in English language and literacy as they engage in learning academic content based on these new, rigorous standards. ELs face an additional challenge in developing literacy in English since they must develop oral proficiency in English—including depth and breadth of vocabulary—at the same time that they are learning to read and write (see chapter 6 for more details). In recognition of the need for new English language development standards to clarify what knowledge, skills, and abilities are needed to help ELs engage with and master the state's content standards, including college- and career-readiness standards, Assembly Bill 124 was enacted on October 8, 2011. It required the State Superintendent of Public Instruction, in consultation with the SBE, to update, revise, and align the current California English Language Development Standards (CA ELD Standards), by grade level, with the state's English Language Arts (ELA) Standards.

In response to this legislation, the California Department of Education (CDE), with the assistance of the California Comprehensive Assistance Center at WestEd in partnership with WestEd's Assessment and Standards Development Services Program, conducted an extensive and robust process to develop and validate new CA ELD Standards that correspond to the CA CCSS for ELA/Literacy and address English language and literacy skills that ELs need in key content areas. This process was grounded in two core principles: (1) transparency toward and input from the field and (2) development based on sound theory and empirical research. The first principle included comprehensive guidance and review provided by the CDE, statewide focus groups, and a state-appointed panel of experts, as well as comments on a draft of the standards received from the public through hearings and written feedback. Public commenters included teachers, principals, staff in district and county offices of education, advocacy groups, education scholars, and other educational community members. For the second principle, three overlapping guidance areas were analyzed: (1) theoretical foundations; (2) current empirical research and research reviews; and (3) additional relevant guidance documents, such as policy documents.

---

1. Common Core State Standards Initiative, "Application of Common Core State Standards for English Language Learners." http://www.corestandards.org/assets/application-for-english-learners.pdf (accessed October 2, 2013).

Organization of This Publication

This publication is intended to assist in building awareness and understanding of how the CA ELD Standards correspond to the CA CCSS for ELA/Literacy. The CA CCSS for ELA/Literacy served as the core foundation for developing the CA ELD Standards, which are intended to guide teachers in supporting the English language development of ELs who are learning rigorous academic content. This section introduces the organization of the CA ELD Standards, which were posted on the CDE Web site in November 2012, and provides a description of each chapter.

After adoption in November 2012, the CA ELD Standards were posted on the CDE Web page at http://www.cde.ca.gov/sp/el/er/eldstandards.asp for the public to consult as a resource. The CA ELD Standards, posted on the CDE Web page, were organized as follows: ELD Overview and Proficiency Level Descriptors; ELD standards for kindergarten through grade 12; appendixes A through D; and the Glossary of Key Terms. In preparation for print publication, the online materials were reorganized to be suitable for publication. An introduction was added, appendixes A through D became chapters, and the CA ELD standards were placed within a single chapter. It is important to note that no changes were made to the content of the CA ELD Standards for this print publication. The following specifies the rearrangement undertaken for those familiar with the original CDE Web page materials.

The Acknowledgments recognize the efforts of all the organizations and individuals who contributed to the development of the CA ELD Standards and the completion of the printed publication. The Acknowledgements were originally a section of the ELD Overview and Proficiency Level Descriptors.

The Introduction provides the background of the standards and an explanation of the organization of the printed publication with a description of each chapter. The Introduction was originally the beginning section of the ELD Overview and Proficiency Level Descriptors.

The publication is divided into two sections, each of which contains three chapters. The first section, which consists of chapters 1–3, is titled "The English Language Development Proficiency Level Descriptors and Standards." It provides an overview of the standards and describes the structure of the ELD standards for kindergarten through grade 12. The second section, comprising chapters 4–6, is titled "Professional Learning for Successful Implementation of the English Language Development Standards." It provides the theoretical foundations and research base of the CA ELD standards, including the implications for understanding how English works and pedagogical considerations for foundational literacy skills for ELs.

The English Language Development Proficiency Level Descriptors and Standards

Chapter 1, "Purposes, Development, and Structure of the California English Language Development Standards," provides a definition of the CA ELD Standards and the purposes for the design of the standards. It describes the rationale for the three proficiency levels and the organization, including the components of the standards. Chapter 1 was originally appendix D.

Chapter 2, "Proficiency Level Descriptors for the California English Language Development Standards," provides an overview of the stages of English language development through which ELs are expected to progress. It depicts the student knowledge, skills, and abilities as a continuum, identifying what ELs know and can do at early stages and upon exit from each of three proficiency levels: Emerging, Expanding, and Bridging. Chapter 2 was originally a section in the ELD Overview and Proficiency Level Descriptors.

Chapter 3, "The Standards: Kindergarten Through Grade 12," presents the CA ELD Standards for each grade level in kindergarten through grade 8 and for grades 9–10 and 11–12, as is done for the CA CCSS for ELA/Literacy.

Professional Learning for Successful Implementation of the English Language Development Standards

Chapter 4, "Theoretical Foundations and the Research Base of the California English Language Development Standards," discusses research evidence and theory that informed the development of the CA ELD Standards. These theoretical foundations and the research ensured that the CA ELD Standards coherently conceptualized, presented, and explained the corresponding language demands of the CA CCSS for ELA/Literacy that are necessary for developing academic uses of English and academic success across the disciplines. Chapter 4 was originally appendix C.

Chapter 5, "Learning About How English Works," offers teachers a new perspective on how to support ELs in understanding academic English and gaining proficiency in using it. The chapter aims to help teachers support ELs in ways that are appropriate to each student's grade level and English proficiency level. Chapter 5 was originally appendix B.

Chapter 6, "Foundational Literacy Skills for English Learners," provides a research summary of key findings with implications for foundational literacy skills instruction for ELs. This chapter also outlines general guidance on providing instruction for ELs on foundational literacy skills, which are now wholly contained in the CA CCSS for ELA/Literacy. Chapter 6 was originally appendix A.

The Glossary of Key Terms at the end of this publication, as in its original online format, provides definitions and examples of key terms used in the CA ELD Standards, the CA CCSS for ELA/Literacy, and in related chapters.

The English Language Development Proficiency Level Descriptors and Standards

Chapter 1

The California English Language Development Standards (CA ELD Standards) reflect recent and emerging research and theory and are intended to support language development as English learners (ELs) engage in rigorous academic content. The CA ELD Standards provide a foundation for ELs in kindergarten through grade 12 (K–12) in California schools so that each EL is able to gain access to academic subjects, engage with them, and meet the state's subject-matter standards for college and career readiness.

Definition of the Standards

The CA ELD Standards describe the key knowledge, skills, and abilities that students who are learning English as a new language need in order to access, engage with, and achieve in grade-level academic content. The CA ELD Standards, in particular, align with the key knowledge, skills, and abilities for achieving college and career readiness described in the California Common Core State Standards for English Language Arts and Literacy in History/Social Studies, Science, and Technical Subjects (CA CCSS for ELA/Literacy). However, the CA ELD Standards do not repeat the CA CCSS for ELA/Literacy, nor do they represent ELA content at lower levels of achievement or rigor. Instead, the CA ELD Standards are designed to provide challenging content in English language development for ELs to gain proficiency in a range of rigorous academic English language skills. **The CA ELD Standards are not intended to replace the CA CCSS for ELA/Literacy.** Instead, they amplify the language knowledge, skills, and abilities of these standards, which are essential for ELs to succeed in school while they are developing their English.

Purposes and Intended Users

The CA ELD Standards are designed to meet the needs of a variety of intended users for different purposes. The CA ELD Standards are designed to:

- reflect expectations of what ELs should know and be able to do with the English language in various contexts;

- set clear developmental benchmarks that reflect ELs' English language proficiency at various developmental stages in a variety of cognitive and linguistic tasks;

- provide teachers with a foundation for delivering rich instruction for ELs so that they can help their students develop English proficiency and prepare ELs to meet grade-level academic achievement standards;

- provide parents, guardians, families, and other caretakers with a tool for discussing learning progress so that they can continue to support their children's language and cognitive development at home;

- provide curriculum developers with guidance on creating rigorous, linguistically and academically rich curriculum and instructional materials for ELs;

- provide a framework to guide development of ELD assessment systems that help California educators ensure that all ELs make progress in the English language knowledge, skills, and abilities needed to become college- and career-ready.

California's English Learner Students

ELs come to California schools from all over the world, and from within California. They come with a range of cultural and linguistic backgrounds, experiences with formal schooling, levels of native language and English literacy, immigrant experiences, and socioeconomic levels, as well as other experiences in the home, school, and community. How educators support ELs to achieve school success through the CA ELD Standards and the academic content standards depends on educators' understanding of the following key factors:

- *Stages of cognitive development.* It is important to note the stages of ELs' cognitive development. Students in the primary grades are "learning to read" while also engaging in challenging content learning. In contrast, students in the intermediate and secondary grades are "reading to learn" in various content areas. ELs entering kindergarten, for example, will benefit from participation in the same instructional activities in literacy as their non-EL peers, along with additional differentiated support based on student need. EL students who enter California schools in the secondary grades may need additional support (depending on the level and extent of previous schooling they have received) to master certain linguistic and cognitive skills and thus fully engage in intellectually challenging academic tasks.

- **Native language literacy.** Adolescent ELs who enter California schools after the primary grades have different levels of native language foundations in literacy. All students can draw upon knowledge of oral vocabulary and structures (e.g., recognition of cognates) to inform their English language learning to some extent, depending on their oral proficiency in the native language and how closely their native language is related to English. Students with established literacy in their native language and content knowledge can transfer these skills and knowledge to English with appropriate instructional support. (See chapter 6, "Foundational Literacy Skills for English Learners," for additional information.) Nevertheless, even with strong native language foundations, some adolescent ELs may still struggle to master disciplinary literacy, given the accelerated time frame in which they are expected to meet grade-level content-area expectations.

- **Long-term English learners.** Many ELs may not have received the support they need to continually progress in English language development and academic subjects (typically English language arts), giving rise to the "long-term English learner" phenomenon. These long-term ELs have been schooled in the United States for six or more years but have not made sufficient linguistic and academic progress to meet redesignation criteria and exit English learner status.[1] Fluent in social/conversational English but challenged by literacy tasks, particularly disciplinary literacy tasks, these students find it difficult to engage meaningfully in increasingly rigorous course work. Long-term ELs face considerable challenges succeeding in

---

1. For a discussion of the term "long-term English learners," see Laurie Olsen, *Reparable Harm: Fulfilling the Unkept Promise of Educational Opportunity for California's Long Term English Learners* (Long Beach, CA: Californians Together, 2010). The publication is available at http://www.californianstogether.org/reports/ (accessed July 28, 2014).

school as the amount and complexity of the academic texts they encounter rapidly increase. Regardless of the challenges ELs face, they are expected to achieve the same core academic standards as their non-EL peers.

- **Programs and services for English learners.** California's ELs are enrolled in a variety of school and instructional settings that influence the application of the CA ELD Standards. An EL might be in a newcomer program, a structured English immersion program, a mainstream program where ELs receive specialized ELD instruction, a separate ELD class, or a bilingual/ dual-language program. The CA ELD Standards apply to all of these settings and are designed to be used **by all teachers of academic content and of ELD in all these settings,** albeit in ways that are appropriate to the setting and identified student needs. For example, they are the focal standards in settings specifically designed for English language development—such as an ELD class where ELs are grouped by English language proficiency level. Additionally, the CA ELD Standards are designed and intended to be used *in tandem with other academic content standards* to support ELs in mainstream academic content classrooms. These settings could include, for example, a self-contained third-grade classroom during ELA, social studies, math, and science instruction; a middle school math class; or a high school science class.

Goals of the California English Language Development Standards

ELs must have full access to high-quality English language arts, mathematics, science, and social studies content, as well as other subjects, at the same time that they are progressing through the ELD-level continuum. The CA ELD Standards correspond with the CA CCSS for ELA/Literacy and are designed to apply to English language and literacy skills across all academic content areas, in addition to classes specifically designed for English language development. The CA CCSS for ELA/Literacy raise expectations for all students in California. Among other things, students are expected to participate in sustained dialogue on a variety of topics and content areas; explain their thinking and build on others' ideas; construct arguments and justify their positions persuasively with sound evidence; and effectively produce written and oral texts in a variety of informational and literary text types. ELs must successfully engage in these challenging academic activities while simultaneously developing proficiency in advanced English. The CA ELD Standards are intended to support this dual endeavor by providing fewer, clearer, and higher standards:

- **Fewer:** Those standards that are necessary and essential for development and success

- **Clearer:** A coherent body of standards that have clear links to curriculum and assessments

- **Higher:** Alignment with the elevated standards of the CA CCSS for ELA/Literacy

The CA ELD Standards achieve this goal of fewer, clearer, and higher standards in two ways. First, the CA ELD Standards highlight and amplify those CA CCSS for ELA/Literacy that promote ELs' abilities to *interact in meaningful ways* during rich instruction so that they develop both English and content knowledge. Second, the CA ELD Standards guide teachers to build ELs' *knowledge about how the English language works* in different contexts to achieve specific communicative purposes. The CA ELD Standards emphasize specific linguistic processes (e.g., structuring cohesive texts) and linguistic resources (e.g., expanding sentences) that ELs need to develop in the context of rigorous academic learning for successful academic achievement.

By focusing on these two areas, educators can more effectively support all ELs to:

- read, analyze, interpret, and create a variety of literary and informational text types;

- develop an understanding of how language is a complex, dynamic, and social resource for making meaning and how content is organized in different text types and disciplines using text structure, language features, and vocabulary, depending on purpose and audience;

- be aware that different languages and variations of English exist and recognize their home languages and cultures as resources to value and draw upon in building proficiency in English;

- contribute actively to class and group discussions, asking questions, responding appropriately, and providing useful feedback;

- demonstrate knowledge of content through oral and multimedia presentations, writing, and collaborative conversations;

- develop proficiency in shifting register based on context.

Unintended and Inappropriate Uses of the Standards

Although the CA ELD Standards are a powerful tool for supporting ELs' linguistic and academic development, they are insufficient when used alone to achieve the goals outlined in the previous section. Therefore, it is important to state explicitly the following purposes for which the standards are not intended and uses that would be inappropriate:

- **The CA ELD Standards *are not to be used in isolation* from the CA CCSS for ELA/Literacy and other content standards during academic content instruction.** Instead, they are designed, and should be used, as a *complement* to the CA CCSS for ELA/Literacy and other academic content standards. It is fully expected that all ELs will receive high-quality instruction based on both the CA CCSS for ELA/Literacy and the CA ELD Standards.

- **The CA ELD Standards are *not to be used piecemeal* at a given proficiency level.** To be used appropriately and effectively, standards articulated in both "Part I: Interacting in Meaningful Ways" and "Part II: Learning About How English Works" should be used in tandem in strategic and purposeful ways.

- **The CA ELD Standards *do not provide an exhaustive list of all the linguistic processes and resources that ELs need to develop* in order to be successful in school.** This is especially the case with regard to disciplinary literacy. The CA ELD Standards do, however, provide descriptions of knowledge and skills that are essential and critical for development, which teachers and curriculum developers can both unpack and expand upon in order to provide a comprehensive instructional program for ELs.

- **The CA ELD Standards *are not a curriculum or a curriculum framework.*** The CA ELD Standards describe what ELs should be able to accomplish if they receive high-quality instruction with appropriate scaffolding and instructional materials. The standards do not name a teaching method or the instructional materials to use.

  Note: **Examples** provided in particular standards are shared ***only as illustrative possibilities*** and should not be misinterpreted as the only objectives of instruction or as the only types of language ELs might or should be able to understand or produce.

  Curriculum and assessment frameworks provide more specific guidance for implementation of these standards via instructional and assessment practices. *The California ELA/ELD Framework* (forthcoming) is intended to incorporate and support the CA CCSS for ELA/Literacy and the CA ELD Standards. It reflects current research on ELA instruction, and it also addresses appropriate and effective ELD instruction. Curriculum frameworks provide guidance to teachers, administrators, and parents on how a standards-based curriculum is implemented in the classroom.

Rationale for Three Proficiency Levels

The CA ELD Standards adopted in 2012 define three proficiency levels: Emerging, Expanding, and Bridging. These levels are intended to serve instructional purposes and do not necessarily represent the full range of performance levels in English language proficiency that may be determined by a standardized ELD assessment. A rigorous standard-setting process applied to actual assessment results may identify a different number of *performance levels* at various cut points along the proficiency level continuum; it is these performance levels that will be used to support determinations of placement, progress, and redesignation of ELs for diagnostic and accountability purposes.

The decision to define three overarching proficiency levels for the CA ELD Standards was based on available research and existing practice. Because there is currently no empirical evidence to establish a particular number of ELD proficiency levels as optimal, the proficiency level descriptors (PLDs),

as well as the three proficiency levels described in the CA ELD Standards, were determined in light of the following sources:

- **Input from Statewide Focus Groups and a Panel of Experts**

  Recommendations from practitioners, administrators, and academic researchers throughout the state confirmed that while ELs may progress through multiple stages of ELD (which may vary in number according to the skills being developed and the ways in which the skills are defined or measured), students are typically grouped into three separate levels for the purposes of instruction.

- **Existing California English Language Development Test (CELDT) Performance Levels and Descriptors for CA ELD Standards**

  Previous CA ELD standards drew distinctions between early intermediate and intermediate levels, as well as between early advanced and advanced levels. The CELDT performance levels were established directly from these distinctions. The descriptors for the entry/early and exit stages in the new ELD Proficiency Level Continuum are consistent with the previous five levels used in the state for instruction and assessment of ELs, providing continuity with current expectations of what ELs know and can do as their English skills progress. As previously noted, a standard-setting process involving expert groups of educators and based on results of an assessment aligned with the new CA ELD Standards will determine which points along the continuum represent meaningful distinctions among student performances. The process may yield more than three performance levels to further delineate measurement of the three proficiency levels described in the CA ELD Standards.

- **Proficiency Level Descriptors from Other English Language Development Standards**

  The number, range, and type of descriptors were informed by consultation and consideration of other widely used or respected national and state ELD standards, such as those of the World-Class Instructional Design and Assessment (WIDA) Standards (http://www.wida.us/standards/eld.aspx) and the Kansas Curricular Standards for English for Speakers of Other Languages (ESOL).[2] Additional frameworks (which delineate three proficiency levels) drawn upon include the *Framework for English Language Proficiency Development Standards Corresponding to the Common Core State Standards and the Next Generation Science Standards* (Council of Chief State School Officers 2012); and the *Common European Framework of Reference for Languages: Learning, Teaching, Assessment* (Council of Europe, n.d.). See chapter 4, "Theoretical Foundations and the Research Base of the English Language Development Standards," for a complete list of sources consulted.

The CA ELD Standards describe the knowledge, skills, and abilities in English as a new language that are expected *upon exit from each proficiency level,* with the highest level, Bridging, being aligned with the CA CCSS for ELA/Literacy. These exit descriptors signal high expectations for ELs to progress through all levels and to attain the academic English language they need to access and engage with grade-level content in all content areas. As previously noted, the PLDs include specifications at "early stages" and upon "exit" for each of the three levels, providing valuable information that can be used in the standard-setting process for determining meaningful distinctions in performance levels.

Legislation and Process for Development and Validation

Assembly Bill 124 (Fuentes, Chapter 605, Statutes of 2011), signed into law on October 8, 2011, required the State Superintendent of Public Instruction (SSPI), in consultation with the State Board of Education (SBE), to update, revise, and align the state's current ELD standards, by grade level, with the state's ELA standards, by November 2012. This legislation directed the SSPI to complete revised CA ELD Standards for SBE review no later than August 31, 2012.

To accomplish this work in the required time frame, the California Department of Education (CDE) requested the assistance of the California Comprehensive

Assistance Center at WestEd. Specifically, WestEd's California Comprehensive Center, in partnership with the Assessment and Standards Development Services program at WestEd, worked at the request of the CDE to conduct an independent analysis of the state's current ELD standards relative to the new CA ELA Standards. Under the CDE's direction, WestEd reviewed information from other states' (e.g., Arizona, Kansas) and organizations' (e.g., WIDA) ELD standards revision and alignment efforts; analyzed statewide public and expert input on revision parameters; drafted the proposed CA ELD Standards; and revised them as needed based on stakeholder review and feedback.

To provide initial input on the CA ELD Standards, the SSPI convened five focus groups in the winter/spring of 2012, which included 10 to 15 educators who were selected to ensure a balanced representation of regions, types of schools, and experience. Focus-group members were recruited from across California, and focus groups were conducted at the following locations: California Department of Education, Sacramento; Ventura County Office of Education, Camarillo; Alameda County Office of Education, Hayward; Los Angeles County Office of Education, Downey; and San Diego County Office of Education, San Diego.

The SSPI also convened a panel consisting of experts in English language instruction, curriculum, and assessment in order to provide ongoing input and guidance on the CA ELD Standards, the PLDs, and accompanying chapters. The panel included school site principals, school district or county office of education administrators overseeing programs and support for ELs, faculty of teacher training programs and researchers with EL expertise at institutions of higher education, and curriculum and instructional specialists with extensive EL experience. The panel of experts, composed of 21 individuals from across California, met five times (two one-day meetings and three two-day meetings, all of which were open to the public) between March and August of 2012, to review initial and revised drafts of the CA ELD Standards and PLDs and to provide guidance for ongoing development. These meetings were recorded, and transcripts were made available, along with shared materials, on the California Comprehensive Center and CDE Web sites.

---

2. The Kansas Curricular Standards for ESOL are posted at http://www.ksde.org/Default.aspx-?tabid=4694 (accessed October 8, 2013).

Before each meeting with the panel of experts, WestEd staff members met with CDE staff members from the following divisions: English Learner Support; Curriculum Frameworks and Instructional Resources; Professional Learning Support; and Assessment Development and Administration. The collaborative meetings resulted in further revisions and refinements to the drafts of the CA ELD Standards, informed by the specific expertise of CDE staff members.

The CDE also held two public hearings and invited the public to provide written feedback on the CA ELD Standards during a one-month public comment period that ended on August 6, 2012. The extensive oral and written comments and suggestions provided by multiple stakeholders—including teachers, principals, district and county offices of education, advocacy groups, educational scholars, and other educational community members—were thoroughly reviewed and analyzed. A final revised draft was presented to the SBE in September 2012. At the request of the SBE, the CDE, in conjunction with SBE staff, oversaw minor technical revisions to the CA ELD Standards and PLDs, as well as refinements to chapters 4, 5, and 6, and a glossary, created by WestEd.

Organization of the Standards

The CA ELD Standards have two main sections common to all grade levels.

Section 1: Overview

This section provides a foundation for and an orientation to the standards via the following components:

- A Goal statement for all English learners in California

- Critical Principles for Developing Language and Cognition in Academic Contexts

- An "at-a-glance" overview of parts I–III of the CA ELD Standards, with corresponding grade-level CA CCSS for ELA/Literacy indicated

This section is generally consistent across all grades, with some terminology variations in the grade spans for K–8, 9–10, and 11–12 indicating relevant cognitive differences. Each component is explained below.

Goal: An overarching goal statement crystallizes what all educators in California want for English learners' development of academic English proficiency: success with grade-level disciplinary content and broader awareness of language.

Critical Principles for Developing Language and Cognition in Academic Contexts. This component further details the goal statement by defining the critical and meaningful experiences and knowledge that English learners need to reach each goal. The Critical Principles also provide the foundation for most of the CA ELD Standards document and introduce parts I–III, indicating the key principles that will be detailed in the remainder of the document.

Parts I–III Overview ("At a Glance"). Because content and language are inextricably linked, the three parts of the CA ELD Standards—"Interacting in Meaningful Ways," "Learning About How English Works," and "Using Foundational Literacy Skills"—should be interpreted as complementary and interrelated dimensions of what must be addressed in a robust instructional program for English learners. Parts I and II are intentionally presented separately in order to call attention to the need for both a focus on meaning and interaction and a focus on building knowledge about the linguistic features and structure of English. Part III outlines foundational literacy skills ELs may need, depending on their previous literacy and educational experiences.

Just as teachers focus on meaningful and engaging activities designed to build content knowledge before strategically delving into specifics about how language is structured, the CA ELD Standards are organized with the focus on meaning and interaction first and the focus on knowledge about the English language and how it works afterward. *Accordingly, the standards in Part II should not be used in isolation; instead, they should be used in the context of fostering intellectually and discourse-rich, meaningful interactions outlined in Part I.*

Parts I and II in the CA ELD Standards are further delineated by headings, represented by letters, which cluster standards together. Below each heading is a set of ELD content *strands,* represented by a number. In Part 1, "Interacting in Meaningful Ways," the headings identify *communicative modes:* Collaborative, Interpretive, and Productive.

Part I: Interacting in Meaningful Ways

A. Collaborative (engagement in dialogue with others)

1. Exchanging information and ideas via oral communication and conversations

2. Interacting via written English (print and multimedia)

3. Offering opinions and negotiating with or persuading others

4. Adapting language choices to various contexts

B. Interpretive (comprehension and analysis of written and spoken texts)

5. Listening actively and asking or answering questions about what was heard

6. Reading closely and explaining interpretations and ideas from reading

7. Evaluating how well writers and speakers use language to present or support ideas

8. Analyzing how writers use vocabulary and other language resources

C. Productive (creation of oral presentations and written texts)

9. Expressing information and ideas in oral presentations

10. Writing literary and informational texts

11. Supporting opinions or justifying arguments and evaluating others' opinions or arguments

12. Selecting and applying varied and precise vocabulary and other language resources

In Part II, "Learning About How English Works," the headings identify key *language processes:* "Structuring Cohesive Texts," "Expanding and Enriching Ideas," and "Connecting and Condensing Ideas."

Part II: Learning About How English Works

A. Structuring Cohesive Texts

1. *Understanding text structure* and organization based on purpose, text type, and discipline

2. *Understanding cohesion* and how language resources across a text contribute to the way a text unfolds and flows

B. Expanding and Enriching Ideas

3. *Using verbs and verb phrases* to create precision and clarity in different text types

4. *Using nouns and noun phrases* to expand ideas and provide more detail

5. *Modifying to add details* to provide more information and create precision

C. Connecting and Condensing Ideas

6. *Connecting ideas* within sentences by combining clauses

7. *Condensing ideas* within sentences using a variety of language resources

Part III: Using Foundational Literacy Skills

Considerations for instruction in foundational literacy at each grade level (K–5) and the grade span 6–12 are outlined here.

Corresponding CA CCSS for ELA/Literacy. The right-hand column of the Overview of the CA ELD Standards shows the correspondence[3] of the CA ELD Standards to the CA CCSS for ELA/Literacy. The CCSS are identified by strand, grade, and number (or number and letter, where applicable), so that RI.4.3, for example, stands for Reading, Informational Text, grade 4, standard 3, and

---

3. As noted previously, because the CA ELD Standards are not intended to repeat content from the CA CCSS for ELA/Literacy, individual ELD and ELA standards *correspond* to each other in terms of knowledge, skills, abilities, and rigor rather than match exactly.

W.5.1a stands for Writing, grade 5, standard 1a. Strand designations from the CA CCSS for ELA/Literacy are indicated in the CA ELD Standards as follows:

RL: Reading Standards for Literature (K–12)

RI: Reading Standards for Informational Text (K–12)

RF: Reading Standards for Foundational Literacy Skills (K–5)

RH: Reading Standards for Literacy in History/Social Studies (6–12)

RST: Reading Standards for Literacy in Science and Technical Subjects (6–12)

SL: Speaking and Listening Standards (K–12)

L: Language Standards (K–12)

W: Writing Standards (K–12)

WHST: Writing Standards for Literacy in History/Social Studies, Science, and Technical Subjects (6–12)

Section 2: Elaboration on Critical Principles for Developing Language and Cognition in Academic Contexts

This section extends the Critical Principles and provides detailed, grade-level CA ELD Standards, with corresponding CA CCSS for ELA/Literacy indicated, in three parts:

Part I: Interacting in Meaningful Ways

Part II: Learning About How English Works

Part III: Using Foundational Literacy Skills

The section unpacks the Critical Principles via a set of ELD standards for each grade level (K–8) and for the grade spans 9–10 and 11–12. These standards provide descriptions of expectations for English learners *upon exit* from each of the three proficiency levels along the ELD continuum—*Emerging, Expanding,* and *Bridging*—by each ELD standard strand. These expectations are appropriate if ELs are provided with an appropriate curriculum, effective instruction, and strategic levels of scaffolding. The components are explained in the following section.

Texts and Discourse in Context. This column emphasizes language as a complex and social meaning-making resource to be fostered via intellectually challenging, interactive, and dialogue-rich contexts focused on content knowledge and linguistic development. *Texts* may be written, spoken, or multimodal and in print or digital form. *Discourse* is, in broad terms, communication of meaning in any modality (e.g., spoken, written, visual). The language choices students make, including which grammatical and lexical resources to use, are influenced by *context,* which includes the communicative purpose, audience, text type, and discipline or content area. Students use their knowledge of the English language in the context of intellectually engaging instruction in which the primary focus is on comprehending and making meaning. This column highlights some of the variables teachers need to consider when designing and implementing instruction for English learners:

The corresponding CA CCSS for ELA/Literacy are provided first so that teachers see the interconnected nature of the CA ELD Standards and the CA CCSS for ELA/Literacy.

Purposes for Using Language. These are purposes for using language that are featured prominently in the CA CCSS for ELA/Literacy and, correspondingly, in the CA ELD Standards. Teachers support ELs to develop an awareness of these purposes as students progress in language proficiency and through the grades.

Text Types. Provided in the CA CCSS for ELA/Literacy, each text type has particular language features, based on the discipline, content, purpose, and audience. Teachers help ELs develop an awareness of text types and language features as ELs progress through the grades. Informational text types are presented first to emphasize their importance in college and career readiness, as well as in developing content knowledge.

Audiences. As they use language, ELs need to consider the audience, which might be a peer in a one-to-one conversation about a social topic; a group of peers engaged in an academic conversation (one to a group); an entire class, such as when a student makes an academic oral presentation or completes a written task (one to many); and other types of audience.

Teachers help ELs develop an awareness of audience as ELs progress through the grades.

ELD Proficiency Level Continuum. This continuum, explained previously in the "Rationale for Three Proficiency Levels," distinguishes the three overall English language development levels: *Emerging, Expanding, and Bridging.* Gradations and spiraling of acquisition of knowledge and skills between levels, as well as variation within levels, are expected.

Part I: Interacting in Meaningful Ways. Part I provides grade-level CA ELD Standards that set expectations for English learners to participate in meaningful, relevant, and intellectually challenging ways in various contexts and disciplines in three modes: *collaborative, interpretive, and productive.*

Part II: Learning About How English Works. Part II focuses on the ways in which English learners develop awareness of language resources available to them, how English is structured and organized, and how meaning is made through language choices. Instruction about English is designed to improve ELs' ability to comprehend and produce academic texts in various content areas. Part II is organized into the following ways of using language: *structuring cohesive texts, expanding and enriching ideas, and connecting and condensing ideas.*

Part III: Using Foundational Literacy Skills. Part III is presented separately in order to highlight for teachers the potential need to provide ELs with specialized instruction to support the development of foundational literacy skills. This specialized instruction is designed by adapting, in particular, the Reading Standards in Foundational Literacy Skills (K–5) in the CA CCSS for ELA/Literacy based on the age, cognitive level, and previous literacy or educational experiences of ELs. Because the Reading Standards in Foundational Literacy Skills are intended to guide instruction for students in kindergarten through grade 5, these standards need to be adapted—using appropriate instructional strategies and materials—to meet the particular pedagogical and literacy needs of ELs at the secondary level, including the need to teach foundational literacy skills in an accelerated time frame.

References

Assessment and Accountability Comprehensive Center. 2009. *Framework for High-Quality English Language Proficiency Standards and Assessments.* San Francisco, CA: WestEd.

Council of Chief State School Officers (CCSSO). 2012. *Framework for English Language Proficiency Development Standards Corresponding to the Common Core State Standards and the Next Generation Science Standards.* Washington, DC: CCSSO. http://www.ccsso.org/Resources/Publications/The_Common_Core_and_English_Language_Learners.html (accessed September 30, 2013).

Council of Europe, Language Policy Unit. N.d. *Common European Framework of Reference for Languages: Learning, Teaching, Assessment.* Cambridge, UK: Cambridge University Press.

Gottlieb, M. 2006. *Assessing English Language Learners: Bridges from Language Proficiency to Academic Achievement.* Thousand Oaks, CA: Corwin Press.

Olsen, L. 2010. *Reparable Harm: Fulfilling the Unkept Promise of Educational Opportunity for California's Long Term English Learners.* Long Beach, CA: Californians Together. http://www.californianstogether.org/.

Chapter 2

Proficiency Level Descriptors for the California English Language Development Standards

The Proficiency Level Descriptors (PLDs) provide an overview of the stages of English language development through which English learners (ELs) are expected to progress as they gain increasing proficiency in English as a new language. The PLDs depict student knowledge, skills, and abilities across a continuum, identifying what ELs know and can do at early stages and upon exit from each of three proficiency levels: Emerging, Expanding, and Bridging.[1] These descriptors are intended to be used as a guide for teachers and curriculum developers to provide ELs with targeted instruction in English language development as well as differentiated instruction in academic content areas.

It is important to note that while the PLDs describe an aligned set of knowledge, skills, and abilities at each proficiency level that reflect a linear progression across the levels, this is done for purposes of presentation and understanding. Actual second language acquisition does not necessarily occur in a linear fashion within or across proficiency levels. An EL, at any given point along his or her trajectory of English learning, may exhibit some abilities (e.g., speaking skills) at a higher proficiency level, while at the same time exhibiting other abilities (e.g., writing skills) at a lower proficiency level.[2] Additionally, a student may successfully perform a particular skill at a lower proficiency level (such as reading and analyzing an informational text) and, at the next higher proficiency level,

need review in the same reading and analysis skills when presented with a new or more complex type of informational text. Thus, while a student may be identified—based on state assessment results and other state and local criteria—as being eligible for English language services appropriate to a particular proficiency level, the student's actual abilities may vary by language domain (e.g., listening, speaking, reading, and writing). For the same reason, a proficiency level does not identify a student (e.g., "Emerging student"), but rather identifies what a student knows and can do at a particular stage of English language development—for example, "a student at the Emerging level" or "a student whose listening comprehension ability is at the Emerging level."

The California English Language Development Standards (CA ELD Standards) describe the knowledge, skills, and abilities that students who are learning English as a new language are expected to exhibit upon *exit from each proficiency level,* with the highest level, Bridging, corresponding with the California Common Core State Standards for English Language Arts and Literacy in History/Social Studies, Science, and Technical Subjects (CA CCSS for ELA/Literacy). These exit descriptors signal high expectations for ELs to progress through all levels and to attain the academic English necessary to access and engage with grade-level content in all subject areas. Note also that the PLDs include specifications at "early stages" and upon "exit" for each of the three levels, providing valuable information that can be used for determining meaningful performance level distinctions based on assessment results.

Organization of the Proficiency Level Descriptors

The organization of the PLDs represents English language development as a continuum of increasing proficiency in language learning and use, starting with *native language* competencies that students possess when they enter school, and concluding (though not ending) with *lifelong language learning* that all

---

1. As there is currently no available empirical evidence to support a particular number of ELD proficiency levels as optimal, the development and design of the PLDs for the CA ELD Standards was based on common practices in the state of grouping ELs into three levels for purposes of instruction. These practices were confirmed by practitioners, administrators, and academic researchers throughout the state as part of the ELD standards validation process, as well as by guidance documents such as the *Framework for English Language Proficiency Development Standards Corresponding to the Common Core State Standards and the Next Generation Science Standards* (Council of Chief State School Officers 2012).

2. See the discussion in Margo Gottlieb's *Assessing English Language Learners: Bridges from Language Proficiency to Academic Achievement* (Thousand Oaks, CA: Corwin Press, 2006), 26–27.

language users engage in.[3] The three levels represent the stages of English language development, describing expectations for how well students can understand and use the English language at each level as they continue to build on existing language skills and knowledge.

Emerging: Students at this level typically progress very quickly, learning to use English for immediate needs as well as beginning to understand and use academic vocabulary and other features of academic language.

Expanding: Students at this level are challenged to increase their English skills in more contexts and learn a greater variety of vocabulary and linguistic structures, applying their growing language skills in more sophisticated ways that are appropriate to their age and grade level.

Bridging: Students at this level continue to learn and apply a range of high-level English language skills in a wide variety of contexts, including comprehension and production of highly technical texts. The "bridge" alluded to is the transition to full engagement in grade-level academic tasks and activities in a variety of content areas without the need for specialized ELD instruction. However, ELs at all levels of English language proficiency fully participate in grade-level tasks in *all* content areas with varying degrees of scaffolding in order to develop both content knowledge and English.

The PLDs emphasize that ELs at all proficiency levels are capable of high-level thinking and can engage in complex, cognitively demanding social and academic activities requiring language, as long as they are provided appropriate linguistic support. The *extent of support needed varies depending on the familiarity and complexity of the task and topic, as well as on the student's English language proficiency level.* Within the PLDs, three general levels of support are identified: Substantial, Moderate, and Light. The descriptors for these general levels of support are intended to signal the extent of linguistic scaffolding most likely needed for appropriately implementing the CA ELD Standards at each proficiency level; however, the descriptors are not intended to explain how to provide support or differentiate instruction for ELs at each level.

Each PLD includes the following:

- Overall Proficiency: A general descriptor of ELs' abilities at *entry to, progress through,* and *exit from* the level

- Early Stages: Descriptors of abilities in English language that ELs have *at the early stages* of the level

- Exit Stages: Descriptors of abilities in English language students have *at exit from* the level

The descriptors for early and exit stages of each proficiency level are detailed across three modes of communication:

A. **Collaborative:** Engagement in dialogue with others

B. **Interpretive:** Comprehension and analysis of written and spoken texts

C. **Productive:** Creation of oral presentations and written texts

Two dimensions of knowledge of language are described:

Metalinguistic Awareness: The extent of language awareness and self-monitoring that students have at the level

Accuracy of Production: The extent of accuracy in production ELs can be expected to exhibit at the level; ELs increase in accuracy of linguistic production as they develop proficiency in English. *Accuracy may vary within a level depending on context, such as extent of cognitive demand or familiarity of a task.*

---

3. Note that the concept of "lifelong language learning" for proficient users of English (as well as other languages) is distinct from that of "long-term English learners" who have not been supported to progress to full proficiency in English.

Proficiency Level Descriptors

Student Capacities	ELD Proficiency Level Continuum						Lifelong Language Learning
	→ Emerging →		→ Expanding →		→ Bridging →		
Native Language English learners come to school possessing a wide range of competencies in their native language appropriate to their age. They may have varying levels of literacy in their native language, depending on their prior experiences in the home, community, and school. As learners of English as a new language, they gain metacognitive awareness of what language is and how it is used and apply this awareness in their language learning strategies, including drawing upon knowledge of their native language.	English learners *enter* the Emerging level having limited receptive and productive English skills. As they *progress through* the Emerging level, they start to respond to more varied communication tasks using learned words and phrases with increasing ease.	Upon *exit* from the Emerging level, students have basic English communication skills in social and academic contexts.	As English learners *progress through* the Expanding level, they move from being able to refashion learned phrases and sentences in English to meet their immediate communication and learning needs toward being able to increasingly engage in using the English language in more complex, cognitively demanding situations.	Upon exit from the Expanding level, students can use English to learn and communicate about a range of topics and academic content areas.	As English learners *progress through* the Bridging level, they move from being able to communicate in ways that are appropriate to different tasks, purposes, and audiences in a variety of social and academic contexts toward being able to refine and enhance their English language competencies in a broader range of contexts.	Upon *exit* from the Bridging level, students can communicate effectively with various audiences on a wide range of familiar and new topics to meet academic demands in a variety of disciplines.	Students who have reached "proficiency" in the English language (as determined by state and/or local criteria) continue to build increasing breadth, depth, and complexity in comprehending and communicating in English in a wide variety of contexts.
High-Level Thinking with Linguistic Support English learners possess cognitive abilities appropriate to their age and experience. In order to communicate about their thinking as they learn English, they may need *varying linguistic support, depending on the linguistic and cognitive demand of the task.*	**General Extent of Support**						
	Substantial Students at the *early stages* of the Emerging level can engage in complex, cognitively demanding social and academic activities requiring language when provided **substantial** linguistic support; as they develop more familiarity and ease with understanding and using English, support may be **moderate or light** for familiar tasks or topics.		**Moderate** Students at the *early stages* of the Expanding level can engage in complex, cognitively demanding social and academic activities requiring language when provided **moderate** linguistic support; as they develop increasing ease with understanding and using English in a variety of contexts, support may be **light** for familiar tasks or topics.		**Light** Students at the *early stages* of the Bridging level can engage in complex, cognitively demanding social and academic activities requiring language when provided **light** linguistic support; as they develop increasing ease with understanding and using highly technical English, support may not be necessary for familiar tasks or topics using everyday English.		**Occasional** Students who have *exited* the Bridging level benefit from **occasional** linguistic support in their ongoing learning of English.

Proficiency Level Descriptors

Mode of Communication	ELD Proficiency Level Continuum			
	Emerging →		Expanding →	
	At the *early stages* of the Emerging level, students are able to perform the following tasks:	Upon *exit* from the Emerging level, students are able to perform the following tasks:	At the *early stages* of the Expanding level, students are able to perform the following tasks:	Upon *exit* from the Expanding level, students are able to perform the following tasks:
Collaborative	• Express basic personal and safety needs and ideas, and respond to questions on social and academic topics with gestures and words or short phrases. • Use basic social conventions to participate in conversations.	• Express basic personal and safety needs and ideas, and respond to questions on social and academic topics with phrases and short sentences. • Participate in simple, face-to-face conversations with peers and others.	• Express a variety of personal needs, ideas, and opinions and respond to questions using short sentences. • Initiate simple conversations on social and academic topics.	• Express more complex feelings, needs, ideas, and opinions using extended oral and written production; respond to questions using extended discourse. • Participate actively in collaborative conversations in all content areas with moderate to light support as appropriate.
Interpretive	• Comprehend frequently occurring words and basic phrases in immediate physical surroundings. • Read very brief grade-appropriate text with simple sentences and familiar vocabulary, supported by graphics or pictures. • Comprehend familiar words, phrases, and questions drawn from content areas.	• Comprehend a sequence of information on familiar topics as presented through stories and face-to-face conversation. • Read brief grade-appropriate text with simple sentences and mostly familiar vocabulary, supported by graphics or pictures. • Demonstrate understanding of words and phrases from previously learned content material.	• Comprehend information on familiar topics and on some unfamiliar topics in contextualized settings. • Read independently a variety of grade-appropriate text with simple sentences. • Read more complex text supported by graphics or pictures. • Comprehend basic concepts in content areas.	• Comprehend detailed information with fewer contextual clues on unfamiliar topics. • Read increasingly complex grade-level text while relying on context and prior knowledge to obtain meaning from print. • Read technical text on familiar topics supported by pictures or graphics.
Productive	• Produce learned words and phrases and use gestures to communicate basic information. • Express ideas using visuals such as drawings, charts, or graphic organizers. • Write or use familiar words and phrases related to everyday and academic topics.	• Produce basic statements and ask questions in direct informational exchanges on familiar and routine subjects. • Express ideas using information and short responses within structured contexts. • Write or use learned vocabulary drawn from academic content areas.	• Produce sustained informational exchanges with others on an expanding variety of topics. • Express ideas in highly structured and scaffolded academic interactions. • Write or use expanded vocabulary to provide information and extended responses in contextualized settings.	• Produce, initiate, and sustain spontaneous interactions on a variety of topics. • Write and express ideas to meet most social and academic needs through the recombination of learned vocabulary and structures with support.

Proficiency Level Descriptors *(continued)*

Mode of Communication	ELD Proficiency Level Continuum	
	→ Bridging ————————————————→	
	At the *early stages* of the Bridging level, students are able to perform the following tasks:	Upon *exit* from the Bridging level, students are able to perform the following tasks:
Collaborative	• Express increasingly complex feelings, needs, ideas, and opinions in a variety of settings; respond to questions using extended and more elaborate discourse. • Initiate and sustain dialogue on a variety of grade-level academic and social topics.	• Participate fully in all collaborative conversations in all content areas at grade level, with occasional support as necessary. • Participate fully in both academic and non-academic settings requiring English.
Interpretive	• Comprehend concrete and many abstract topics and begin to recognize language subtleties in a variety of communication settings. • Read increasingly complex text at grade level. • Read technical text supported by pictures or graphics.	• Comprehend concrete and abstract topics and recognize language subtleties in a variety of communication settings. • Read, with limited comprehension difficulty, a variety of grade-level and technical texts in all content areas.
Productive	• Produce, initiate, and sustain interactions with increasing awareness of tailoring language to specific purposes and audiences. • Write and express ideas to meet increasingly complex academic demands for specific purposes and audiences.	• Produce, initiate, and sustain extended interactions tailored to specific purposes and audiences. • Write and express ideas to meet a variety of social needs and academic demands for specific purposes and audiences.

Proficiency Level Descriptors

Knowledge of Language	ELD Proficiency Level Continuum			
	→ Emerging →		→ Expanding →	
	At the *early stages* of the Emerging level, students are able to perform the following tasks:	Upon *exit* from the Emerging level, students are able to perform the following tasks:	At the *early stages* of the Expanding level, students are able to perform the following tasks:	Upon *exit* from the Expanding level, students are able to perform the following tasks:
Metalinguistic Awareness	Apply to their learning of English an emerging awareness of: • differences and similarities between their native language and English; • ways in which different kinds of language are appropriate for different tasks, purposes, and audiences; • how to intentionally and purposefully use a limited range of everyday vocabulary, phrases, and memorized statements and questions in English.	Apply to their learning of English an awareness of: • differences and similarities between their native language and English; • ways in which different kinds of language are appropriate for different tasks, purposes, and audiences; • how to intentionally and purposefully use mostly everyday and a limited range of general academic vocabulary and domain-specific vocabulary, phrases, and memorized statements and questions in English related mostly to familiar topics.	Apply to their learning of English an expanding awareness of: • differences and similarities between their native language and English; • ways in which language may be different based on task, purpose, and audience; • how to intentionally and purposefully use mostly everyday vocabulary, and an expanding range of general academic and domain-specific vocabulary in English related mostly to familiar topics; • how to extend discourse in limited ways in a range of conversations; • how to recognize language differences and engage in some self-monitoring.	Apply to their learning of English an awareness of: • differences and similarities between their native language and English; • ways in which language may be different based on task, purpose, and audience; • how to intentionally and purposefully use both everyday vocabulary and a range of general academic and domain-specific vocabulary in English related to familiar and new topics; • how to extend discourse in a variety of ways in a range of conversations; • how to recognize language differences, engage in self-monitoring, and adjust oral and written language.
Accuracy of Production	• Be comprehensible when using memorized or copied words or phrases. • Produce English but may exhibit **frequent errors** in pronunciation, grammar, and writing conventions that **often** impede meaning.	• Be comprehensible when using simple or learned phrases and sentences. • Produce English but may exhibit **frequent errors** in pronunciation, grammar, and writing conventions that **sometimes** impede meaning.	• Be comprehensible when using simple and some expanded sentences and discourse or texts. • Produce English but may exhibit **fairly frequent errors** in pronunciation, grammar, and writing conventions that **may sometimes** impede meaning.	• Be comprehensible when using expanded sentences, discourse, or texts. • Produce English but may exhibit **fairly frequent errors** in pronunciation, grammar, and writing conventions that **usually do not** impede meaning.

Proficiency Level Descriptors *(continued)*

Knowledge of Language	ELD Proficiency Level Continuum	
	→ Bridging →	
	At the *early stages* of the Bridging level, students are able to perform the following tasks:	Upon *exit* from the Bridging level, students are able to perform the following tasks:
Metalinguistic Awareness	Apply to their learning of English a sophisticated awareness of: ● differences and similarities between their native language and English; ● ways in which language may be different based on task, purpose, and audience; ● how to intentionally and purposefully use a range of precise and varied grade-level general academic and domain-specific vocabulary in English related to new topics; ● how to extend grade-level academic discourse in a variety of ways in a range of conversations and written texts of varying lengths and complexities; ● how to recognize language differences, engage in self-monitoring, and adjust oral and written language in a range of contexts.	Apply to their learning of English a sophisticated awareness of: ● differences and similarities between their native language and English; ● ways in which language may be different based on task, purpose, and audience; ● how to intentionally and purposefully use a range of precise and varied grade-level general academic and domain-specific vocabulary in English related to new topics across the disciplines; ● how to extend grade-level academic discourse in a variety of ways in a range of conversations and written texts of varying lengths and complexities across disciplines; ● how to recognize language differences, engage in self-monitoring, and adjust oral and written language in a range of contexts across disciplines.
Accuracy of Production	● Be comprehensible when using a variety of grade-level expanded discourse or texts. ● Produce English but may exhibit **some errors** in pronunciation, grammar, and writing conventions that **usually do not** impede meaning.	● Be comprehensible when using a variety of grade-level expanded discourse or texts on a variety of topics. ● Produce English but may exhibit **some minor errors** in pronunciation, grammar, and writing conventions that **do not** impede meaning.

Chapter 3

The Standards: Kindergarten Through Grade 12

Section 1: Overview

Goal: English learners read, analyze, interpret, and create a variety of literary and informational text types. They develop an understanding of how language is a complex, dynamic, and social resource for making meaning, as well as how content is organized in different text types and across disciplines using text structure, language features, and vocabulary depending on purpose and audience. They are aware that different languages and variations of English exist, and they recognize their home languages and cultures as resources to value in their own right and to draw upon in order to build proficiency in English. English learners contribute actively to class and group discussions, asking questions, responding appropriately, and providing useful feedback. They demonstrate knowledge of content through oral presentations, writing tasks, collaborative conversations, and multimedia. They develop proficiency in shifting language use based on task, purpose, audience, and text type.

Critical Principles for Developing Language and Cognition in Academic Contexts: While advancing along the continuum of English language development levels, English learners at all levels engage in intellectually challenging literacy, disciplinary, and disciplinary literacy tasks. They use language in meaningful and relevant ways appropriate to grade level, content area, topic, purpose, audience, and text type in English language arts, mathematics, science, social studies, and the arts. Specifically, they use language to gain and exchange information and ideas in three communicative modes (collaborative, interpretive, and productive), and they apply knowledge of language to academic tasks via three cross-mode language processes (structuring cohesive texts, expanding and enriching ideas, and connecting and condensing ideas) using various linguistic resources.

Part I: Interacting in Meaningful Ways	Corresponding CA CCSS for ELA/Literacy*
A. Collaborative	
1. Exchanging information and ideas with others through oral collaborative conversations on a range of social and academic topics	• SL.K.1, 6; L.K.1, 6
2. Interacting with others in written English in various communicative forms (print, communicative technology, and multimedia)	• W.K.6; L.K.1, 6
3. Offering and supporting opinions and negotiating with others in communicative exchanges	• SL.K.1, 6; L.K.1, 6
4. Adapting language choices to various contexts (based on task, purpose, audience, and text type)	• Not applicable at kindergarten

*The California English Language Development Standards correspond to the California Common Core State Standards for English Language Arts and Literacy in History/Social Science and Technical Subjects (CA CCSS for ELA/Literacy). English learners should have full access to opportunities to learn ELA, mathematics, science, history/social studies, and other content at the same time they are progressing toward full proficiency in English.

Part I: Interacting in Meaningful Ways	Corresponding CA CCSS for ELA/Literacy
B. Interpretive	
5. Listening actively to spoken English in a range of social and academic contexts	• SL.K.1–3
6. Reading closely literary and informational texts and viewing multimedia to determine how meaning is conveyed explicitly and implicitly through language	• RL.K.1–7, 9, 10; RI.K.1–7, 9–10; SL.K.2–3; L.K.4, 6
7. Evaluating how well writers and speakers use language to support ideas and opinions with details or reasons depending on modality, text type, purpose, audience, topic, and content area	• RL.K.3–4, 6; RI.K.2, 6, 8; L.K.4–6
8. Analyzing how writers and speakers use vocabulary and other language resources for specific purposes (to explain, persuade, entertain, etc.) depending on modality, text type, purpose, audience, topic, and content area	• RL.K.4–5; RI.K.4; L.K.4–6
C. Productive	
9. Expressing information and ideas in formal oral presentations on academic topics	• SL.K.4–6; L.K.1, 6
10. Composing/writing literary and informational texts to present, describe, and explain ideas and information, using appropriate technology	• W.K.1–3, 5–8; L.K.1–2, 6
11. Supporting own opinions and evaluating others' opinions in speaking and writing	• W.K.1; SL.K.4, 6; L.K.1–2, 6
12. Selecting and applying varied and precise vocabulary and language structures to effectively convey ideas	• W.K.5; SL.K.4, 6; L.K.1, 5–6
Part II: Learning About How English Works	**Corresponding CA CCSS for ELA/Literacy**
A. Structuring Cohesive Texts	
1. Understanding text structure	• RL.K.5; RI.K.5; W.K.1–3, 5; SL.K.4
2. Understanding cohesion	• RL.K.5; RI.K.5; W.K.1–3,5; SL.K.4; L.K.1
B. Expanding and Enriching Ideas	
3. Using verbs and verb phrases	• W.K.5; SL.K.6; L.K.1, 6
4. Using nouns and noun phrases	• W.K.5; SL.K.6; L.K.1, 6
5. Modifying to add details	• W.K.5; SL.K.4, 6; L.K.1, 6
C. Connecting and Condensing Ideas	
6. Connecting ideas	• W.K.1–3, 5; SL.K.4, 6; L.K.1, 6
7. Condensing ideas	• Not applicable at kindergarten
Part III: Using Foundational Literacy Skills	• RF.K.1–4

Note: **Examples** provided in specific standards are offered *only as illustrative possibilities* and should not be misinterpreted as the only objectives of instruction or as the only types of language that English learners might or should be able to understand or produce.

Section 2: Elaboration on Critical Principles for Developing Language and Cognition in Academic Contexts
Part I: Interacting in Meaningful Ways

Texts and Discourse in Context		ELD Proficiency Level Continuum		
		→ Emerging →	→ Expanding →	→ Bridging →
Part I, strands 1–4, corresponding to the CA CCSS for ELA/Literacy 1. SL.K.1; 6; L.K.1, 6 2. W.K.6; L.K.1, 6 3. SL.K.1; 6; L.K.1, 6 4. Not applicable at kindergarten **Purposes for using language include but are not limited to:** Describing, entertaining, informing, interpreting, analyzing, recounting, explaining, persuading, negotiating, justifying, evaluating, and so on. **Informational text types include but are not limited to:** Description (e.g., science log entry), procedure (e.g., how to solve a mathematics problem), recount (e.g., autobiography, science experiment results), information report (e.g., science or history report), explanation (e.g., how or why something happened), exposition (e.g., opinion), response (e.g., literary analysis), and so on. **Literary text types include but are not limited to:** Stories (e.g., fantasy, legends, fables), drama (e.g., readers' theater), poetry, retelling a story, and so on. **Audiences include but are not limited to:** Peers (one to one) Small group (one to a group) Whole group (one to many)	**A. Collaborative**	*1. Exchanging information and ideas* Contribute to conversations and express ideas by asking and answering *yes-no* and *wh-* questions and responding using gestures, words, and simple phrases. *2. Interacting via written English* Collaborate with the teacher and peers on joint composing projects of short informational and literary texts that include minimal writing (labeling with a few words), using technology, where appropriate, for publishing, graphics, and the like. *3. Offering opinions* Offer opinions and ideas in conversations using a small set of learned phrases (e.g., *I think X*), as well as open responses. *4. Adapting language choices* No standard for kindergarten.	*1. Exchanging information and ideas* Contribute to class, group, and partner discussions by listening attentively, following turn-taking rules, and asking and answering questions. *2. Interacting via written English* Collaborate with the teacher and peers on joint composing projects of informational and literary texts that include some writing (e.g., short sentences), using technology, where appropriate, for publishing, graphics, and the like. *3. Offering opinions* Offer opinions in conversations using an expanded set of learned phrases (e.g., *I think/don't think X. I agree with X*), as well as open responses, in order to gain and/or hold the floor. *4. Adapting language choices* No standard for kindergarten.	*1. Exchanging information and ideas* Contribute to class, group, and partner discussions by listening attentively, following turn-taking rules, and asking and answering questions. *2. Interacting via written English* Collaborate with the teacher and peers on joint composing projects of informational and literary texts that include a greater amount of writing (e.g., a very short story), using technology, where appropriate, for publishing, graphics, and the like. *3. Offering opinions* Offer opinions in conversations using an expanded set of learned phrases (e.g., *I think/don't think X. I agree with X, but . . .*), as well as open responses, in order to gain and/or hold the floor or add information to an idea. *4. Adapting language choices* No standard for kindergarten.

Section 2: Elaboration on Critical Principles for Developing Language and Cognition in Academic Contexts
Part I: Interacting in Meaningful Ways

Texts and Discourse in Context		ELD Proficiency Level Continuum		
		→ Emerging →	→ Expanding →	→ Bridging →
Part I, strands 5–8, corresponding to the CA CCSS for ELA/Literacy 5. SL.K.1–3 6. RL.K.1–7, 9–10; RI.K.1–7, 9–10; SL.K.2–3; L.K.4, 6 7. RL.K.3–4, 6; RI.K.2, 6, 8; L.K.4–6 8. RL.K.4–5; RI.K.4; L.K.4–6 **Purposes for using language include but are not limited to:** Describing, entertaining, informing, interpreting, analyzing, recounting, explaining, persuading, negotiating, justifying, evaluating, and so on. **Informational text types include but are not limited to:** Description (e.g., science log entry), procedure (e.g., how to solve a mathematics problem), recount (e.g., autobiography, science experiment results), information report (e.g., science or history report), explanation (e.g., how or why something happened), exposition (e.g., opinion), response (e.g., literary analysis), and so on. **Literary text types include but are not limited to:** Stories (e.g., fantasy, legends, fables), drama (e.g., readers' theater), poetry, retelling a story, and so on. **Audiences include but are not limited to:** Peers (one to one) Small group (one to a group) Whole group (one to many)	**B. Interpretive**	*5. Listening actively* Demonstrate active listening to read-alouds and oral presentations by asking and answering *yes-no* and *wh-* questions with oral sentence frames and substantial prompting and support. *6. Reading/viewing closely* Describe ideas, phenomena (e.g., parts of a plant), and text elements (e.g., characters) based on understanding of a select set of grade-level texts and viewing of multimedia, with substantial support. *7. Evaluating language choices* Describe the language an author uses to present an idea (e.g., the words and phrases used when a character is introduced), with prompting and substantial support. *8. Analyzing language choices* Distinguish how two different frequently used words (e.g., describing an action with the verb *walk* versus *run*) produce a different effect.	*5. Listening actively* Demonstrate active listening to read-alouds and oral presentations by asking and answering questions with oral sentence frames and occasional prompting and support. *6. Reading/viewing closely* Describe ideas, phenomena (e.g., how butterflies eat), and text elements (e.g., setting, characters) in greater detail based on understanding of a variety of grade-level texts and viewing of multimedia, with moderate support. *7. Evaluating language choices* Describe the language an author uses to present an idea (e.g., the adjectives used to describe a character), with prompting and moderate support. *8. Analyzing language choices* Distinguish how two different words with similar meaning (e.g., describing an action as *walk* versus *march*) produce shades of meaning and a different effect.	*5. Listening actively* Demonstrate active listening to read-alouds and oral presentations by asking and answering detailed questions, with minimal prompting and light support. *6. Reading/viewing closely* Describe ideas, phenomena (e.g., insect metamorphosis), and text elements (e.g., major events, characters, setting) using key details based on understanding of a variety of grade-level texts and viewing of multimedia, with light support. *7. Evaluating language choices* Describe the language an author uses to present or support an idea (e.g., the vocabulary used to describe people and places), with prompting and light support. *8. Analyzing language choices* Distinguish how multiple different words with similar meaning (e.g., *walk, march, strut, prance*) produce shades of meaning and a different effect.

Texts and Discourse in Context		ELD Proficiency Level Continuum		
		→ Emerging →	→ Expanding →	→ Bridging →
Part I, strands 9–12, corresponding to the CA CCSS for ELA/Literacy 9. SL.K.4–6; L.K.1, 6 10. W.K.1-3, 5–8; L.K.1–2, 6 11. W.K.1; SL.K.4, 6; L.K.1–2, 6 12. W.K.5; SL.K.4, 6; L.K.1, 5–6 **Purposes for using language include but are not limited to:** Describing, entertaining, informing, interpreting, analyzing, recounting, explaining, persuading, negotiating, justifying, evaluating, and so on. **Informational text types include but are not limited to:** Description (e.g., science log entry), procedure (e.g., how to solve a mathematics problem), recount (e.g., autobiography, science experiment results), information report (e.g., science or history report), explanation (e.g., how or why something happened), exposition (e.g., opinion), response (e.g., literary analysis), and so on. **Literary text types include but are not limited to:** Stories (e.g., fantasy, legends, fables), drama (e.g., readers' theater), poetry, retelling a story, and so on. **Audience include but are not limited to:** Peers (one to one) Small group (one to a group) Whole group (one to many)	**C. Productive**	**9. Presenting** Plan and deliver very brief oral presentations (e.g., show and tell, describing a picture). **10. Composing/Writing** Draw, dictate, and write to compose very short literary texts (e.g., story) and informational texts (e.g., a description of a dog), using familiar vocabulary collaboratively in shared language activities with an adult (e.g., joint construction of texts), with peers, and sometimes independently. **11. Supporting opinions** Offer opinions and provide good reasons (e.g., *My favorite book is X because X.*) referring to the text or to relevant background knowledge. **12. Selecting language resources** a. Retell texts and recount experiences using a select set of key words. b. Use a select number of general academic and domain-specific words to add detail (e.g., adding the word *spicy* to describe a favorite food, using the word *larva* when explaining insect metamorphosis) while speaking and composing.	**9. Presenting** Plan and deliver brief oral presentations on a variety of topics (e.g., show and tell, author's chair, recounting an experience, describing an animal). **10. Composing/Writing** Draw, dictate, and write to compose short literary texts (e.g., story) and informational texts (e.g., a description of dogs), collaboratively with an adult (e.g., joint construction of texts), with peers, and with increasing independence. **11. Supporting opinions** Offer opinions and provide good reasons and some textual evidence or relevant background knowledge (e.g., paraphrased examples from text or knowledge of content). **12. Selecting language resources** a. Retell texts and recount experiences using complete sentences and key words. b. Use a growing number of general academic and domain-specific words in order to add detail or to create shades of meaning (e.g., using the word *scurry* versus *run*) while speaking and composing.	**9. Presenting** Plan and deliver longer oral presentations on a variety of topics in a variety of content areas (e.g., retelling a story, describing a science experiment). **10. Composing/Writing** Draw, dictate, and write to compose longer literary texts (e.g., story) and informational texts (e.g., an information report on dogs), collaboratively with an adult (e.g., joint construction of texts), with peers, and independently using appropriate text organization. **11. Supporting opinions** Offer opinions and provide good reasons with detailed textual evidence or relevant background knowledge (e.g., specific examples from text or knowledge of content). **12. Selecting language resources** a. Retell texts and recount experiences using increasingly detailed complete sentences and key words. b. Use a wide variety of general academic and domain-specific words, synonyms, antonyms, and non-literal language to create an effect (e.g., using the word *suddenly* to signal a change) or to create shades of meaning (e.g., The cat's fur was *as white as snow*) while speaking and composing.

Section 2: Elaboration on Critical Principles for Developing Language and Cognition in Academic Contexts
Part II: Learning About How English Works

Texts and Discourse in Context		ELD Proficiency Level Continuum		
		→ Emerging →	→ Expanding →	→ Bridging →
Part II, strands 1–2, corresponding to the CA CCSS for ELA/Literacy 1. RL.K.5; RI.K.5; W.K.1–3, 5; SL.K.4 2. RL.K.5; RI.K.5; W.K.1–3, 5; SL.K.4; L.K.1 **Purposes for using language include but are not limited to:** Describing, entertaining, informing, interpreting, analyzing, recounting, explaining, persuading, negotiating, justifying, evaluating, and so on. **Informational text types include but are not limited to:** Description (e.g., science log entry), procedure (e.g., how to solve a mathematics problem), recount (e.g., autobiography, science experiment results), information report (e.g., science or history report), explanation (e.g., how or why something happened), exposition (e.g., opinion), response (e.g., literary analysis), and so on. **Literary text types include but are not limited to:** Stories (e.g., fantasy, legends, fables), drama (e.g., readers' theater), poetry, retelling a story, and so on. **Audiences include but are not limited to:** Peers (one to one) Small group (one to a group) Whole group (one to many)	**A. Structuring Cohesive Texts**	*1. Understanding text structure* Apply understanding of how text types are organized (e.g., how a story is organized by a sequence of events) to comprehending and composing texts in shared language activities guided by the teacher, with peers, and sometimes independently. *2. Understanding cohesion* Apply basic understanding of how ideas, events, or reasons are linked throughout a text using more everyday connecting words or phrases (e.g., *one time, then*) to comprehending texts and composing texts in shared language activities guided by the teacher, with peers, and sometimes independently.	*1. Understanding text structure* Apply understanding of how different text types are organized to express ideas (e.g., how a story is organized sequentially with predictable stages versus how an informative text is organized by topic and details) to comprehending texts and composing texts in shared language activities guided by the teacher, collaboratively with peers, and with increasing independence. *2. Understanding cohesion* Apply understanding of how ideas, events, or reasons are linked throughout a text using a growing number of connecting words or phrases (e.g., *next, after a long time*) to comprehending texts and composing texts in shared language activities guided by the teacher, collaboratively with peers, and with increasing independence.	*1. Understanding text structure* Apply understanding of how different text types are organized predictably (e.g., a narrative text versus an informative text versus an opinion text) to comprehending texts and composing texts in shared language activities guided by the teacher, with peers, and independently. *2. Understanding cohesion* Apply understanding of how ideas, events, or reasons are linked throughout a text using a variety of connecting words or phrases (e.g., *first/second/third, once, at the end*) to comprehending texts and composing texts in shared language activities guided by the teacher, with peers, and independently.

Texts and Discourse in Context		ELD Proficiency Level Continuum		
		→ Emerging →	→ Expanding →	→ Bridging →
Part II, strands 3–5, corresponding to the CA CCSS for ELA/Literacy 3. W.K.5; SL.K.6; L.K.1, 6 4. W.K.5; SL.K.6; L.K.1, 6 5. W.K.5; SL.K.4, 6; L.K.1, 6 **Purposes for using language include but are not limited to:** Describing, entertaining, informing, interpreting, analyzing, recounting, explaining, persuading, negotiating, justifying, evaluating, and so on. **Informational text types include but are not limited to:** Description (e.g., science log entry), procedure (e.g., how to solve a mathematics problem), recount (e.g., autobiography, science experiment results), information report (e.g., science or history report), explanation (e.g., how or why something happened), exposition (e.g., opinion), response (e.g., literary analysis), and so on. **Literary text types include but are not limited to:** Stories (e.g., fantasy, legends, fables), drama (e.g., readers' theater), poetry, retelling a story, and so on. **Audiences include but are not limited to:** Peers (one to one) Small group (one to a group) Whole group (one to many)	**B. Expanding and Enriching Ideas**	*3. Using verbs and verb phrases* a. Use frequently used verbs (e.g., go, eat, run) and verb types (e.g., doing, saying, being/having, thinking/feeling) in shared language activities guided by the teacher and with increasing independence. b. Use simple verb tenses appropriate for the text type and discipline to convey time (e.g., simple past for recounting an experience) in shared language activities guided by the teacher and with increasing independence. *4. Using nouns and noun phrases* Expand noun phrases in simple ways (e.g., adding a familiar adjective to describe a noun) in order to enrich the meaning of sentences and add details about ideas, people, things, and so on, in shared language activities guided by the teacher and sometimes independently. *5. Modifying to add details* Expand sentences with frequently used prepositional phrases (such as *in the house, on the boat*) to provide details (e.g., time, manner, place, cause) about a familiar activity or process in shared language activities guided by the teacher and sometimes independently.	*3. Using verbs and verb phrases* a. Use a growing number of verbs and verb types (e.g., doing, saying, being/having, thinking/feeling) in shared language activities guided by the teacher and independently. b. Use a growing number of verb tenses appropriate for the text type and discipline to convey time (e.g., simple past tense for retelling, simple present for a science description) in shared language activities guided by the teacher and independently. *4. Using nouns and noun phrases* Expand noun phrases in a growing number of ways (e.g., adding a newly learned adjective to a noun) in order to enrich the meaning of sentences and add details about ideas, people, things, and so on, in shared language activities guided by the teacher and with increasing independence. *5. Modifying to add details* Expand sentences with prepositional phrases to provide details (e.g., time, manner, place, cause) about a familiar or new activity or process in shared language activities guided by the teacher and with increasing independence.	*3. Using verbs and verb phrases* a. Use a wide variety of verbs and verb types (e.g., doing, saying, being/having, thinking/feeling) in shared language activities guided by the teacher and independently. b. Use a wide variety of verb tenses appropriate for the text type and discipline to convey time (e.g., simple present for a science description, simple future to predict) in shared language activities guided by the teacher and independently. *4. Using nouns and noun phrases* Expand noun phrases in a wide variety of ways (e.g., adding a variety of adjectives to noun phrases) in order to enrich the meaning of phrases/sentences and add details about ideas, people, things, and so on, in shared language activities guided by the teacher and independently. *5. Modifying to add details* Expand simple and compound sentences with prepositional phrases to provide details (e.g., time, manner, place, cause) in shared language activities guided by the teacher and independently.

Section 2: Elaboration on Critical Principles for Developing Language and Cognition in Academic Contexts
Part II: Learning About How English Works

Texts and Discourse in Context		ELD Proficiency Level Continuum		
		→ Emerging →	→ Expanding →	→ Bridging →
Part II, strands 6–7, corresponding to the CA CCSS for ELA/Literacy 6. W.K.1–3, 5; SL.K.4, 6; L.K.1, 6 7. Not applicable at kindergarten **Purposes for using language include but are not limited to:** Describing, entertaining, informing, interpreting, analyzing, recounting, explaining, persuading, negotiating, justifying, evaluating, and so on. **Informational text types include but are not limited to:** Description (e.g., science log entry), procedure (e.g., how to solve a mathematics problem), recount (e.g., autobiography, science experiment results), information report (e.g., science or history report), explanation (e.g., how or why something happened), exposition (e.g., opinion), response (e.g., literary analysis), and so on. **Literary text types include but not limited to:** Stories (e.g., fantasy, legends, fables), drama (e.g., readers' theater), poetry, retelling a story, and so on. **Audiences include but are not limited to:** Peers (one to one) Small group (one to a group) Whole group (one to many)	**C. Connecting and Condensing Ideas**	*6. Connecting ideas* Combine clauses in a few basic ways to make connections between and join ideas (e.g., creating compound sentences using *and, but, so*) in shared language activities guided by the teacher and sometimes independently. *7. Condensing ideas* No standard for kindergarten.	*6. Connecting ideas* Combine clauses in an increasing variety of ways to make connections between and join ideas, for example, to express cause/effect (e.g., *She jumped because the dog barked*) in shared language activities guided by the teacher and with increasing independence. *7. Condensing ideas* No standard for kindergarten.	*6. Connecting ideas* Combine clauses in a wide variety of ways (e.g., rearranging complete simple sentences to form compound sentences) to make connections between and join ideas (e.g., *The boy was hungry. The boy ate a sandwich.* → *The boy was hungry so he ate a sandwich*) in shared language activities guided by the teacher and independently. *7. Condensing ideas* No standard for kindergarten.

Section 2: Elaboration on Critical Principles for Developing Language and Cognition in Academic Contexts
Part III: Using Foundational Literacy Skills

Foundational literacy skills in an alphabetic writing system ● Print concepts ● Phonological awareness ● Phonics and word recognition ● Fluency	See chapter 6 for information on teaching foundational reading skills to English learners of various profiles based on age, native language, native language writing system, schooling experience, and literacy experience and proficiency. Some considerations are as follows: ● Native language and literacy (e.g., phoneme awareness or print concept skills in native language) should be assessed for potential transference to English language and literacy. ● Similarities between the native language and English should be highlighted (e.g., phonemes or letters that are the same in both languages). ● Differences between the native language and English should be highlighted (e.g., some phonemes in English may not exist in the student's native language; native language syntax may be different from English syntax).

Grade 1

Goal: English learners read, analyze, interpret, and create a variety of literary and informational text types. They develop an understanding of how language is a complex, dynamic, and social resource for making meaning, as well as how content is organized in different text types and across disciplines using text structure, language features, and vocabulary depending on purpose and audience. They are aware that different languages and variations of English exist, and they recognize their home languages and cultures as resources to value in their own right and to draw upon in order to build proficiency in English. English learners contribute actively to class and group discussions, asking questions, responding appropriately, and providing useful feedback. They demonstrate knowledge of content through oral presentations, writing tasks, collaborative conversations, and multimedia. They develop proficiency in shifting language use based on task, purpose, audience, and text type.

Critical Principles for Developing Language and Cognition in Academic Contexts: While advancing along the continuum of English language development levels, English learners at all levels engage in intellectually challenging literacy, disciplinary, and disciplinary literacy tasks. They use language in meaningful and relevant ways appropriate to grade level, content area, topic, purpose, audience, and text type in English language arts, mathematics, science, social studies, and the arts. Specifically, they use language to gain and exchange information and ideas in three communicative modes (collaborative, interpretive, and productive), and they apply knowledge of language to academic tasks via three cross-mode language processes (structuring cohesive texts, expanding and enriching ideas, and connecting and condensing ideas) using various linguistic resources.

Part I: Interacting in Meaningful Ways	Corresponding CA CCSS for ELA/Literacy*
A. Collaborative	
1. Exchanging information and ideas with others through oral collaborative conversations on a range of social and academic topics	• SL.1.1, 6; L.1.1, 6
2. Interacting with others in written English in various communicative forms (print, communicative technology, and multimedia)	• W.1.6; L.1.1, 6
3. Offering and supporting opinions and negotiating with others in communicative exchanges	• SL.1.1, 6; L.1.1, 6
4. Adapting language choices to various contexts (based on task, purpose, audience, and text type)	• Not applicable at grade 1

*The California English Language Development Standards correspond to the California Common Core State Standards for English Language Arts and Literacy in History/Social Science and Technical Subjects (CA CCSS for ELA/Literacy). English learners should have full access to opportunities to learn ELA, mathematics, science, history/social studies, and other content at the same time they are progressing toward full proficiency in English.

Part I: Interacting in Meaningful Ways	Corresponding CA CCSS for ELA/Literacy
B. Interpretive	
5. Listening actively to spoken English in a range of social and academic contexts	• SL.1.1–3
6. Reading closely literary and informational texts and viewing multimedia to determine how meaning is conveyed explicitly and implicitly through language	• RL.1.1–7, 9, 10; RI.1.1–7, 9–10; SL.1.2–3; L.1.4, 6
7. Evaluating how well writers and speakers use language to support ideas and opinions with details or reasons depending on modality, text type, purpose, audience, topic, and content area	• RL.1.3–4, 6; RI.1.2, 6, 8; L.1.4–6
8. Analyzing how writers and speakers use vocabulary and other language resources for specific purposes (to explain, persuade, entertain, etc.) depending on modality, text type, purpose, audience, topic, and content area	• RL.1.4–5; RI.1.4; L.1.4–6
C. Productive	
9. Expressing information and ideas in formal oral presentations on academic topics	• SL.1.4–6; L.1.1, 6
10. Writing literary and informational texts to present, describe, and explain ideas and information, using appropriate technology	• W.1.1–3, 5–8; L.1.1–2, 6
11. Supporting own opinions and evaluating others' opinions in speaking and writing	• W.1.1; SL.1.4, 6; L.1.1–2, 6
12. Selecting and applying varied and precise vocabulary and language structures to effectively convey ideas	• W.1.5; SL.1.4, 6; L.1.1, 5–6
Part II: Learning About How English Works	**Corresponding CA CCSS for ELA/Literacy**
A. Structuring Cohesive Texts	
1. Understanding text structure	• RL.1.5; RI.1.5; W.1.1–3, 5; SL.1.4
2. Understanding cohesion	• RL.1.5; RI.1.5; W.1.1–3, 5; SL.1.4; L.1.1
B. Expanding and Enriching Ideas	
3. Using verbs and verb phrases	• W.1.5; SL.1.6; L.1.1, 6
4. Using nouns and noun phrases	• W.1.5; SL.1.6; L.1.1, 6
5. Modifying to add details	• W.1.5; SL.1.4, 6; L.1.1, 6
C. Connecting and Condensing Ideas	
6. Connecting ideas	• W.1.1–3, 5; SL.1.4, 6; L.1.1, 6
7. Condensing ideas	• W.1.1–3, 5; SL.1.4, 6; L.1.1, 6
Part III: Using Foundational Literacy Skills	• RF.K-1.1–4 (as appropriate)

Note: **Examples** provided in specific standards are offered ***only as illustrative possibilities*** and should not be misinterpreted as the only objectives of instruction or as the only types of language that English learners might or should be able to understand or produce.

Section 2: Elaboration on Critical Principles for Developing Language and Cognition in Academic Contexts
Part I: Interacting in Meaningful Ways

Texts and Discourse in Context		ELD Proficiency Level Continuum		
		→ Emerging →	→ Expanding →	→ Bridging →
Part I, strands 1–4, corresponding to the CA CCSS for ELA/Literacy 1. SL.1.1, 6; L.1.1, 6 2. W.1.6; L.1.1, 6 3. SL.1.1, 6; L.1.1, 6 4. Not applicable at grade 1 **Purposes for using language include but are not limited to:** Describing, entertaining, informing, interpreting, analyzing, recounting, explaining, persuading, negotiating, justifying, evaluating, and so on. **Informational text types include but are not limited to:** Description (e.g., science log entry), procedure (e.g., how to solve a mathematics problem), recount (e.g., autobiography, science experiment results), information report (e.g., science or history report), explanation (e.g., how or why something happened), exposition (e.g., opinion), response (e.g., literary analysis), and so on. **Literary text types include but are not limited to:** Stories (e.g., fantasy, legends, fables), drama (e.g., readers' theater), poetry, retelling a story, and so on. **Audiences include but are not limited to:** Peers (one to one) Small group (one to a group) Whole group (one to many)	**A. Collaborative**	*1. Exchanging information and ideas* Contribute to conversations and express ideas by asking and answering *yes-no* and *wh-* questions and responding using gestures, words, and simple phrases. *2. Interacting via written English* Collaborate with teacher and peers on joint writing projects of short informational and literary texts, using technology where appropriate for publishing, graphics, and the like. *3. Offering opinions* Offer opinions and ideas in conversations using a small set of learned phrases (e.g., *I think X*), as well as open responses in order to gain and/or hold the floor. *4. Adapting language choices* No standard for grade 1.	*1. Exchanging information and ideas* Contribute to class, group, and partner discussions by listening attentively, following turn-taking rules, and asking and answering questions. *2. Interacting via written English* Collaborate with peers on joint writing projects of longer informational and literary texts, using technology where appropriate for publishing, graphics, and the like. *3. Offering opinions* Offer opinions and negotiate with others in conversations using an expanded set of learned phrases (e.g., *I think/don't think X. I agree with X*), as well as open responses in order to gain and/or hold the floor, elaborate on an idea, and so on. *4. Adapting language choices* No standard for grade 1.	*1. Exchanging information and ideas* Contribute to class, group, and partner discussions by listening attentively, following turn-taking rules, and asking and answering questions. *2. Interacting via written English* Collaborate with peers on joint writing projects of longer informational and literary texts, using technology where appropriate for publishing, graphics, and the like. *3. Offering opinions* Offer opinions and negotiate with others in conversations using an expanded set of learned phrases (e.g., *I think/don't think X. I agree with X*), and open responses in order to gain and/or hold the floor, elaborate on an idea, provide different opinions, and so on. *4. Adapting language choices* No standard for grade 1.

Section 2: Elaboration on Critical Principles for Developing Language and Cognition in Academic Contexts
Part I: Interacting in Meaningful Ways

Texts and Discourse in Context		ELD Proficiency Level Continuum		
		→ Emerging →	→ Expanding →	→ Bridging →
Part I, strands 5–8, corresponding to the CA CCSS for ELA/Literacy 5. SL.1.1–3 6. RL.1.1–7, 9, 10; RI.1.1–7, 9–10; SL.1.2–3; L.1.4, 6 7. RL.1.3–4, 6; RI.1.2, 6, 8; L.1.4–6 8. RL.1.4–5; RI.1.4; L.1.4–6 **Purposes for using language include but are not limited to:** Describing, entertaining, informing, interpreting, analyzing, recounting, explaining, persuading, negotiating, justifying, evaluating, and so on. **Informational text types include but are not limited to:** Description (e.g., science log entry), procedure (e.g., how to solve a mathematics problem), recount (e.g., autobiography, science experiment results), information report (e.g., science or history report), explanation (e.g., how or why something happened), exposition (e.g., opinion), response (e.g., literary analysis), and so on. **Literary text types include but are not limited to:** Stories (e.g., fantasy, legends, fables), drama (e.g., readers' theater); poetry, retelling a story, and so on. **Audiences include but are not limited to:** Peers (one to one) Small group (one to a group) Whole group (one to many)	**B. Interpretive**	**5. Listening actively** Demonstrate active listening to read-alouds and oral presentations by asking and answering yes-no and wh- questions with oral sentence frames and substantial prompting and support. **6. Reading/viewing closely** Describe ideas, phenomena (e.g., plant life cycle), and text elements (e.g., characters) based on understanding of a select set of grade-level texts and viewing of multimedia, with substantial support. **7. Evaluating language choices** Describe the language writers or speakers use to present an idea (e.g., the words and phrases used to describe a character), with prompting and substantial support. **8. Analyzing language choices** Distinguish how two different frequently used words (e.g., *large* versus *small*) produce a different effect on the audience.	**5. Listening actively** Demonstrate active listening to read-alouds and oral presentations by asking and answering questions, with oral sentence frames and occasional prompting and support. **6. Reading/viewing closely** Describe ideas, phenomena (e.g., how earthworms eat), and text elements (e.g., setting, main idea) in greater detail based on understanding of a variety of grade-level texts and viewing of multimedia, with moderate support. **7. Evaluating language choices** Describe the language writers or speakers use to present or support an idea (e.g., the adjectives used to describe people and places), with prompting and moderate support. **8. Analyzing language choices** Distinguish how two different words with similar meaning (e.g., *large* versus *enormous*) produce shades of meaning and a different effect on the audience.	**5. Listening actively** Demonstrate active listening to read-alouds and oral presentations by asking and answering detailed questions, with minimal prompting and light support. **6. Reading/viewing closely** Describe ideas, phenomena (e.g., erosion), and text elements (e.g., central message, character traits) using key details based on understanding of a variety of grade-level texts and viewing of multimedia, with light support. **7. Evaluating language choices** Describe the language writers or speakers use to present or support an idea (e.g., the author's choice of vocabulary to portray characters, places, or real people) with prompting and light support. **8. Analyzing language choices** Distinguish how multiple different words with similar meaning (e.g., *big, large, huge, enormous, gigantic*) produce shades of meaning and a different effect on the audience.

Texts and Discourse in Context		ELD Proficiency Level Continuum		
		→ Emerging →	→ Expanding →	→ Bridging →
Part I, strands 9–12, corresponding to the CA CCSS for ELA/Literacy 9. SL.1.4–6; L.1.1, 6 10. W.1.1–3, 5–8; L.1.1–2, 6 11. W.1.1; SL.1.4, 6; L.1.1–2, 6 12. W.1.5; SL.1.4, 6; L.1.1, 5–6 **Purposes for using language include but are not limited to:** Describing, entertaining, informing, interpreting, analyzing, recounting, explaining, persuading, negotiating, justifying, evaluating, and so on. **Informational text types include but are not limited to:** Description (e.g., science log entry), procedure (e.g., how to solve a mathematics problem), recount (e.g., autobiography, science experiment results), information report (e.g., science or history report), explanation (e.g., how or why something happened), exposition (e.g., opinion), response (e.g., literary analysis), and so on. **Literary text types include but are not limited to:** Stories (e.g., fantasy, legends, fables), drama (e.g., readers' theater), poetry, retelling a story, and so on. **Audiences include but are not limited to:** Peers (one to one) Small group (one to a group) Whole group (one to many)	**C. Productive**	*9. Presenting* Plan and deliver very brief oral presentations (e.g., show and tell, describing a picture). *10. Writing* Write very short literary texts (e.g., story) and informational texts (e.g., a description of an insect) using familiar vocabulary collaboratively with an adult (e.g., joint construction of texts), with peers, and sometimes independently. *11. Supporting opinions* Offer opinions and provide good reasons (e.g., *My favorite book is X because X*) referring to the text or to relevant background knowledge. *12. Selecting language resources* a. Retell texts and recount experiences, using key words. b. Use a select number of general academic and domain-specific words to add detail (e.g., adding the word *scrumptious* to describe a favorite food, using the word *thorax* to refer to insect anatomy) while speaking and writing.	*9. Presenting* Plan and deliver brief oral presentations on a variety of topics (e.g., show and tell, author's chair, recounting an experience, describing an animal, and the like). *10. Writing* Write short literary texts (e.g., a story) and informational texts (e.g., an informative text on the life cycle of an insect) collaboratively with an adult (e.g., joint construction of texts), with peers, and with increasing independence. *11. Supporting opinions* Offer opinions and provide good reasons and some textual evidence or relevant background knowledge (e.g., paraphrased examples from text or knowledge of content). *12. Selecting language resources* a. Retell texts and recount experiences, using complete sentences and key words. b. Use a growing number of general academic and domain-specific words in order to add detail, create an effect (e.g., using the word *suddenly* to signal a change), or create shades of meaning (e.g., *prance versus walk*) while speaking and writing.	*9. Presenting* Plan and deliver longer oral presentations on a variety of topics in a variety of content areas (e.g., retelling a story, describing a science experiment). *10. Writing* Write longer literary texts (e.g., a story) and informational texts (e.g., an informative text on the life cycle of insects) collaboratively with an adult (e.g., joint construction), with peers, and independently. *11. Supporting opinions* Offer opinions and provide good reasons with detailed textual evidence or relevant background knowledge (e.g., specific examples from text or knowledge of content). *12. Selecting language resources* a. Retell texts and recount experiences, using increasingly detailed complete sentences and key words. b. Use a wide variety of general academic and domain-specific words, synonyms, antonyms, and non-literal language (e.g., The dog was *as big as a house*) to create an effect, precision, and shades of meaning while speaking and writing.

Texts and Discourse in Context		ELD Proficiency Level Continuum		
		→ Emerging →	→ Expanding →	→ Bridging →
Part II, strands 1–2, corresponding to the CA CCSS for ELA/Literacy 1. RL.1.5; RI.1.5; W.1.1–3, 5; SL.1.4 2. RL.1.5; RI.1.5; W.1.1–3, 5; SL.1.4; L.1.1 **Purposes for using language include but are not limited to:** Describing, entertaining, informing, interpreting, analyzing, recounting, explaining, persuading, negotiating, justifying, evaluating, and so on. **Informational text types include but are not limited to:** Description (e.g., science log entry), procedure (e.g., how to solve a mathematics problem), recount (e.g., autobiography, science experiment results), information report (e.g., science or history report), explanation (e.g., how or why something happened), exposition (e.g., opinion), response (e.g., literary analysis), and so on. **Literary text types include but are not limited to:** Stories (e.g., fantasy, legends, fables), drama (e.g., readers' theater), poetry, retelling a story, and so on. **Audiences include but are not limited to:** Peers (one to one) Small group (one to a group) Whole group (one to many)	**A. Structuring Cohesive Texts**	*1. Understanding text structure* Apply understanding of how text types are organized (e.g., how a story is organized by a sequence of events) to comprehending texts and composing basic texts with substantial support (e.g., using drawings, through joint construction with a peer or teacher) to comprehending texts and writing texts in shared language activities guided by the teacher, with peers, and sometimes independently. *2. Understanding cohesion* Apply basic understanding of how ideas, events, or reasons are linked throughout a text using more everyday connecting words or phrases (e.g., *one day, after, then*) to comprehending texts and writing texts in shared language activities guided by the teacher, with peers, and sometimes independently.	*1. Understanding text structure* Apply understanding of how different text types are organized to express ideas (e.g., how a story is organized sequentially with predictable stages versus how an informative text is organized by topic and details) to comprehending texts and writing texts in shared language activities guided by the teacher and with increasing independence. *2. Understanding cohesion* Apply understanding of how ideas, events, or reasons are linked throughout a text using a growing number of connecting words or phrases (e.g., *a long time ago, suddenly*) to comprehending texts and writing texts in shared language activities guided by the teacher and with increasing independence.	*1. Understanding text structure* Apply understanding of how different text types are organized predictably to express ideas (e.g., how a story is organized versus an informative/ explanatory text versus an opinion text) to comprehending texts and writing texts in shared language activities guided by the teacher and independently. *2. Understanding cohesion* Apply understanding of how ideas, events, or reasons are linked throughout a text using a variety of connecting words or phrases (e.g., *for example, after that, first/ second/third*) to comprehending texts and writing texts in shared language activities guided by the teacher and independently.

Section 2: Elaboration on Critical Principles for Developing Language and Cognition in Academic Contexts
Part II: Learning About How English Works

Texts and Discourse in Context		ELD Proficiency Level Continuum		
		→ Emerging →	→ Expanding →	→ Bridging →
Part II, strands 3–5, corresponding to the CA CCSS for ELA/Literacy 3. W.1.5; SL.1.6; L.1.1, 6 4. W.1.5; SL.1.6; L.1.1, 6 5. W.1.5; SL.1.4, 6; L.1.1, 6 **Purposes for using language include but are not limited to:** Describing, entertaining, informing, interpreting, analyzing, recounting, explaining, persuading, negotiating, justifying, evaluating, and so on. **Informational text types include but are not limited to:** Description (e.g., science log entry), procedure (e.g., how to solve a mathematics problem), recount (e.g., autobiography, science experiment results), information report (e.g., science or history report), explanation (e.g., how or why something happened), exposition (e.g., opinion), response (e.g., literary analysis), and so on. **Literary text types include but are not limited to:** Stories (e.g., fantasy, legends, fables), drama (e.g., readers' theater), poetry, retelling a story, and so on. **Audiences include but are not limited to:** Peers (one to one) Small group (one to a group) Whole group (one to many)	**B. Expanding and Enriching Ideas**	***3. Using verbs and verb phrases*** a. Use frequently used verbs (e.g., go, eat, run) and verb types (e.g., doing, saying, being/having, thinking/feeling) in shared language activities guided by the teacher and sometimes independently. b. Use simple verb tenses appropriate for the text type and discipline to convey time (e.g., simple past for recounting an experience) in shared language activities guided by the teacher and sometimes independently. ***4. Using nouns and noun phrases*** Expand noun phrases in simple ways (e.g., adding a familiar adjective to describe a noun) in order to enrich the meaning of sentences and add details about ideas, people, things, and the like, in shared language activities guided by the teacher and sometimes independently. ***5. Modifying to add details*** Expand sentences with frequently used prepositional phrases (such as *in the house, on the boat*) to provide details (e.g., time, manner, place, cause) about a familiar activity or process in shared language activities guided by the teacher and sometimes independently.	***3. Using verbs and verb phrases*** a. Use a growing number of verbs and verb types (e.g., doing, saying, being/having, thinking/feeling) in shared language activities guided by the teacher and with increasing independence. b. Use a growing number of verb tenses appropriate for the text type and discipline to convey time (e.g., simple past tense for retelling, simple present for a science description) in shared language activities guided by the teacher and with increasing independence. ***4. Using nouns and noun phrases*** Expand noun phrases in a growing number of ways (e.g., adding a newly learned adjective to a noun) to enrich the meaning of sentences and add details about ideas, people, things, and the like, in shared language activities guided by the teacher and with increasing independence. ***5. Modifying to add details*** Expand sentences with prepositional phrases to provide details (e.g., time, manner, place, cause) about a familiar or new activity or process in shared language activities guided by the teacher and with increasing independence.	***3. Using verbs and verb phrases*** a. Use a wide variety of verbs and verb types (e.g., doing, saying, being/having, thinking/feeling) in shared language activities guided by the teacher and independently. b. Use a wide variety of verb tenses appropriate for the text type and discipline to convey time (e.g., simple present for a science description, simple future to predict) in shared language activities guided by the teacher and independently. ***4. Using nouns and noun phrases*** Expand noun phrases in a wide variety of ways (e.g., adding a variety of adjectives to noun phrases) in order to enrich the meaning of phrases/ sentences and add details about ideas, people, things, and the like, in shared language activities guided by the teacher and independently. ***5. Modifying to add details*** Expand simple and compound sentences with prepositional phrases to provide details (e.g., time, manner, place, cause) in shared language activities guided by the teacher and independently.

Section 2: Elaboration on Critical Principles for Developing Language and Cognition in Academic Contexts
Part II: Learning About How English Works

Texts and Discourse in Context	ELD Proficiency Level Continuum		
	→ Emerging →	→ Expanding →	→ Bridging →
Part II, strands 6–7, corresponding to the CA CCSS for ELA/Literacy 6. W.1.1–3, 5; SL.1.4, 6; L.1.1, 6 7. W.1.1–3, 5; SL.1.4, 6; L.1.1, 6 **Purposes for using language include but are not limited to:** Describing, entertaining, informing, interpreting, analyzing, recounting, explaining, persuading, negotiating, justifying, evaluating, and so on. **Informational text types include but are not limited to:** Description (e.g., science log entry), procedure (e.g., how to solve a mathematics problem), recount (e.g., autobiography, science experiment results), information report (e.g., science or history report), explanation (e.g., how or why something happened), exposition (e.g., opinion), response (e.g., literary analysis), and so on. **Literary text types include but are not limited to:** Stories (e.g., fantasy, legends, fables), drama (e.g., readers' theater), poetry, retelling a story, and so on. **Audiences include but are not limited to:** Peers (one to one) Small group (one to a group) Whole group (one to many)	**C. Connecting and Condensing Ideas**		
	6. Connecting ideas Combine clauses in a few basic ways to make connections between and to join ideas (e.g., creating compound sentences using *and, but, so*) in shared language activities guided by the teacher and sometimes independently.	*6. Connecting ideas* Combine clauses in an increasing variety of ways to make connections between and to join ideas, for example, to express cause/effect (e.g., *She jumped because the dog barked*), in shared language activities guided by the teacher and with increasing independence.	*6. Connecting ideas* Combine clauses in a wide variety of ways (e.g., rearranging complete, simple-to-form compound sentences) to make connections between and to join ideas (e.g., *The boy was hungry. The boy ate a sandwich.* → *The boy was hungry so he ate a sandwich*) in shared language activities guided by the teacher and independently.
	7. Condensing ideas Condense clauses in simple ways (e.g., changing: *I like blue. I like red. I like purple* → *I like blue, red, and purple*) to create precise and detailed sentences in shared language activities guided by the teacher and sometimes independently.	*7. Condensing ideas* Condense clauses in a growing number of ways (e.g., through embedded clauses as in, *She's a doctor. She saved the animals.* → *She's the doctor who saved the animals*) to create precise and detailed sentences in shared language activities guided by the teacher and with increasing independence.	*7. Condensing ideas* Condense clauses in a variety of ways (e.g., through embedded clauses and other condensing, for example, through embedded clauses as in *She's a doctor. She's amazing. She saved the animals.* → *She's the amazing doctor who saved the animals*) to create precise and detailed sentences in shared language activities guided by the teacher and independently.

Section 2: Elaboration on Critical Principles for Developing Language and Cognition in Academic Contexts
Part III: Using Foundational Literacy Skills

Foundational literacy skills in an alphabetic writing system • Print concepts • Phonological awareness • Phonics and word recognition • Fluency	See chapter 6 for information on teaching foundational reading skills to English learners of various profiles based on age, native language, native language writing system, schooling experience, and literacy experience and proficiency. Some considerations are as follows: • Native language and literacy (e.g., phoneme awareness or print concept skills in native language) should be assessed for potential transference to English language and literacy. • Similarities between the native language and English should be highlighted (e.g., phonemes or letters that are the same in both languages). • Differences between the native language and English should be highlighted (e.g., some phonemes in English may not exist in the student's native language; native language syntax may be different from English syntax).

Section 1: Overview

Goal: English learners read, analyze, interpret, and create a variety of literary and informational text types. They develop an understanding of how language is a complex, dynamic, and social resource for making meaning, as well as how content is organized in different text types and across disciplines using text structure, language features, and vocabulary depending on purpose and audience. They are aware that different languages and variations of English exist, and they recognize their home languages and cultures as resources to value in their own right and to draw upon in order to build proficiency in English. English learners contribute actively to class and group discussions, asking questions, responding appropriately, and providing useful feedback. They demonstrate knowledge of content through oral presentations, writing tasks, collaborative conversations, and multimedia. They develop proficiency in shifting language use based on task, purpose, audience, and text type.

Critical Principles for Developing Language and Cognition in Academic Contexts: While advancing along the continuum of English language development levels, English learners at all levels engage in intellectually challenging literacy, disciplinary, and disciplinary literacy tasks. They use language in meaningful and relevant ways appropriate to grade level, content area, topic, purpose, audience, and text type in English language arts, mathematics, science, social studies, and the arts. Specifically, they use language to gain and exchange information and ideas in three communicative modes (collaborative, interpretive, and productive), and they apply knowledge of language to academic tasks via three cross-mode language processes (structuring cohesive texts, expanding and enriching ideas, and connecting and condensing ideas) using various linguistic resources.

Part I: Interacting in Meaningful Ways	Corresponding CA CCSS for ELA/Literacy*
A. Collaborative	
1. Exchanging information and ideas with others through oral collaborative conversations on a range of social and academic topics	• SL.2.1, 6; L.2.1, 3, 6
2. Interacting with others in written English in various communicative forms (print, communicative technology, and multimedia)	• W.2.6; L.2.1, 3, 6
3. Offering and supporting opinions and negotiating with others in communicative exchanges	• SL.2.1, 6; L.2.1, 3, 6
4. Adapting language choices to various contexts (based on task, purpose, audience, and text type)	• W.2.4–5; SL.2.1, 6; L.2.1, 3, 6

*The California English Language Development Standards correspond to the California Common Core State Standards for English Language Arts and Literacy in History/Social Science and Technical Subjects (CA CCSS for ELA/Literacy). English learners should have full access to opportunities to learn ELA, mathematics, science, history/social studies, and other content at the same time they are progressing toward full proficiency in English.

Part I: Interacting in Meaningful Ways	Corresponding CA CCSS for ELA/Literacy
B. Interpretive	
5. Listening actively to spoken English in a range of social and academic contexts	• SL.2.1–3; L.2.3
6. Reading closely literary and informational texts and viewing multimedia to determine how meaning is conveyed explicitly and implicitly through language	• RL.2.1–7, 9–10; RI.2.1–7, 9–10; SL.2.2–3; L.2.3, 4, 6
7. Evaluating how well writers and speakers use language to support ideas and opinions with details or reasons depending on modality, text type, purpose, audience, topic, and content area	• RL.2.3–4, 6; RI.2.2, 6, 8; SL.2.3; L.2.3–6
8. Analyzing how writers and speakers use vocabulary and other language resources for specific purposes (to explain, persuade, entertain, etc.) depending on modality, text type, purpose, audience, topic, and content area	• RL.2.4–5; RI.2.4–5; SL.2.3; L.2.3–6
C. Productive	
9. Expressing information and ideas in formal oral presentations on academic topics	• SL.2.4–6; L.2.1, 3, 6
10. Writing literary and informational texts to present, describe, and explain ideas and information, using appropriate technology	• W.2.1–8, 10; L.2.1–3, 6
11. Supporting own opinions and evaluating others' opinions in speaking and writing	• W.2.1, 4, 10; SL.2.4, 6; L.2.1–3, 6
12. Selecting and applying varied and precise vocabulary and language structures to effectively convey ideas	• W.2.4–5; SL.2.4, 6; L.2.1, 3, 5–6
Part II: Learning About How English Works	**Corresponding CA CCSS for ELA/Literacy**
A. Structuring Cohesive Texts	
1. Understanding text structure	• RL.2.5; RI.2.5; W.2.1–5; SL.2.4
2. Understanding cohesion	• RL.2.5; RI.2.5; W.2.1–4; SL.2.4; L.2.1, 3
B. Expanding and Enriching Ideas	
3. Using verbs and verb phrases	• W.2.5; SL.2.6; L.2.1, 3, 6
4. Using nouns and noun phrases	• W.2.5; SL.2.6; L.2.1, 3, 6
5. Modifying to add details	• W.2.5; SL.2.4, 6; L.2.1, 3, 6
C. Connecting and Condensing Ideas	
6. Connecting ideas	• W.2.1–3, 5; SL.2.4, 6; L.2.1, 3, 6
7. Condensing ideas	• W.2.1–3, 5; SL.2.4, 6; L.2.1, 3, 6
Part III: Using Foundational Literacy Skills	• RF.K–1.1–4; RF.2.3–4 (as appropriate)

Note: **Examples** provided in specific standards are offered *only as illustrative possibilities* and should not be misinterpreted as the only objectives of instruction or as the only types of language that English learners might or should be able to understand or produce.

Section 2: Elaboration on Critical Principles for Developing Language and Cognition in Academic Contexts
Part I: Interacting in Meaningful Ways

Texts and Discourse in Context		ELD Proficiency Level Continuum		
		→ Emerging →	→ Expanding →	→ Bridging →
Part I, strands 1–4, corresponding to the CA CCSS for ELA/Literacy 1. SL.2.1, 6; L.2.1, 3, 6 2. W.2.6; L.2.1, 3, 6 3. SL.2.1, 6; L.2.1, 3, 6 4. W.2.4–5; SL.2.1, 6; L.2.1, 3, 6 **Purposes for using language include but are not limited to:** Describing, entertaining, informing, interpreting, analyzing, recounting, explaining, persuading, negotiating, justifying, evaluating, and so on. **Informational text types include but are not limited to:** Description (e.g., science log entry), procedure (e.g., how to solve a mathematics problem), recount (e.g., autobiography, science experiment results), information report (e.g., science or history report), explanation (e.g., how or why something happened), exposition (e.g., opinion), response (e.g., literary analysis), and so on. **Literary text types include but are not limited to:** Stories (e.g., fantasy, legends, fables), drama (e.g., readers' theater), poetry, retelling a story, and so on. **Audiences include but are not limited to:** Peers (one to one) Small group (one to a group) Whole group (one to many)	**A. Collaborative**	*1. Exchanging information and ideas* Contribute to conversations and express ideas by asking and answering *yes-no* and *wh-* questions and responding using gestures, words, and learned phrases. *2. Interacting via written English* Collaborate with peers on joint writing projects of short informational and literary texts, using technology where appropriate for publishing, graphics, and the like. *3. Offering opinions* Offer opinions and negotiate with others in conversations using learned phrases (e.g., *I think X.*), as well as open responses, in order to gain and/or hold the floor. *4. Adapting language choices* Recognize that language choices (e.g., vocabulary) vary according to social setting (e.g., playground versus classroom), with substantial support from peers or adults.	*1. Exchanging information and ideas* Contribute to class, group, and partner discussions, including sustained dialogue, by listening attentively, following turn-taking rules, asking relevant questions, affirming others, and adding relevant information. *2. Interacting via written English* Collaborate with peers on joint writing projects of longer informational and literary texts, using technology where appropriate for publishing, graphics, and the like. *3. Offering opinions* Offer opinions and negotiate with others in conversations using an expanded set of learned phrases (e.g., *I agree with X, but X.*), as well as open responses, in order to gain and/or hold the floor, provide counterarguments, and the like. *4. Adapting language choices* Adjust language choices (e.g., vocabulary, use of dialogue, and so on) according to purpose (e.g., persuading, entertaining), task, and audience (e.g., peers versus adults), with moderate support from peers or adults.	*1. Exchanging information and ideas* Contribute to class, group, and partner discussions, including sustained dialogue, by listening attentively, following turn-taking rules, asking relevant questions, affirming others, adding pertinent information, building on responses, and providing useful feedback. *2. Interacting via written English* Collaborate with peers on joint writing projects of a variety of longer informational and literary texts, using technology where appropriate for publishing, graphics, and the like. *3. Offering opinions* Offer opinions and negotiate with others in conversations using a variety of learned phrases (e.g., *That's a good idea, but X*), as well as open responses, in order to gain and/or hold the floor, provide counterarguments, elaborate on an idea, and the like. *4. Adapting language choices* Adjust language choices according to purpose (e.g., persuading, entertaining), task, and audience (e.g., peer-to-peer versus peer-to-teacher), with light support from peers or adults.

Section 2: Elaboration on Critical Principles for Developing Language and Cognition in Academic Contexts
Part I: Interacting in Meaningful Ways

Texts and Discourse in Context		ELD Proficiency Level Continuum		
		→ Emerging →	→ Expanding →	→ Bridging →
Part I, strands 5–8, corresponding to the CA CCSS for ELA/Literacy 5. SL.2.1–3; L.2.3 6. RL.2.1–7, 9–10; RI.2.1–7, 9–10; SL.2.2–3; L.2.3, 4, 6 7. RL.2.3–4, 6; RI.2.2, 6, 8; SL.2.3; L.2.3–6 8. RL.2.4–5; RI.2.4–5; SL.2.3; L.2.3–6 **Purposes for using language include but are not limited to:** Describing, entertaining, informing, interpreting, analyzing, recounting, explaining, persuading, negotiating, justifying, evaluating, and so on. **Informational text types include but are not limited to:** Description (e.g., science log entry), procedure (e.g., how to solve a mathematics problem), recount (e.g., autobiography, science experiment results), information report (e.g., science or history report), explanation (e.g., how or why something happened), exposition (e.g., opinion), response (e.g., literary analysis), and so on. **Literary text types include but are not limited to:** Stories (e.g., fantasy, legends, fables), drama (e.g., readers' theater); poetry; retelling a story, and so on. **Audiences include but are not limited to:** Peers (one to one) Small group (one to a group) Whole group (one to many)	**B. Interpretive**	**5. Listening actively** Demonstrate active listening to read-alouds and oral presentations by asking and answering basic questions, with oral sentence frames and substantial prompting and support. **6. Reading/viewing closely** Describe ideas, phenomena (e.g., plant life cycle), and text elements (e.g., main idea, characters, events) based on understanding of a select set of grade-level texts and viewing of multimedia, with substantial support. **7. Evaluating language choices** Describe the language writers or speakers use to present an idea (e.g., the words and phrases used to describe a character), with prompting and substantial support. **8. Analyzing language choices** Distinguish how two different frequently used words (e.g., describing a character as *happy* versus *angry*) produce a different effect on the audience.	**5. Listening actively** Demonstrate active listening to read-alouds and oral presentations by asking and answering detailed questions, with oral sentence frames and occasional prompting and support. **6. Reading/viewing closely** Describe ideas, phenomena (e.g., how earthworms eat), and text elements (e.g., setting, events) in greater detail based on understanding of a variety of grade-level texts and viewing of multimedia, with moderate support. **7. Evaluating language choices** Describe the language writers or speakers use to present or support an idea (e.g., the author's choice of vocabulary or phrasing to portray characters, places, or real people), with prompting and moderate support. **8. Analyzing language choices** Distinguish how two different words with similar meaning (e.g., describing a character as *happy* versus *ecstatic*) produce shades of meaning and different effects on the audience.	**5. Listening actively** Demonstrate active listening to read-alouds and oral presentations by asking and answering detailed questions, with minimal prompting and light support. **6. Reading/viewing closely** Describe ideas, phenomena (e.g., erosion), and text elements (e.g., central message, character traits) using key details based on understanding of a variety of grade-level texts and viewing of multimedia, with light support. **7. Evaluating language choices** Describe how well writers or speakers use specific language resources to support an opinion or present an idea (e.g., whether the vocabulary used to present evidence is strong enough), with light support. **8. Analyzing language choices** Distinguish how multiple different words with similar meaning (e.g., *pleased versus happy versus ecstatic, heard* or *knew* versus *believed*) produce shades of meaning and different effects on the audience.

Section 2: Elaboration on Critical Principles for Developing Language and Cognition in Academic Contexts
Part I: Interacting in Meaningful Ways

Texts and Discourse in Context		ELD Proficiency Level Continuum		
		→ Emerging →	→ Expanding →	→ Bridging →
Part I, strands 9–12, corresponding to the CA CCSS for ELA/Literacy 9. SL.2.4–6; L.2.1, 3, 6 10. W.2.1-8, 10; L.2.1-3, 6 11. W.2.1, 4, 10; SL.2.4, 6; L.2.1-3, 6 12. W.2.4-5; SL.2.4, 6; L.2.1, 3, 5-6 **Purposes for using language include but are not limited to:** Describing, entertaining, informing, interpreting, analyzing, recounting, explaining, persuading, negotiating, justifying, evaluating, and so on. **Informational text types include but are not limited to:** Description (e.g., science log entry), procedure (e.g., how to solve a mathematics problem), recount (e.g., autobiography, science experiment results), information report (e.g., science or history report), explanation (e.g., how or why something happened), exposition (e.g., opinion), response (e.g., literary analysis), and so on. **Literary text types include but are not limited to:** Stories (e.g., fantasy, legends, fables), drama (e.g., readers' theater), poetry, retelling a story, and so on. **Audiences include but are not limited to:** Peers (one to one) Small group (one to a group) Whole group (one to many)	**C. Productive**	*9. Presenting* Plan and deliver very brief oral presentations (e.g., recounting an experience, retelling a story, describing a picture). *10. Writing* Write very short literary texts (e.g., story) and informational texts (e.g., a description of a volcano) using familiar vocabulary collaboratively with an adult (e.g., joint construction of texts), with peers, and sometimes independently. *11. Supporting opinions* Support opinions by providing good reasons and some textual evidence or relevant background knowledge (e.g., referring to textual evidence or knowledge of content). *12. Selecting language resources* a. Retell texts and recount experiences by using key words. b. Use a select number of general academic and domain-specific words to add detail (e.g., adding the word *generous* to describe a character, using the word *lava* to explain volcanic eruptions) while speaking and writing.	*9. Presenting* Plan and deliver brief oral presentations on a variety of topics (e.g., retelling a story, describing an animal). *10. Writing* Write short literary texts (e.g., a story) and informational texts (e.g., an explanatory text explaining how a volcano erupts) collaboratively with an adult (e.g., joint construction of texts), with peers, and with increasing independence. *11. Supporting opinions* Support opinions by providing good reasons and increasingly detailed textual evidence (e.g., providing examples from the text) or relevant background knowledge about the content. *12. Selecting language resources* a. Retell texts and recount experiences using complete sentences and key words. b. Use a growing number of general academic and domain-specific words in order to add detail, create an effect (e.g., using the word *suddenly* to signal a change), or create shades of meaning (e.g., *scurry* versus *dash*) while speaking and writing.	*9. Presenting* Plan and deliver longer oral presentations on a variety of topics and content areas (e.g., retelling a story, recounting a science experiment, describing how to solve a mathematics problem). *10. Writing* Write longer literary texts (e.g., a story) and informational texts (e.g., an explanatory text explaining how a volcano erupts) collaboratively with an adult (e.g., joint construction), with peers and independently. *11. Supporting opinions* Support opinions or persuade others by providing good reasons and detailed textual evidence (e.g., specific events or graphics from text) or relevant background knowledge about the content. *12. Selecting language resources* a. Retell texts and recount experiences using increasingly detailed complete sentences and key words. b. Use a wide variety of general academic and domain-specific words, synonyms, antonyms, and non-literal language (e.g., He was *as quick as a cricket*) to create an effect, precision, and shades of meaning while speaking and writing.

Texts and Discourse in Context		ELD Proficiency Level Continuum		
		→ Emerging →	→ Expanding →	→ Bridging →
Part II, strands 1–2, corresponding to the CA CCSS for ELA/Literacy 1. RL.2.5; RI.2.5; W.2.1–5; SL.2.4 2. RL.2.5; RI.2.5; W.2.1–4; SL.2.4; L.2.1, 3 **Purposes for using language include but are not limited to:** Describing, entertaining, informing, interpreting, analyzing, recounting, explaining, persuading, negotiating, justifying, evaluating, and so on. **Informational text types include but are not limited to:** Description (e.g., science log entry), procedure (e.g., how to solve a mathematics problem), recount (e.g., autobiography, science experiment results), information report (e.g., science or history report), explanation (e.g., how or why something happened), exposition (e.g., opinion), response (e.g., literary analysis), and so on. **Literary text types include but are not limited to:** Stories (e.g., fantasy, legends, fables), drama (e.g., readers' theater), poetry, retelling a story, and so on. **Audiences include but are not limited to:** Peers (one to one) Small group (one to a group) Whole group (one to many)	**A. Structuring Cohesive Texts**	*1. Understanding text structure* Apply understanding of how different text types are organized to express ideas (e.g., how a story is organized sequentially) to comprehending and composing texts in shared language activities guided by the teacher, with peers, and sometimes independently. *2. Understanding cohesion* Apply basic understanding of how ideas, events, or reasons are linked throughout a text using more everyday connecting words or phrases (e.g., *today, then*) to comprehending and composing texts in shared language activities guided by the teacher, with peers, and sometimes independently.	*1. Understanding text structure* Apply understanding of how different text types are organized to express ideas (e.g., how a story is organized sequentially with predictable stages versus how an information report is organized by topic and details) to comprehending texts and composing texts with increasing independence *2. Understanding cohesion* Apply understanding of how ideas, events, or reasons are linked throughout a text using a growing number of connecting words or phrases (e.g., *after a long time, first/next*) to comprehending texts and writing texts with increasing independence.	*1. Understanding text structure* Apply understanding of how different text types are organized predictably to express ideas (e.g., a narrative versus an informative/explanatory text versus an opinion text) to comprehending and writing texts independently. *2. Understanding cohesion* Apply understanding of how ideas, events, or reasons are linked throughout a text using a variety of connecting words or phrases (e.g., *for example, after that, suddenly*) to comprehending and writing texts independently.

Section 2: Elaboration on Critical Principles for Developing Language and Cognition in Academic Contexts
Part II: Learning About How English Works

Texts and Discourse in Context		ELD Proficiency Level Continuum		
		→ Emerging →	→ Expanding →	→ Bridging →
Part II, strands 3–5, corresponding to the CA CCSS for ELA/Literacy 3. W.2.5; SL.2.6; L.2.1, 3, 6 4. W.2.5; SL.2.6; L.2.1, 3, 6 5. W.2.5; SL.2.4, 6; L.2.1, 3, 6 **Purposes for using language include but are not limited to:** Describing, entertaining, informing, interpreting, analyzing, recounting, explaining, persuading, negotiating, justifying, evaluating, and so on. **Informational text types include but are not limited to:** Description (e.g., science log entry), procedures (e.g., how to solve a mathematics problem), recount (e.g., autobiography, science experiment results), information report (e.g., science or history report), explanation (e.g., how or why something happened), exposition (e.g., opinion), response (e.g., literary analysis), and so on. **Literary text types include but are not limited to:** Stories (e.g., fantasy, legends, fables), drama (e.g., readers' theater); poetry, retelling a story, and so on. **Audiences include but are not limited to:** Peers (one to one) Small group (one to a group) Whole group (one to many)	**B. Expanding and Enriching Ideas**	*3. Using verbs and verb phrases* a. Use frequently used verbs (e.g., walk, run) and verb types (e.g., doing, saying, being/having, thinking/feeling) in shared language activities guided by the teacher and sometimes independently. b. Use simple verb tenses appropriate to the text type and discipline to convey time (e.g., simple past tense for recounting an experience) in shared language activities guided by the teacher and sometimes independently. *4. Using nouns and noun phrases* Expand noun phrases in simple ways (e.g., adding a familiar adjective to describe a noun) in order to enrich the meaning of sentences and to add details about ideas, people, things, and the like, in shared language activities guided by the teacher and sometimes independently. *5. Modifying to add details* Expand sentences with frequently used adverbials (e.g., prepositional phrases, such as *at school, with my friend*) to provide details (e.g., time, manner, place, cause) about a familiar activity or process in shared language activities guided by the teacher and sometimes independently.	*3. Using verbs and verb phrases* a. Use a growing number of verb types (e.g., doing, saying, being/having, thinking/feeling) with increasing independence. b. Use a growing number of verb tenses appropriate to the text type and discipline to convey time (e.g., simple past tense for retelling, simple present for a science description) with increasing independence. *4. Using nouns and noun phrases* Expand noun phrases in a growing number of ways (e.g., adding a newly learned adjective to a noun) in order to enrich the meaning of sentences and to add details about ideas, people, things, and the like, with increasing independence. *5. Modifying to add details* Expand sentences with a growing number of adverbials (e.g., adverbs, prepositional phrases) to provide details (e.g., time, manner, place, cause) about a familiar or new activity or process with increasing independence.	*3. Using verbs and verb phrases* a. Use a variety of verb types (e.g., doing, saying, being/having, thinking/feeling) independently. b. Use a wide variety of verb tenses appropriate to the text type and discipline to convey time (e.g., simple present tense for a science description, simple future to predict) independently. *4. Using nouns and noun phrases* Expand noun phrases in a variety of ways (e.g., adding comparative/superlative adjectives to nouns) in order to enrich the meaning of phrases/sentences and to add details about ideas, people, things, and the like, independently. *5. Modifying to add details* Expand sentences with a variety of adverbials (e.g., adverbs, adverb phrases, prepositional phrases) to provide details (e.g., time, manner, place, cause) independently.

Texts and Discourse in Context		ELD Proficiency Level Continuum		
		→ Emerging →	→ Expanding →	→ Bridging →
Part II, strands 6–7, corresponding to the CA CCSS for ELA/Literacy 6. W.2.1–3, 5; SL.2.4, 6; L.2.1, 3, 6 7. W.2.1–3, 5; SL.2.4, 6; L.2.1, 3, 6 **Purposes for using language include but are not limited to:** Describing, entertaining, informing, interpreting, analyzing, recounting, explaining, persuading, negotiating, justifying, evaluating, and so on. **Informational text types include but are not limited to:** Description (e.g., science log entry), procedure (e.g., how to solve a mathematics problem), recount (e.g., autobiography, science experiment results), information report (e.g., science or history report), explanation (e.g., how or why something happened), exposition (e.g., opinion), response (e.g., literary analysis), and so on. **Literary text types include but are not limited to:** Stories (e.g., fantasy, legends, fables), drama (e.g., readers' theater); poetry, retelling a story, and so on. **Audiences include but are not limited to:** Peers (one to one) Small group (one to a group) Whole group (one to many)	**C. Connecting and Condensing Ideas**	*6. Connecting ideas* Combine clauses in a few basic ways to make connections between and to join ideas (e.g., creating compound sentences using *and, but, so*) in shared language activities guided by the teacher and sometimes independently. *7. Condensing ideas* Condense clauses in simple ways (e.g., changing: *It's green. It's red.* → *It's green and red*) to create precise and detailed sentences in shared language activities guided by the teacher and sometimes independently.	*6. Connecting ideas* Combine clauses in an increasing variety of ways to make connections between and to join ideas, for example, to express cause/effect (e.g., *She jumped because the dog barked*) with increasing independence. *7. Condensing ideas* Condense clauses in a growing number of ways (e.g., through embedded clauses as in, *It's a plant. It's found in the rain forest.* → *It's a green and red plant that's found in the rain forest*) to create precise and detailed sentences with increasing independence.	*6. Connecting ideas* Combine clauses in a wide variety of ways (e.g., rearranging complete simple to form compound sentences) to make connections between and to join ideas (e.g., *The boy was hungry. The boy ate a sandwich.* → *The boy was hungry so he ate a sandwich*) independently. *7. Condensing ideas* Condense clauses in a variety of ways (e.g., through embedded clauses and other condensing as in, *It's a plant. It's green and red. It's found in the tropical rain forest.* → *It's a green and red plant that's found in the tropical rain forest*) to create precise and detailed sentences independently.

Section 2: Elaboration on Critical Principles for Developing Language and Cognition in Academic Contexts
Part III: Using Foundational Literacy Skills

Foundational literacy skills in an alphabetic writing system • Print concepts • Phonological awareness • Phonics and word recognition • Fluency	See chapter 6 for information on teaching foundational reading skills to English learners of various profiles based on age, native language, native language writing system, schooling experience, and literacy experience and proficiency. Some considerations are as follows: • Native language and literacy (e.g., phoneme awareness or print concept skills in native language) should be assessed for potential transference to English language and literacy. • Similarities between the native language and English should be highlighted (e.g., phonemes or letters that are the same in both languages). • Differences between the native language and English should be highlighted (e.g., some phonemes in English may not exist in the student's native language; native language syntax may be different from English syntax).

Section 1: Overview

Goal: English learners read, analyze, interpret, and create a variety of literary and informational text types. They develop an understanding of how language is a complex, dynamic, and social resource for making meaning, as well as how content is organized in different text types and across disciplines using text structure, language features, and vocabulary depending on purpose and audience. They are aware that different languages and variations of English exist, and they recognize their home languages and cultures as resources to value in their own right and also to draw upon in order to build proficiency in English. English learners contribute actively to class and group discussions, asking questions, responding appropriately, and providing useful feedback. They demonstrate knowledge of content through oral presentations, writing tasks, collaborative conversations, and multimedia. They develop proficiency in shifting language use based on task, purpose, audience, and text type.

Critical Principles for Developing Language and Cognition in Academic Contexts: While advancing along the continuum of English language development levels, English learners at all levels engage in intellectually challenging literacy, disciplinary, and disciplinary literacy tasks. They use language in meaningful and relevant ways appropriate to grade level, content area, topic, purpose, audience, and text type in English language arts, mathematics, science, social studies, and the arts. Specifically, they use language to gain and exchange information and ideas in three communicative modes (collaborative, interpretive, and productive), and they apply knowledge of language to academic tasks via three cross-mode language processes (structuring cohesive texts, expanding and enriching ideas, and connecting and condensing ideas) using various linguistic resources.

Part I: Interacting in Meaningful Ways	Corresponding CA CCSS for ELA/Literacy*
A. Collaborative	
1. Exchanging information and ideas with others through oral collaborative discussions on a range of social and academic topics	• SL.3.1, 6; L.3.1, 3, 6
2. Interacting with others in written English in various communicative forms (print, communicative technology, and multimedia)	• W.3.6; L.3.1, 3, 6
3. Offering and supporting opinions and negotiating with others in communicative exchanges	• SL.3.1, 6; L.3.1, 3, 6
4. Adapting language choices to various contexts (based on task, purpose, audience, and text type)	• W.3.4–5; SL.3.1, 6; L.3.1, 3, 6

---

*The California English Language Development Standards correspond to the California Common Core State Standards for English Language Arts and Literacy in History/Social Science and Technical Subjects (CA CCSS for ELA/Literacy). English learners should have full access to opportunities to learn ELA, mathematics, science, history/social studies, and other content at the same time they are progressing toward full proficiency in English.

Part I: Interacting in Meaningful Ways	Corresponding CA CCSS for ELA/Literacy
B. Interpretive	
5. Listening actively to spoken English in a range of social and academic contexts	• SL.3.1–3; L.3.3
6. Reading closely literary and informational texts and viewing multimedia to determine how meaning is conveyed explicitly and implicitly through language	• RL.3.1–7,9–10; RI.3.1–7,9–10; SL.3.2–3; L.3.3, 4, 6
7. Evaluating how well writers and speakers use language to support ideas and opinions with details or reasons depending on modality, text type, purpose, audience, topic, and content area	• RL.3.3–4, 6; RI.3.2, 6, 8; SL.3.3; L.3.3–6
8. Analyzing how writers and speakers use vocabulary and other language resources for specific purposes (to explain, persuade, entertain, etc.) depending on modality, text type, purpose, audience, topic, and content area	• RL.3.4–5; RI.3.4–5; SL.3.3; L.3.3–6
C. Productive	
9. Expressing information and ideas in formal oral presentations on academic topics	• SL.3.4–6; L.3.1, 3, 6
10. Writing literary and informational texts to present, describe, and explain ideas and information, using appropriate technology	• W.3.1–8, 10; L.3.1–3, 6
11. Supporting own opinions and evaluating others' opinions in speaking and writing	• W.3.1, 4, 10; SL.3.4, 6; L.3.1–3, 6
12. Selecting and applying varied and precise vocabulary and language structures to effectively convey ideas	• W.3.4–5; SL.3.4, 6; L.3.1, 3, 5–6

Part II: Learning About How English Works	Corresponding CA CCSS for ELA/Literacy
A. Structuring Cohesive Texts	
1. Understanding text structure	• RL.3.5; RI.3.5; W.3.1–5; SL.3.4
2. Understanding cohesion	• RL.3.5; RI.3.5; W.3.1–4; SL.3.4; L.3.1, 3
B. Expanding and Enriching Ideas	
3. Using verbs and verb phrases	• W.3.5; SL.3.6; L.3.1, 3, 6
4. Using nouns and noun phrases	• W.3.5; SL.3.6; L.3.1, 3, 6
5. Modifying to add details	• W.3.5; SL.3.4, 6; L.3.1, 3, 6
C. Connecting and Condensing Ideas	
6. Connecting ideas	• W.3.1–3, 5; SL.3.4, 6; L.3.1, 3, 6
7. Condensing ideas	• W.3.1–3, 5; SL.3.4, 6; L.3.1, 3, 6
Part III: Using Foundational Literacy Skills	• RF.K–3.1–4 (as appropriate)

Note: **Examples** provided in specific standards are offered *only as illustrative possibilities* and should not be misinterpreted as the only objectives of instruction or as the only types of language that English learners might or should be able to understand or produce.

Texts and Discourse in Context		ELD Proficiency Level Continuum		
		→ Emerging →	→ Expanding →	→ Bridging →
Part I, strands 1–4, corresponding to the CA CCSS for ELA/Literacy 1. SL.3.1,6; L.3.1, 3, 6 2. W.3.6; L.3.1, 3, 6 3. SL.3.1,6; L.3.1, 3, 6 4. W.3.4–5; SL.3.1, 6; L.3.1, 3, 6 **Purposes for using language include but are not limited to:** Describing, entertaining, informing, interpreting, analyzing, recounting, explaining, persuading, negotiating, justifying, evaluating, and so on. **Informational text types include but are not limited to:** Description (e.g., science log entry), procedure (e.g., how to solve a mathematics problem), recount (e.g., autobiography, science experiment results), information report (e.g., science or history report), explanation (e.g., how or why something happened), exposition (e.g., opinion), response (e.g., literary analysis), and so on. **Literary text types include but are not limited to:** Stories (e.g., fantasy, legends, fables), drama (e.g., readers' theater), poetry, retelling a story, and so on. **Audiences include but are not limited to:** Peers (one to one) Small group (one to a group) Whole group (one to many)	A. Collaborative	*1. Exchanging information and ideas* Contribute to conversations and express ideas by asking and answering *yes-no* and *wh-* questions and responding using short phrases. *2. Interacting via written English* Collaborate with peers on joint writing projects of short informational and literary texts, using technology where appropriate for publishing, graphics, and the like. *3. Offering opinions* Offer opinions and negotiate with others in conversations using basic learned phrases (e.g., *I think . . .*), as well as open responses in order to gain and/or hold the floor. *4. Adapting language choices* Recognize that language choices (e.g., vocabulary) vary according to social setting (e.g., playground versus classroom), with substantial support from peers or adults.	*1. Exchanging information and ideas* Contribute to class, group, and partner discussions, including sustained dialogue, by following turn-taking rules, asking relevant questions, affirming others, and adding relevant information. *2. Interacting via written English* Collaborate with peers on joint writing projects of longer informational and literary texts, using technology where appropriate for publishing, graphics, and the like. *3. Offering opinions* Offer opinions and negotiate with others in conversations using an expanded set of learned phrases (e.g., *I agree with X, and . . .*), as well as open responses in order to gain and/or hold the floor, provide counterarguments, and the like. *4. Adapting language choices* Adjust language choices (e.g., vocabulary, use of dialogue, and the like) according to purpose (e.g., persuading, entertaining), social setting, and audience (e.g., peers versus adults), with moderate support from peers or adults.	*1. Exchanging information and ideas* Contribute to class, group, and partner discussions, including sustained dialogue, by following turn-taking rules, asking relevant questions, affirming others, adding relevant information, building on responses, and providing useful feedback. *2. Interacting via written English* Collaborate with peers on joint writing projects of a variety of longer informational and literary texts, using technology where appropriate for publishing, graphics, and the like. *3. Offering opinions* Offer opinions and negotiate with others in conversations using a variety of learned phrases (e.g., *That's a good idea, but . . .*), as well as open responses in order to gain and/or hold the floor, provide counterarguments, elaborate on an idea, and the like. *4. Adapting language choices* Adjust language choices according to purpose (e.g., persuading, entertaining), task, and audience (e.g., peer-to-peer versus peer-to-teacher), with light support from peers or adults.

Texts and Discourse in Context		ELD Proficiency Level Continuum		
		→ Emerging →	→ Expanding →	→ Bridging →
Part I, strands 5–8, corresponding to the CA CCSS for ELA/Literacy: 5. SL.3.1-3; L.3.3 6. RL.3.1-7, 9-10; RI.3.1-7, 9-10; SL.3.2-3; L.3.3, 4, 6 7. RL.3.3-4, 6; RI.3.2, 6, 8; SL.3.3; L.3.3-6 8. RL.3.4-5; RI.3.4-5; SL.3.3; L.3.3-6 **Purposes for using language include but are not limited to:** Describing, entertaining, informing, interpreting, analyzing, recounting, explaining, persuading, negotiating, justifying, evaluating, and so on. **Informational text types include but are not limited to:** Description (e.g., science log entry), procedure (e.g., how to solve a mathematics problem), recount (e.g., autobiography, science experiment results), information report (e.g., science or history report) explanation (e.g., how or why something happened), exposition (e.g., opinion), response (e.g., literary analysis), and so on. **Literary text types include but are not limited to:** Stories (e.g., fantasy, legends, fables), drama (e.g., readers' theater), poetry, retelling a story, and so on. **Audiences include but are not limited to:** Peers (one to one) Small group (one to a group) Whole group (one to many)	**B. Interpretive**	***5. Listening actively*** Demonstrate active listening to read-alouds and oral presentations by asking and answering basic questions, with prompting and substantial support. ***6. Reading/viewing closely*** Describe ideas, phenomena (e.g., insect metamorphosis), and text elements (e.g., main idea, characters, setting) based on understanding of a select set of grade-level texts and viewing of multimedia, with substantial support. ***7. Evaluating language choices*** Describe the language writers or speakers use to support an opinion or present an idea (e.g., by identifying the phrases or words in the text that provide evidence), with prompting and substantial support. ***8. Analyzing language choices*** Distinguish how different words produce different effects on the audience (e.g., describing a character as *happy* versus *sad*).	***5. Listening actively*** Demonstrate active listening to read-alouds and oral presentations by asking and answering detailed questions, with occasional prompting and moderate support. ***6. Reading/viewing closely*** Describe ideas, phenomena (e.g., how cows digest food), and text elements (e.g., main idea, characters, events) in greater detail based on understanding of a variety of grade-level texts and viewing of multimedia, with moderate support. ***7. Evaluating language choices*** Describe the specific language writers or speakers use to present or support an idea (e.g., the specific vocabulary or phrasing used to provide evidence), with prompting and moderate support. ***8. Analyzing language choices*** Distinguish how different words with similar meanings (e.g., describing a character as *happy* versus *ecstatic*) produce shades of meaning and different effects on the audience.	***5. Listening actively*** Demonstrate active listening to read-alouds and oral presentations by asking and answering detailed questions, with minimal prompting and light support. ***6. Reading/viewing closely*** Describe ideas, phenomena (e.g., volcanic eruptions), and text elements (e.g., central message, character traits, major events) using key details based on understanding of a variety of grade-level texts and viewing of multimedia, with light support. ***7. Evaluating language choices*** Describe how well writers or speakers use specific language resources to support an opinion or present an idea (e.g., whether the vocabulary or phrasing used to provide evidence is strong enough), with light support. ***8. Analyzing language choices*** Distinguish how multiple different words with similar meanings (e.g., *pleased* versus *happy* versus *ecstatic, heard* versus knew versus *believed*) produce shades of meaning and different effects on the audience.

Section 2: Elaboration on Critical Principles for Developing Language and Cognition in Academic Contexts
Part I: Interacting in Meaningful Ways

Texts and Discourse in Context		ELD Proficiency Level Continuum		
		→ Emerging →	→ Expanding →	→ Bridging →
Part I, strands 9–12, corresponding to the CA CCSS for ELA/Literacy: 9. SL.3.4–6; L.3.1, 3, 6 10. W.3.1–8, 10; L.3.1–3, 11. W.3.1, 4, 10; SL.3.4, 6; L.3.1–3, 6 12. W.3.4–5; SL.3.4, 6; L.3.1, 3, 5–6 **Purposes for using language include but are not limited to:** Describing, entertaining, informing, interpreting, analyzing, recounting, explaining, persuading, negotiating, justifying, evaluating, and so on. **Informational text types include but are not limited to:** Description (e.g., science log entry), procedure (e.g., how to solve a mathematics problem), recount (e.g., autobiography, science experiment results), information report (e.g., science or history report), explanation (e.g., how or why something happened), exposition (e.g., opinion), response (e.g., literary analysis), and so on. **Literary text types include but are not limited to:** Stories (e.g., fantasy, legends, fables), drama (e.g., readers' theater), poetry, retelling a story, and so on. **Audiences include but are not limited to:** Peers (one to one) Small group (one to a group) Whole group (one to many)	**C. Productive**	*9. Presenting* Plan and deliver very brief oral presentations (e.g., retelling a story, describing an animal, and the like). *10. Writing* a. Write short literary and informational texts (e.g., a description of a flashlight) collaboratively (e.g., joint construction of texts with an adult or with peers) and sometimes independently. b. Paraphrase texts and recount experiences using key words from notes or graphic organizers. *11. Supporting opinions* Support opinions by providing good reasons and some textual evidence or relevant background knowledge (e.g., referring to textual evidence or knowledge of content). *12. Selecting language resources* Use a select number of general academic and domain-specific words to add detail (e.g., adding the word *dangerous* to describe a place, using the word *habitat* when describing animal behavior) while speaking and writing.	*9. Presenting* Plan and deliver brief oral presentations on a variety of topics and content areas (e.g., retelling a story, explaining a science process, and the like). *10. Writing* a. Write longer literary and informational texts (e.g., an explanatory text on how flashlights work) collaboratively (e.g., joint construction of texts with an adult or with peers) and with increasing independence using appropriate text organization. b. Paraphrase texts and recount experiences using complete sentences and key words from notes or graphic organizers. *11. Supporting opinions* Support opinions by providing good reasons and increasingly detailed textual evidence (e.g., providing examples from the text) or relevant background knowledge about the content. *12. Selecting language resources* Use a growing number of general academic and domain-specific words in order to add detail, create an effect (e.g., using the word *suddenly* to signal a change), or create shades of meaning (e.g., *scurry* versus *dash*) while speaking and writing.	*9. Presenting* Plan and deliver longer oral presentations on a variety of topics and content areas (e.g., retelling a story, explaining a science process or historical event, and the like). *10. Writing* a. Write longer and more detailed literary and informational texts (e.g., an explanatory text on how flashlights work) collaboratively (e.g., joint construction of texts with an adult or with peers) and independently using appropriate text organization and growing understanding of register. b. Paraphrase texts and recount experiences using increasingly detailed complete sentences and key words from notes or graphic organizers. *11. Supporting opinions* Support opinions or persuade others by providing good reasons and detailed textual evidence (e.g., specific events or graphics from text) or relevant background knowledge about the content. *12. Selecting language resources* Use a wide variety of general academic and domain-specific words, synonyms, antonyms, and non-literal language to create an effect, precision, and shades of meaning while speaking and writing.

Section 2: Elaboration on Critical Principles for Developing Language and Cognition in Academic Contexts
Part II: Learning About How English Works

Texts and Discourse in Context		ELD Proficiency Level Continuum		
		→ Emerging →	→ Expanding →	→ Bridging →
Part II, strands 1–2, corresponding to the CA CCSS for ELA/Literacy 1. RL.3.5; RI.3.5; W.3.1–5; SL.3.4 2. RL.3.5; RI.3.5; W.3.1–4; SL.3.4; L.3.1, 3 **Purposes for using language include but are not limited to:** Describing, entertaining, informing, interpreting, analyzing, recounting, explaining, persuading, negotiating, justifying, evaluating, and so on. **Informational text types include but are not limited to:** Description (e.g., science log entry), procedure (e.g., how to solve a mathematics problem), recount (e.g., autobiography, science experiment results), information report (e.g., science or history report), explanation (e.g., how or why something happened), exposition (e.g., opinion), response (e.g., literary analysis), and so on. **Literary text types include but are not limited to:** Stories (e.g., fantasy, legends, fables), drama (e.g., readers' theater); poetry, retelling a story, and so on. **Audiences include but are not limited to:** Peers (one to one) Small group (one to a group) Whole group (one to many)	**A. Structuring Cohesive Texts**	*1. Understanding text structure* Apply understanding of how different text types are organized to express ideas (e.g., how a story is organized sequentially) to comprehending texts and writing basic texts. *2. Understanding cohesion* a. Apply basic understanding of language resources that refer the reader back or forward in text (e.g., how pronouns refer back to nouns in text) to comprehending texts and writing basic texts. b. Apply basic understanding of how ideas, events, or reasons are linked throughout a text using everyday connecting words or phrases (e.g., *then, next*) to comprehending texts and writing basic texts.	*1. Understanding text structure* Apply understanding of how different text types are organized to express ideas (e.g., how a story is organized sequentially with predictable stages) to comprehending texts and writing texts with increasing cohesion. *2. Understanding cohesion* a. Apply growing understanding of language resources that refer the reader back or forward in text (e.g., how pronouns refer back to nouns in text) to comprehending texts and writing texts with increasing cohesion. b. Apply growing understanding of how ideas, events, or reasons are linked throughout a text using a variety of connecting words or phrases (e.g., *at the beginning/end, first/next*) to comprehending texts and writing texts with increasing cohesion.	*1. Understanding text structure* Apply understanding of how different text types are organized to express ideas (e.g., how a story is organized sequentially with predictable stages versus how opinion/arguments are structured logically, grouping related ideas) to comprehending texts and writing cohesive texts. *2. Understanding cohesion* a. Apply increasing understanding of language resources that refer the reader back or forward in text (e.g., how pronouns or synonyms refer back to nouns in text) to comprehending and writing cohesive texts. b. Apply increasing understanding of how ideas, events, or reasons are linked throughout a text using an increasing variety of connecting and transitional words or phrases (e.g., *for example, afterward, first/next/last*) to comprehending texts and writing cohesive texts.

Section 2: Elaboration on Critical Principles for Developing Language and Cognition in Academic Contexts
Part II: Learning About How English Works

Texts and Discourse in Context		ELD Proficiency Level Continuum		
		→ Emerging →	→ Expanding →	→ Bridging →
Part II, strands 3–5, corresponding to the CA CCSS for ELA/Literacy 3. W.3.5; SL.3.6; L.3.1, 3, 6 4. W.3.5; SL.3.6; L.3.1, 3, 6 5. W.3.5; SL.3.4, 6; L.3.1, 3, 6 **Purposes for using language include but are not limited to:** Describing, entertaining, informing, interpreting, analyzing, recounting, explaining, persuading, negotiating, justifying, evaluating, and so on. **Informational text types include but are not limited to:** Description (e.g., science log entry), procedure (e.g., how to solve a mathematics problem), recount (e.g., autobiography, science experiment results), information report (e.g., science or history report), explanation (e.g., how or why something happened), exposition (e.g., opinion), response (e.g., literary analysis), and so on. **Literary text types include but are not limited to:** Stories (e.g., fantasy, legends, fables), drama (e.g., readers' theater), poetry, retelling a story, and so on. **Audiences include but are not limited to:** Peers (one to one) Small group (one to a group) Whole group (one to many)	**B. Expanding and Enriching Ideas**	*3. Using verbs and verb phrases* Use frequently used verbs, different verb types (e.g., doing, saying, being/having, thinking/feeling), and verb tenses appropriate to the text type and discipline to convey time (e.g., simple past for recounting an experience). *4. Using nouns and noun phrases* Expand noun phrases in simple ways (e.g., adding an adjective to a noun) in order to enrich the meaning of sentences and add details about ideas, people, things, and the like. *5. Modifying to add details* Expand sentences with adverbials (e.g., adverbs, adverb phrases, prepositional phrases) to provide details (e.g., time, manner, place, cause, and the like) about a familiar activity or process (e.g., They walked *to the soccer field*).	*3. Using verbs and verb phrases* Use a growing number of verb types (e.g., doing, saying, being/having, thinking/feeling) and verb tenses appropriate to the text type and discipline to convey time (e.g., simple past for retelling, simple present for a science description). *4. Using nouns and noun phrases* Expand noun phrases in a growing number of ways (e.g., adding comparative/superlative adjectives to nouns) in order to enrich the meaning of sentences and add details about ideas, people, things, and the like. *5. Modifying to add details* Expand sentences with adverbials (e.g., adverbs, adverb phrases, prepositional phrases) to provide details (e.g., time, manner, place, cause, and the like) about a familiar or new activity or process (e.g., They worked *quietly;* they ran *across the soccer field*).	*3. Using verbs and verb phrases* Use a variety of verb types (e.g., doing, saying, being/having, thinking/feeling) and verb tenses appropriate to the text type and discipline to convey time (e.g., simple present for a science description, simple future to predict). *4. Using nouns and noun phrases* Expand noun phrases in a variety of ways (e.g., adding comparative/ superlative adjectives to noun phrases, simple clause embedding) in order to enrich the meaning of sentences and add details about ideas, people, things, and the like. *5. Modifying to add details* Expand sentences with adverbials (e.g., adverbs, adverb phrases, prepositional phrases) to provide details (e.g., time, manner, place, cause, and the like) about a range of familiar and new activities or processes (e.g., They worked *quietly all night in their room*).

Texts and Discourse in Context	ELD Proficiency Level Continuum		
	→ Emerging →	→ Expanding →	→ Bridging →
Part II, strands 6–7, corresponding to the CA CCSS for ELA/Literacy 6. W.3.1-3,5; SL.3.4,6; L.3.1, 3, 6 7. W.3.1-3,5; SL.3.4,6; L.3.1, 3, 6 **Purposes for using language include but are not limited to:** Describing, entertaining, informing, interpreting, analyzing, recounting, explaining, persuading, negotiating, justifying, evaluating, and so on. **Informational text types include but are not limited to:** Description (e.g., science log entry), procedure (e.g., how to solve a mathematics problem), recount (e.g., autobiography, science experiment results), information report (e.g., science or history report), explanation (e.g., how or why something happened), exposition (e.g., opinion), response (e.g., literary analysis), and so on. **Literary text types include but are not limited to:** Stories (e.g., fantasy, legends, fables), drama (e.g., readers' theater), poetry, retelling a story, and so on. **Audiences include but are not limited to:** Peers (one to one) Small group (one to a group) Whole group (one to many)	**C. Connecting and Condensing Ideas**		
	6. Connecting ideas Combine clauses in a few basic ways to make connections between and join ideas (e.g., creating compound sentences using *and, but, so*).	*6. Connecting ideas* Combine clauses in an increasing variety of ways (e.g., creating compound and complex sentences) to make connections between and join ideas, for example, to express cause/effect (e.g., *The deer ran because the mountain lion came*) or to make a concession (e.g., *She studied all night even though she wasn't feeling well*).	*6. Connecting ideas* Combine clauses in a wide variety of ways (e.g., creating compound and complex sentences) to make connections between and join ideas, for example, to express cause/effect (e.g., *The deer ran because the mountain lion approached them*), to make a concession (e.g., *She studied all night even though she wasn't feeling well*), or to link two ideas that happen at the same time (e.g., *The cubs played while their mother hunted*).
	7. Condensing ideas Condense clauses in simple ways (e.g., changing: *It's green. It's red.* → *It's green and red*) to create precise and detailed sentences.	*7. Condensing ideas* Condense clauses in a growing number of ways (e.g., through embedded clauses as in, *It's a plant. It's found in the rain forest.* → *It's a green and red plant that's found in the tropical rain forest*) to create precise and detailed sentences.	*7. Condensing ideas* Condense clauses in a variety of ways (e.g., through embedded clauses and other condensing as in, *It's a plant. It's green and red. It's found in the tropical rain forest.* → *It's a green and red plant that's found in the tropical rain forest*) to create precise and detailed sentences.

Section 2: Elaboration on Critical Principles for Developing Language and Cognition in Academic Contexts
Part III: Using Foundational Literacy Skills

Foundational literacy skills in an alphabetic writing system • Print concepts • Phonological awareness • Phonics and word recognition • Fluency	See chapter 6 for information on teaching foundational reading skills to English learners of various profiles based on age, native language, native language writing system, schooling experience, and literacy experience and proficiency. Some considerations are as follows: • Native language and literacy (e.g., phoneme awareness or print concept skills in native language) should be assessed for potential transference to English language and literacy. • Similarities between the native language and English should be highlighted (e.g., phonemes or letters that are the same in both languages). • Differences between the native language and English should be highlighted (e.g., some phonemes in English may not exist in the student's native language; native language syntax may be different from English syntax).

Section 1: Overview

Goal: English learners read, analyze, interpret, and create a variety of literary and informational text types. They develop an understanding of how language is a complex, dynamic, and social resource for making meaning, as well as how content is organized in different text types and across disciplines using text structure, language features, and vocabulary depending on purpose and audience. They are aware that different languages and variations of English exist, and they recognize their home languages and cultures as resources to value in their own right and also to draw upon in order to build proficiency in English. English learners contribute actively to class and group discussions, asking questions, responding appropriately, and providing useful feedback. They demonstrate knowledge of content through oral presentations, writing tasks, collaborative conversations, and multimedia. They develop proficiency in shifting language use based on task, purpose, audience, and text type.

Critical Principles for Developing Language and Cognition in Academic Contexts: While advancing along the continuum of English language development levels, English learners at all levels engage in intellectually challenging literacy, disciplinary, and disciplinary literacy tasks. They use language in meaningful and relevant ways appropriate to grade level, content area, topic, purpose, audience, and text type in English language arts, mathematics, science, social studies, and the arts. Specifically, they use language to gain and exchange information and ideas in three communicative modes (collaborative, interpretive, and productive), and they apply knowledge of language to academic tasks via three cross-mode language processes (structuring cohesive texts, expanding and enriching ideas, and connecting and condensing ideas) using various linguistic resources.

Part I: Interacting in Meaningful Ways	Corresponding CA CCSS for ELA/Literacy*
A. Collaborative	
1. Exchanging information and ideas with others through oral collaborative discussions on a range of social and academic topics	• SL.4.1, 6; L.4.1, 3, 6
2. Interacting with others in written English in various communicative forms (print, communicative technology, and multimedia)	• W.4.6; L.4.1, 3, 6
3. Offering and supporting opinions and negotiating with others in communicative exchanges	• SL.4.1, 6; L.4.1, 3, 6
4. Adapting language choices to various contexts (based on task, purpose, audience, and text type)	• W.4.4–5; SL.4.1, 6; L.4.1, 3, 6

*The California English Language Development Standards correspond to the California Common Core State Standards for English Language Arts and Literacy in History/Social Science and Technical Subjects (CA CCSS for ELA/Literacy). English learners should have full access to opportunities to learn ELA, mathematics, science, history/social studies, and other content at the same time they are progressing toward full proficiency in English.

Part I: Interacting in Meaningful Ways	Corresponding CA CCSS for ELA/Literacy
B. Interpretive	
5. Listening actively to spoken English in a range of social and academic contexts	• SL.4.1–3; L.4.3
6. Reading closely literary and informational texts and viewing multimedia to determine how meaning is conveyed explicitly and implicitly through language	• RL.4.1–7, 9–10; RI.4.1–7, 9–10; SL.4.2–3; L.4.3, 4, 6
7. Evaluating how well writers and speakers use language to support ideas and opinions with details or reasons depending on modality, text type, purpose, audience, topic, and content area	• RL.4.3–4, 6; RI.4.2, 6, 8; SL.4.3; L.4.3–6
8. Analyzing how writers and speakers use vocabulary and other language resources for specific purposes (to explain, persuade, entertain, etc.) depending on modality, text type, purpose, audience, topic, and content area	• RL.4.4–5; RI.4.4–5; SL.4.3; L.4.3–6
C. Productive	
9. Expressing information and ideas in formal oral presentations on academic topics	• SL.4.4–6; L.4.1, 3, 6
10. Writing literary and informational texts to present, describe, and explain ideas and information, using appropriate technology	• W.4.1–10; L.4.1–3, 6
11. Supporting own opinions and evaluating others' opinions in speaking and writing	• W.4.1, 4, 9–10; SL.4.4, 6; L.4.1–3, 6
12. Selecting and applying varied and precise vocabulary and other language resources to effectively convey ideas	• W.4.4–5; SL.4.4, 6; L.4.1, 3, 5–6
Part II: Learning About How English Works	**Corresponding CA CCSS for ELA/Literacy**
A. Structuring Cohesive Texts	
1. Understanding text structure	• RL.4.5; RI.4.5; W.4.1–5; SL.4.4
2. Understanding cohesion	• RL.4.5; RI.4.5; W.4.1–4; SL.4.4; L.4.1, 3
B. Expanding and Enriching Ideas	
3. Using verbs and verb phrases	• W.4.5; SL.4.6; L.4.1, 3, 6
4. Using nouns and noun phrases	• W.4.5; SL.4.6; L.4.1, 3, 6
5. Modifying to add details	• W.4.5; SL.4.4, 6; L.4.1, 3, 6
C. Connecting and Condensing Ideas	
6. Connecting ideas	• W.4.1–3, 5; SL.4.4, 6; L.4.1, 3, 6
7. Condensing ideas	• W.4.1–3, 5; SL.4.4, 6; L.4.1, 3, 6
Part III: Using Foundational Literacy Skills	• RF.K–1.1–4; RF.2–4.3–4 (as appropriate)

Note: **Examples** provided in specific standards are offered *only as illustrative possibilities* and should not be misinterpreted as the only objectives of instruction or as the only types of language that English learners might or should be able to understand or produce.

Section 2: Elaboration on Critical Principles for Developing Language and Cognition in Academic Contexts
Part I: Interacting in Meaningful Ways

Texts and Discourse in Context		ELD Proficiency Level Continuum		
		→ Emerging →	→ Expanding →	→ Bridging →
Part I, strands 1–4, corresponding to the CA CCSS for ELA/Literacy 1. SL.4.1, 6; L.4.1, 3, 6 2. W.4.6; L.4.1, 3, 6 3. SL.4.1, 6; L.4.1, 3, 6 4. W.4.4–5; SL.4.1, 6; L.4.1, 3, 6 **Purposes for using language include but are not limited to:** Describing, entertaining, informing, interpreting, analyzing, recounting, explaining, persuading, negotiating, justifying, evaluating, and so on. **Informational text types include but are not limited to:** Description (e.g., science log entry), procedure (e.g., how to solve a mathematics problem), recount (e.g., autobiography, science experiment results), information report (e.g., science or history report), explanation (e.g., how or why something happened); exposition (e.g., opinion), response (e.g., literary analysis), and so on. **Literary text types include but are not limited to:** Stories (e.g., fantasy, legends, fables), drama (e.g., readers' theater), poetry, retelling a story, and so on. **Audiences include but are not limited to:** Peers (one to one) Small group (one to a group) Whole group (one to many)	**A. Collaborative**	*1. Exchanging information/ideas* Contribute to conversations and express ideas by asking and answering *yes-no* and *wh-* questions and responding using short phrases. *2. Interacting via written English* Collaborate with peers on joint writing projects of short informational and literary texts, using technology where appropriate for publishing, graphics, and the like. *3. Offering opinions* Negotiate with or persuade others in conversations using basic learned phrases (e.g., *I think . . .*), as well as open responses, in order to gain and/or hold the floor. *4. Adapting language choices* Adjust language choices according to social setting (e.g., playground, classroom) and audience (e.g., peers, teacher), with substantial support.	*1. Exchanging information/ideas* Contribute to class, group, and partner discussions, including sustained dialogue, by following turn-taking rules, asking relevant questions, affirming others, and adding relevant information. *2. Interacting via written English* Collaborate with peers on joint writing projects of longer informational and literary texts, using technology where appropriate for publishing, graphics, and the like. *3. Offering opinions* Negotiate with or persuade others in conversations using an expanded set of learned phrases (e.g., *I agree with X, but . . .*), as well as open responses, in order to gain and/or hold the floor, provide counterarguments, and so on. *4. Adapting language choices* Adjust language choices according to purpose (e.g., persuading, entertaining), task (e.g., telling a story versus explaining a science experiment), and audience, with moderate support.	*1. Exchanging information/ideas* Contribute to class, group, and partner discussions, including sustained dialogue, by following turn-taking rules, asking relevant questions, affirming others, adding relevant information, building on responses, and providing useful feedback. *2. Interacting via written English* Collaborate with peers on joint writing projects of a variety of longer informational and literary texts, using technology where appropriate for publishing, graphics, and the like. *3. Offering opinions* Negotiate with or persuade others in conversations using a variety of learned phrases (e.g., *That's a good idea. However . . .*), as well as open responses, in order to gain and/or hold the floor, provide counterarguments, elaborate on an idea, and so on. *4. Adapting language choices* Adjust language choices according to purpose, task (e.g., facilitating a science experiment), and audience, with light support.

Section 2: Elaboration on Critical Principles for Developing Language and Cognition in Academic Contexts
Part I: Interacting in Meaningful Ways

Texts and Discourse in Context		ELD Proficiency Level Continuum		
		→ Emerging →	→ Expanding →	→ Bridging →
Part I, strands 5–8, corresponding to the CA CCSS for ELA/Literacy: 5. SL.4.1–3; L.4.3 6. RL.4.1–7, 9–10; RI.4.1–7, 9–10; SL.4.2–3; L.4.3, 4, 6 7. RL.4.3–4, 6; RI.4.2, 6, 8; SL.4.3; L.4.3–6 8. RL.4.4–5; RI.4.4–5; SL.4.3; L.4.3–6 **Purposes for using language include but are not limited to:** Describing, entertaining, informing, interpreting, analyzing, recounting, explaining, persuading, negotiating, justifying, evaluating, and so on. **Informational text types include but are not limited to:** Description (e.g., science log entry), procedures (e.g., how to solve a mathematics problem), recount (e.g., autobiography, science experiment results), information report (e.g., science or history report), explanation (e.g., how or why something happened), exposition (e.g., opinion), response (e.g., literary analysis), and so on. **Literary text types include but are not limited to:** Stories (e.g., fantasy, legends, fables), drama (e.g., readers' theater), poetry, retelling a story, and so on. **Audiences include but are not limited to:** Peers (one to one) Small group (one to a group) Whole group (one to many)	**B. Interpretive**	*5. Listening actively* Demonstrate active listening of read-alouds and oral presentations by asking and answering basic questions, with prompting and substantial support. *6. Reading/viewing closely* a. Describe ideas, phenomena (e.g., volcanic eruptions), and text elements (main idea, characters, events, and the like) based on close reading of a select set of grade-level texts, with substantial support. b. Use knowledge of frequently used affixes (e.g., *un-, mis-*) and linguistic context, reference materials, and visual cues to determine the meaning of unknown words on familiar topics. *7. Evaluating language choices* Describe the specific language writers or speakers use to present or support an idea (e.g., the specific vocabulary or phrasing used to provide evidence), with prompting and substantial support. *8. Analyzing language choices* Distinguish how different words with similar meanings produce different effects on the audience (e.g., describing a character's actions as *whined* versus *said*).	*5. Listening actively* Demonstrate active listening of read-alouds and oral presentations by asking and answering detailed questions, with occasional prompting and moderate support. *6. Reading/viewing closely* a. Describe ideas, phenomena (e.g., animal migration), and text elements (main idea, central message, and the like) in greater detail based on close reading of a variety of grade-level texts, with moderate support. b. Use knowledge of morphology (e.g., affixes, roots, and base words), linguistic context, and reference materials to determine the meaning of unknown words on familiar topics. *7. Evaluating language choices* Describe how well writers or speakers use specific language resources to support an opinion or present an idea (e.g., whether the vocabulary or phrasing used to provide evidence is strong enough), with prompting and moderate support. *8. Analyzing language choices* Distinguish how different words with similar meanings (e.g., describing a character as *smart* versus *an expert*) and figurative language (e.g., *as big as a whale*) produce shades of meaning and different effects on the audience.	*5. Listening actively* Demonstrate active listening of read-alouds and oral presentations by asking and answering detailed questions, with minimal prompting and light support. *6. Reading/viewing closely* a. Describe ideas, phenomena (e.g., pollination), and text elements (main idea, character traits, event sequence, and the like) in detail based on close reading of a variety of grade-level texts, with light support. b. Use knowledge of morphology (e.g., affixes, roots, and base words) and linguistic context to determine the meaning of unknown and multiple-meaning words on familiar and new topics. *7. Evaluating language choices* Describe how well writers and speakers use specific language resources to support an opinion or present an idea (e.g., the clarity or appealing nature of language used to present evidence), with prompting and light support. *8. Analyzing language choices* Distinguish how different words with related meanings (e.g., *fun* versus *entertaining* versus *thrilling, possibly* versus *certainly*) and figurative language produce shades of meaning and different effects on the audience.

Section 2: Elaboration on Critical Principles for Developing Language and Cognition in Academic Contexts
Part I: Interacting in Meaningful Ways

Texts and Discourse in Context		ELD Proficiency Level Continuum		
		→ Emerging →	→ Expanding →	→ Bridging →
Part I, strands 9–12, corresponding to the CA CCSS for ELA/Literacy 9. SL.4.4–6; L.4.1, 3, 6 10. W.4.1–10; L.4.1–3, 6 11. W.4.1,4, 9–10; SL.4.4, 6; L.4.1–3, 6 12. W.4.4–5; SL.4.4, 6; L.4.1, 3, 5–6 **Purposes for using language include but are not limited to:** Describing, entertaining, informing, interpreting, analyzing, recounting, explaining, persuading, negotiating, justifying, evaluating, and so on. **Informational text types include but are not limited to:** Description (e.g., science log entry), procedure (e.g., how to solve a mathematics problem), recount (e.g., autobiography, science experiment results), information report (e.g., science or history report), explanation (e.g., how or why something happened), exposition (e.g., opinion), response (e.g., literary analysis), and so on. **Literary text types include but are not limited to:** Stories (e.g., fantasy, legends, fables), drama (e.g., readers' theater), poetry, retelling a story, and so on. **Audiences include but are not limited to:** Peers (one to one) Small group (one to a group) Whole group (one to many)	**C. Productive**	*9. Presenting* Plan and deliver brief oral presentations on a variety of topics and content areas (e.g., retelling a story, explaining a science process, reporting on a current event, recounting a memorable experience, and so on), with substantial support. *10. Writing* a. Write short literary and informational texts (e.g., a description of a flashlight) collaboratively (e.g., joint construction of texts with an adult or with peers) and sometimes independently. b. Write brief summaries of texts and experiences using complete sentences and key words (e.g., from notes or graphic organizers). *11. Supporting opinions* a. Support opinions by expressing appropriate/accurate reasons using textual evidence (e.g., referring to text) or relevant background knowledge about content, with substantial support. b. Express ideas and opinions or temper statements using basic modal expressions (e.g., *can, will, maybe*).	*9. Presenting* Plan and deliver longer oral presentations on a variety of topics and content areas (e.g., retelling a story, explaining a science process, reporting on a current event, recounting a memorable experience, and so on), with moderate support. *10. Writing* a. Write longer literary and informational texts (e.g., an explanatory text on how flashlights work) collaboratively (e.g., joint construction of texts with an adult or with peers) and with increasing independence using appropriate text organization. b. Write increasingly concise summaries of texts and experiences using complete sentences and key words (e.g., from notes or graphic organizers). *11. Supporting opinions* a Support opinions or persuade others by expressing appropriate/accurate reasons using some textual evidence (e.g., paraphrasing facts) or relevant background knowledge about content, with moderate support. b. Express attitude and opinions or temper statements with familiar modal expressions (e.g., *maybe/probably, can/must*).	*9. Presenting* Plan and deliver oral presentations on a variety of topics in a variety of content areas (e.g., retelling a story, explaining a science process, reporting on a current event, recounting a memorable experience, and so on), with light support. *10. Writing* a. Write longer and more detailed literary and informational texts (e.g., an explanatory text on how flashlights work) collaboratively (e.g., joint construction of texts with an adult or with peers) and independently using appropriate text organization and growing understanding of register. b. Write clear and coherent summaries of texts and experiences using complete and concise sentences and key words (e.g., from notes or graphic organizers). *11. Supporting opinions* a. Support opinions or persuade others by expressing appropriate/accurate reasons using detailed textual evidence (e.g., quotations or specific events from text) or relevant background knowledge about content, with light support. b. Express attitude and opinions or temper statements with nuanced modal expressions (e.g., *probably/certainly, should/would*) and phrasing (e.g., *In my opinion . . .*).

Texts and Discourse in Context		ELD Proficiency Level Continuum		
		→ Emerging →	→ Expanding →	→ Bridging →
Part I, strands 9–12, corresponding to the CA CCSS for ELA/Literacy 9. SL.4.4–6; L.4.1, 3, 6 10. W.4.1–10; L.4.1–3, 6 11. W.4.1,4, 9–10; SL.4.4, 6; L.4.1–3, 6 12. W.4.4–5; SL.4.4, 6; L.4.1, 3, 5–6 **Purposes for using language include but are not limited to:** Describing, entertaining, informing, interpreting, analyzing, recounting, explaining, persuading, negotiating, justifying, evaluating, and so on. **Informational text types include but are not limited to:** Description (e.g., science log entry), procedure (e.g., how to solve a mathematics problem), recount (e.g., autobiography, science experiment results), information report (e.g., science or history report), explanation (e.g., how or why something happened), exposition (e.g., opinion), response (e.g., literary analysis), and so on. **Literary text types include but are not limited to:** Stories (e.g., fantasy, legends, fables), drama (e.g., readers' theater), poetry, retelling a story, and so on. **Audiences include but are not limited to:** Peers (one to one) Small group (one to a group) Whole group (one to many)	**C. Productive**	*12. Selecting language resources* a. Use a select number of general academic and domain-specific words to create precision while speaking and writing. b. Select a few frequently used affixes for accuracy and precision (e.g., She walks, I'm *un*happy).	*12. Selecting language resources* a. Use a growing number of general academic and domain-specific words, synonyms, and antonyms to create precision and shades of meaning while speaking and writing. b. Select a growing number of frequently used affixes for accuracy and precision (e.g., She walk*ed*. He likes . . . , I'm *un*happy).	*12. Selecting language resources* a. Use a wide variety of general academic and domain-specific words, synonyms, antonyms, and figurative language to create precision and shades of meaning while speaking and writing. b. Select a variety of appropriate affixes for accuracy and precision (e.g., She's walk*ing*. I'm *un*comfortable. They left reluctant*ly*).

Texts and Discourse in Context		ELD Proficiency Level Continuum		
		→ Emerging →	→ Expanding →	→ Bridging →
Part II, strands 1–2, corresponding to the CA CCSS for ELA/Literacy 1. RL.4.5; RI.4.5; W.4.1–5; SL.4.4 2. RL.4.5; RI.4.5; W.4.1–4; SL.4.4; L.4.1, 3 **Purposes for using language include but are not limited to:** Describing, entertaining, informing, interpreting, analyzing, recounting, explaining, persuading, negotiating, justifying, evaluating, and so on. **Informational text types include but are not limited to:** Description (e.g., science log entry), procedure (e.g., how to solve a mathematics problem), recount (e.g., autobiography, science experiment results), information report (e.g., science or history report); explanation (e.g., how or why something happened), exposition (e.g., opinion), response (e.g., literary analysis), and so on. **Literary text types include but are not limited to:** Stories (e.g., fantasy, legends, fables), drama (e.g., readers' theater), poetry, retelling a story, and so on. **Audiences include but are not limited to:** Peers (one to one) Small group (one to a group) Whole group (one to many)	**A. Structuring Cohesive Texts**	*1. Understanding text structure* Apply understanding of how different text types are organized to express ideas (e.g., how a narrative is organized sequentially) to comprehending texts and writing basic texts. *2. Understanding cohesion* a. Apply basic understanding of language resources for referring the reader back or forward in text (e.g., how pronouns refer back to nouns in text) to comprehending texts and writing basic texts. b. Apply basic understanding of how ideas, events, or reasons are linked throughout a text using everyday connecting words or phrases (e.g., *first, yesterday*) to comprehending texts and writing basic texts.	*1. Understanding text structure* Apply increasing understanding of how different text types are organized to express ideas (e.g., how a narrative is organized sequentially with predictable stages versus how an explanation is organized around ideas) to comprehending texts and writing texts with increasing cohesion. *2. Understanding cohesion* a. Apply growing understanding of language resources for referring the reader back or forward in text (e.g., how pronouns or synonyms refer back to nouns in text) to comprehending texts and writing texts with increasing cohesion. b. Apply growing understanding of how ideas, events, or reasons are linked throughout a text using a variety of connecting words or phrases (e.g., *since, next, for example*) to comprehending texts and writing texts with increasing cohesion.	*1. Understanding text structure* Apply understanding of how different text types are organized to express ideas (e.g., how a narrative is organized sequentially with predictable stages versus how opinions/arguments are structured logically, grouping related ideas) to comprehending texts and writing cohesive texts. *2. Understanding cohesion* a. Apply increasing understanding of language resources for referring the reader back or forward in text (e.g., how pronouns, synonyms, or nominalizations refer back to nouns in text) to comprehending texts and writing cohesive texts. b. Apply increasing understanding of how ideas, events, or reasons are linked throughout a text using an increasing variety of academic connecting and transitional words or phrases (e.g., *for instance, in addition, at the end*) to comprehending texts and writing cohesive texts.

Section 2: Elaboration on Critical Principles for Developing Language and Cognition in Academic Contexts
Part II: Learning About How English Works

Texts and Discourse in Context		ELD Proficiency Level Continuum		
		→ Emerging →	→ Expanding →	→ Bridging →
Part II, strands 3–5, corresponding to the CA CCSS for ELA/Literacy 3. W.4.5; SL.4.6; L.4.1, 3, 6 4. W.4.5; SL.4.6; L.4.1, 3, 6 5. W.4.5; SL.4.4,6; L.4.1, 3, 6 **Purposes for using language include but are not limited to:** Describing, entertaining, informing, interpreting, analyzing, recounting, explaining, persuading, negotiating, justifying, evaluating, and so on. **Informational text types include but are not limited to:** Description (e.g., science log entry), procedure (e.g., how to solve a mathematics problem), recount (e.g., autobiography, science experiment results), information report (e.g., science or history report), explanation (e.g., how or why something happened), exposition (e.g., opinion), response (e.g., literary analysis), and so on. **Literary text types include but are not limited to:** Stories (e.g., fantasy, legends, fables), drama (e.g., readers' theater), poetry, retelling a story, and so on. **Audiences include but are not limited to:** Peers (one to one) Small group (one to a group) Whole group (one to many)	**B. Expanding and Enriching Ideas**	**3. Using verbs and verb phrases** Use various verbs/verb types (e.g., doing, saying, being/having, thinking/feeling) and tenses appropriate to the text type and discipline (e.g., simple past for recounting an experience) for familiar topics. **4. Using nouns and noun phrases** Expand noun phrases in simple ways (e.g., adding an adjective) in order to enrich the meaning of sentences and add details about ideas, people, things, and so on. **5. Modifying to add details** Expand sentences with familiar adverbials (e.g., basic prepositional phrases) to provide details (e.g., time, manner, place, cause, and so on) about a familiar activity or process (e.g., They walked *to the soccer field*).	**3. Using verbs and verb phrases** Use various verbs/verb types (e.g., doing, saying, being/having, thinking/feeling) and tenses appropriate to the task, text type, and discipline (e.g., simple past for retelling, timeless present for science explanation) for an increasing variety of familiar and new topics. **4. Using nouns and noun phrases** Expand noun phrases in a variety of ways (e.g., adding adjectives to noun phrases or simple clause embedding) in order to enrich the meaning of sentences and add details about ideas, people, things, and so on. **5. Modifying to add details** Expand sentences with a growing variety of adverbials (e.g., adverbs, prepositional phrases) to provide details (e.g., time, manner, place, cause, and so on) about a familiar or new activity or process (e.g., They worked *quietly*. They ran *across the soccer field*).	**3. Using verbs and verb phrases** Use various verbs/verb types (e.g., doing, saying, being/having, thinking/feeling) and tenses appropriate to the task and text type (e.g., timeless present for science explanation, mixture of past and present for historical information report) for a variety of familiar and new topics. **4. Using nouns and noun phrases** Expand noun phrases in an increasing variety of ways (e.g., adding general academic adjectives and adverbs to noun phrases or more complex clause embedding) in order to enrich the meaning of sentences and add details about ideas, people, things, and so on. **5. Modifying to add details** Expand sentences with a variety of adverbials (e.g., adverbs, adverb phrases, prepositional phrases) to provide details (e.g., time, manner, place, cause, and so on) about a variety of familiar and new activities and processes (e.g., They worked *quietly all night in their room*).

Texts and Discourse in Context		ELD Proficiency Level Continuum		
		→ Emerging →	→ Expanding →	→ Bridging →
Part II, strands 6–7, corresponding to the CA CCSS for ELA/Literacy 6. W.4.1-3, 5; SL.4.4, 6; L.4.1, 3, 6 7. W.4.1-3, 5; SL.4.4, 6; L.4.1, 3, 6 **Purposes for using language include but are not limited to:** Describing, entertaining, informing, interpreting, analyzing, recounting, explaining, persuading, negotiating, justifying, evaluating, and so on. **Informational text types include but are not limited to:** Description (e.g., science log entry), procedure (e.g., how to solve a mathematics problem), recount (e.g., autobiography, science experiment results), information report (e.g., science or history report), explanation (e.g., how or why something happened), exposition (e.g., opinion), response (e.g., literary analysis), and so on. **Literary text types include but are not limited to:** Stories (e.g., fantasy, legends, fables), drama (e.g., readers' theater), poetry, retelling a story, and so on. **Audiences include but are not limited to:** Peers (one to one) Small group (one to a group) Whole group (one to many)	**C. Connecting and Condensing Ideas**	*6. Connecting ideas* Combine clauses in a few basic ways to make connections between and join ideas in sentences (e.g., creating compound sentences using coordinate conjunctions, such as *and, but, so*). *7. Condensing ideas* Condense clauses in simple ways (e.g., through simple embedded clauses, as in, The woman is a doctor. She helps children. → The woman is a doctor *who helps children*) to create precise and detailed sentences.	*6. Connecting ideas* Combine clauses in an increasing variety of ways (e.g., creating complex sentences using familiar subordinate conjunctions) to make connections between and join ideas in sentences, for example, to express cause/effect (e.g., *The deer ran because the mountain lion came*) or to make a concession (e.g., She studied all night *even though she wasn't feeling well*). *7. Condensing ideas* Condense clauses in an increasing variety of ways (e.g., through a growing number of embedded clauses and other condensing, as in, The dog ate quickly. The dog choked. → The dog ate so quickly *that it choked*) to create precise and detailed sentences.	*6. Connecting ideas* Combine clauses in a wide variety of ways (e.g., creating complex sentences using a variety of subordinate conjunctions) to make connections between and join ideas, for example, to express cause/effect (e.g., *Since the lion was at the waterhole, the deer ran away*), to make a concession, or to link two ideas that happen at the same time (e.g., *The cubs played while their mother hunted*). *7. Condensing ideas* Condense clauses in a variety of ways (e.g., through various types of embedded clauses and other ways of condensing as in, There was a Gold Rush. It began in the 1850s. It brought a lot of people to California. → The Gold Rush *that began in the 1850s* brought a lot of people to California) to create precise and detailed sentences.

Section 2: Elaboration on Critical Principles for Developing Language and Cognition in Academic Contexts
Part III: Using Foundational Literacy Skills

Foundational literacy skills in an alphabetic writing system • Print concepts • Phonological awareness • Phonics and word recognition • Fluency	See chapter 6 for information on teaching foundational reading skills to English learners of various profiles based on age, native language, native language writing system, schooling experience, and literacy experience and proficiency. Some considerations are as follows: • Native language and literacy (e.g., phoneme awareness or print concept skills in native language) should be assessed for potential transference to English language and literacy. • Similarities between the native language and English should be highlighted (e.g., phonemes or letters that are the same in both languages). • Differences between the native language and English should be highlighted (e.g., some phonemes in English may not exist in the student's native language; native language syntax may be different from English syntax).

Grade 5

Section 1: Overview

Goal: English learners read, analyze, interpret, and create a variety of literary and informational text types. They develop an understanding of how language is a complex, dynamic, and social resource for making meaning, as well as how content is organized in different text types and across disciplines using text structure, language features, and vocabulary depending on purpose and audience. They are aware that different languages and variations of English exist, and they recognize their home languages and cultures as resources to value in their own right and also to draw upon in order to build proficiency in English. English learners contribute actively to class and group discussions, asking questions, responding appropriately, and providing useful feedback. They demonstrate knowledge of content through oral presentations, writing tasks, collaborative conversations, and multimedia. They develop proficiency in shifting language use based on task, purpose, audience, and text type.

Critical Principles for Developing Language and Cognition in Academic Contexts: While advancing along the continuum of English language development levels, English learners at all levels engage in intellectually challenging literacy, disciplinary, and disciplinary literacy tasks. They use language in meaningful and relevant ways appropriate to grade level, content area, topic, purpose, audience, and text type in English language arts, mathematics, science, social studies, and the arts. Specifically, they use language to gain and exchange information and ideas in three communicative modes (collaborative, interpretive, and productive), and they apply knowledge of language to academic tasks via three cross-mode language processes (structuring cohesive texts, expanding and enriching ideas, and connecting and condensing ideas) using various linguistic resources.

Part I: Interacting in Meaningful Ways	Corresponding CA CCSS for ELA/Literacy*
A. Collaborative	
1. Exchanging information and ideas with others through oral collaborative discussions on a range of social and academic topics	• SL.5.1, 6; L.5.1, 3, 6
2. Interacting with others in written English in various communicative forms (print, communicative technology, and multimedia)	• W.5.6; L.5.1, 3, 6
3. Offering and supporting opinions and negotiating with others in communicative exchanges	• SL.5.1, 6; L.5.1, 3, 6
4. Adapting language choices to various contexts (based on task, purpose, audience, and text type)	• W.5.4–5; SL.5.1, 6; L.5.1, 3, 6

---

*The California English Language Development Standards correspond to the California Common Core State Standards for English Language Arts and Literacy in History/Social Science and Technical Subjects (CA CCSS for ELA/Literacy). English learners should have full access to opportunities to learn ELA, mathematics, science, history/social studies, and other content at the same time they are progressing toward full proficiency in English.

Part I: Interacting in Meaningful Ways	Corresponding CA CCSS for ELA/Literacy
B. Interpretive	
5. Listening actively to spoken English in a range of social and academic contexts	• SL.5.1–3; L.5.3
6. Reading closely literary and informational texts and viewing multimedia to determine how meaning is conveyed explicitly and implicitly through language	• RL.5.1–7, 9–10; RI.5.1–7, 9–10; SL.5.2–3; L.5.3, 4, 6
7. Evaluating how well writers and speakers use language to support ideas and opinions with details or reasons depending on modality, text type, purpose, audience, topic, and content area	• RL.5.3–4, 6; RI.5.2, 6, 8; SL.5.3; L.5.3–6
8. Analyzing how writers and speakers use vocabulary and other language resources for specific purposes (to explain, persuade, entertain, etc.) depending on modality, text type, purpose, audience, topic, and content area	• RL.5.4–5; RI.5.4–5; SL.5.3; L.5.3–6
C. Productive	
9. Expressing information and ideas in formal oral presentations on academic topics	• SL.5.4–6; L.5.1, 3, 6
10. Writing literary and informational texts to present, describe, and explain ideas and information, using appropriate technology	• W.5.1–10; L.5.1–3, 6
11. Supporting own opinions and evaluating others' opinions in speaking and writing	• W.5.1, 4, 9–10; SL.5.4, 6; L.5.1–3, 6
12. Selecting and applying varied and precise vocabulary and language structures to effectively convey ideas	• W.5.4–5; SL.5.4, 6; L.5.1, 3, 5–6
Part II: Learning About How English Works	**Corresponding CA CCSS for ELA/Literacy**
A. Structuring Cohesive Texts	
1. Understanding text structure	• RL.5.5; RI.5.5; W.5.1–5; SL.5.4
2. Understanding cohesion	• RL.5.5; RI.5.5; W.5.1–4; SL.5.4; L.5.1, 3
B. Expanding and Enriching Ideas	
3. Using verbs and verb phrases	• W.5.5; SL.5.6; L.5.1, 3, 6
4. Using nouns and noun phrases	• W.5.5; SL.5.6; L.5.1, 3, 6
5. Modifying to add details	• W.5.5; SL.5.4, 6; L.5.1, 3, 6
C. Connecting and Condensing Ideas	
6. Connecting ideas	• W.5.1–3, 5; SL.5.4, 6; L.5.1, 3, 6
7. Condensing ideas	• W.5.1–3, 5; SL.5.4, 6; L.5.1, 3, 6
Part III: Using Foundational Literacy Skills	• RF.K–1.1–4; RF.2–5.3–4 (as appropriate)

Note: **Examples** provided in specific standards are offered *only as illustrative possibilities* and should not be misinterpreted as the only objectives of instruction or as the only types of language that English learners might or should be able to understand or produce.

Section 2: Elaboration on Critical Principles for Developing Language and Cognition in Academic Contexts
Part I: Interacting in Meaningful Ways

Texts and Discourse in Context		ELD Proficiency Level Continuum		
		→ Emerging →	→ Expanding →	→ Bridging →
Part I, strands 1–4, corresponding to the CA CCSS for ELA/Literacy 1. SL.5.1, 6; L.5.1, 3, 6 2. W.5.6; L.5.1, 3, 6 3. SL.5.1, 6; L.5.1, 3, 6 4. W.5.4–5; SL.5.1, 6; L.5.1, 3, 6 **Purposes for using language include but are not limited to:** Describing, entertaining, informing, interpreting, analyzing, recounting, explaining, persuading, negotiating, justifying, evaluating, and so on. **Informational text types include but are not limited to:** Description (e.g., science log entry), procedure (e.g., how to solve a mathematics problem), recount (e.g., autobiography, science experiment results), information report (e.g., science or history report), explanation (e.g., how or why something happened), exposition (e.g., opinion), response (e.g., literary analysis), and so on. **Literary text types include but are not limited to:** Stories (e.g., fantasy, legends, fables), drama (e.g., readers' theater), poetry, retelling a story, and so on. **Audiences include but are not limited to:** Peers (one to one) Small group (one to a group) Whole group (one to many)	**A. Collaborative**	*1. Exchanging information/ideas* Contribute to conversations and express ideas by asking and answering *yes-no* and *wh-* questions and responding using short phrases. *2. Interacting via written English* Collaborate with peers on joint writing projects of short informational and literary texts, using technology where appropriate for publishing, graphics, and the like. *3. Offering opinions* Negotiate with or persuade others in conversations using basic learned phrases (e.g., *I think . . .*), as well as open responses, in order to gain and/or hold the floor. *4. Adapting language choices* Adjust language choices according to social setting (e.g., playground, classroom) and audience (e.g., peers, teacher), with substantial support.	*1. Exchanging information/ideas* Contribute to class, group, and partner discussions, including sustained dialogue, by following turn-taking rules, asking relevant questions, affirming others, and adding relevant information. *2. Interacting via written English* Collaborate with peers on joint writing projects of longer informational and literary texts, using technology where appropriate for publishing, graphics, and the like. *3. Offering opinions* Negotiate with or persuade others in conversations using an expanded set of learned phrases (e.g., *I agree with X, but . . .*), as well as open responses, in order to gain and/or hold the floor, provide counterarguments, and so on. *4. Adapting language choices* Adjust language choices according to purpose (e.g., persuading, entertaining), task (e.g., telling a story versus explaining a science experiment), and audience, with moderate support.	*1. Exchanging information/ideas* Contribute to class, group, and partner discussions, including sustained dialogue, by following turn-taking rules, asking relevant questions, affirming others, adding relevant information, building on responses, and providing useful feedback. *2. Interacting via written English* Collaborate with peers on joint writing projects of a variety of longer informational and literary texts, using technology where appropriate for publishing, graphics, and the like. *3. Offering opinions* Negotiate with or persuade others in conversations using a variety of learned phrases (e.g., *That's an interesting idea. However, . . .*), as well as open responses, in order to gain and/or hold the floor, provide counterarguments, elaborate on an idea, and so on. *4. Adapting language choices* Adjust language choices according to purpose, task (e.g., facilitating a science experiment), and audience, with light support.

Texts and Discourse in Context		ELD Proficiency Level Continuum		
		→ Emerging →	→ Expanding →	→ Bridging →
Part I, strands 5–8, corresponding to the CA CCSS for ELA/Literacy 5. SL.5.1–3; L.5.3 6. RL.5.1–7, 9–10; RI.5.1–7, 9–10; SL.5.2–3; L.5.3, 4, 6 7. RL.5.3–4, 6; RI.5.2, 6, 8; SL.5.3; L.5.3–6 8. RL.5.4–5; RI.5.4–5; SL.5.3; L.5.3–6 **Purposes for using language include but are not limited to:** Describing, entertaining, informing, interpreting, analyzing, recounting, explaining, persuading, negotiating, justifying, evaluating, and so on. **Informational text types include but are not limited to:** Description (e.g., science log entry), procedure (e.g., how to solve a mathematics problem), recount (e.g., autobiography, science experiment results), information report (e.g., science or history report), explanation (e.g., how or why something happened), exposition (e.g., opinion), response (e.g., literary analysis); and so on. **Literary text types include but are not limited to:** Stories (e.g., fantasy, legends, fables), drama (e.g., readers' theater), poetry, retelling a story, and so on. **Audiences include but are not limited to:** Peers (one to one) Small group (one to a group) Whole group (one to many)	**B. Interpretive**	**5. Listening actively** Demonstrate active listening of read-alouds and oral presentations by asking and answering basic questions, with prompting and substantial support. **6. Reading/viewing closely** a. Explain ideas, phenomena, processes, and text relationships (e.g., compare/contrast, cause/effect, problem/solution) based on close reading of a variety of grade-level texts and viewing of multimedia, with substantial support. b. Use knowledge of frequently-used affixes (e.g., *un-, mis-*), linguistic context, reference materials, and visual cues to determine the meaning of unknown words on familiar topics. **7. Evaluating language choices** Describe the specific language writers or speakers use to present or support an idea (e.g., the specific vocabulary or phrasing used to provide evidence), with prompting and substantial support. **8. Analyzing language choices** Distinguish how different words with similar meanings produce different effects on the audience (e.g., describing a character as *angry* versus *furious*).	**5. Listening actively** Demonstrate active listening of read-alouds and oral presentations by asking and answering detailed questions, with occasional prompting and moderate support. **6. Reading/viewing closely** a. Explain ideas, phenomena, processes, and text relationships (e.g., compare/contrast, cause/effect, problem/solution) based on close reading of a variety of grade-level texts and viewing of multimedia, with moderate support. b. Use knowledge of morphology (e.g., affixes, roots, and base words), linguistic context, and reference materials to determine the meaning of unknown words on familiar and new topics. **7. Evaluating language choices** Explain how well writers and speakers use language resources to support an opinion or present an idea (e.g., whether the vocabulary used to provide evidence is strong enough, or if the phrasing used to signal a shift in meaning does this well), with moderate support. **8. Analyzing language choices** Distinguish how different words with similar meanings (e.g., describing an event as *sad* versus *tragic*) and figurative language (e.g., *she ran like a cheetah*) produce shades of meaning and different effects on the audience.	**5. Listening actively** Demonstrate active listening of read-alouds and oral presentations by asking and answering detailed questions, with minimal prompting and light support. **6. Reading/viewing closely** a. Explain ideas, phenomena, processes, and text relationships (e.g., compare/contrast, cause/effect, problem/solution) based on close reading of a variety of grade-level texts and viewing of multimedia, with light support. b. Use knowledge of morphology (e.g., affixes, roots, and base words), linguistic context, and reference materials to determine the meaning of unknown words on familiar and new topics. **7. Evaluating language choices** Explain how well writers and speakers use specific language resources to support an opinion or present an idea (e.g., the clarity or appealing nature of language used to provide evidence or describe characters, or if the phrasing used to introduce a topic is appropriate), with light support. **8. Analyzing language choices** Distinguish how different words with related meanings (e.g., *fun* versus *thrilling, possibly* versus *certainly*) and figurative language (e.g., *the stream slithered through the parched land*) produce shades of meaning and different effects on the audience.

Texts and Discourse in Context		ELD Proficiency Level Continuum		
		→ Emerging →	→ Expanding →	→ Bridging →
Part I, strands 9–12, corresponding to the CA CCSS for ELA/Literacy 9. SL.5.4–6; L.5.1, 3, 6 10. W.5.1–10; L.5.1–3, 6 11. W.5.1, 4, 9–10; SL.5.4, 6; L.5.1–3, 6 12. W.5.4–5; SL.5.4, 6; L.5.1, 3, 5–6 **Purposes for using language include but are not limited to:** Describing, entertaining, informing, interpreting, analyzing, recounting, explaining, persuading, negotiating, justifying, evaluating, and so on. **Informational text types include but are not limited to:** Description (e.g., science log entry), procedure (e.g., how to solve a mathematics problem), recount (e.g., autobiography, science experiment results), information report (e.g., science or history report), explanation (e.g., how or why something happened), exposition (e.g., opinion), response (e.g., literary analysis), and so on. **Literary text types include but are not limited to:** Stories (e.g., fantasy, legends, fables), drama (e.g., readers' theater), poetry, retelling a story, and so on. **Audiences include but are not limited to:** Peers (one to one) Small group (one to a group) Whole group (one to many)	**C. Productive**	**9. Presenting** Plan and deliver brief oral presentations on a variety of topics and content areas (e.g., providing a report on a current event, reciting a poem, recounting an experience, explaining a science process), with moderate support, such as graphic organizers. **10. Writing** a. Write short literary and informational texts (e.g., a description of a camel) collaboratively (e.g., joint construction of texts with an adult or with peers) and sometimes independently. b. Write brief summaries of texts and experiences using complete sentences and key words (e.g., from notes or graphic organizers). **11. Supporting opinions** a. Support opinions by expressing appropriate/accurate reasons using textual evidence (e.g., referring to text) or relevant background knowledge about content, with substantial support. b. Express ideas and opinions or temper statements using basic modal expressions (e.g., *can, has to, maybe*).	**9. Presenting** Plan and deliver longer oral presentations on a variety of topics and content areas (e.g., providing an opinion speech on a current event, reciting a poem, recounting an experience, explaining a science process), with moderate support. **10. Writing** a. Write longer literary and informational texts (e.g., an informative report on different kinds of camels) collaboratively (e.g., joint construction of texts with an adult or with peers) and with increasing independence by using appropriate text organization. b. Write increasingly concise summaries of texts and experiences using complete sentences and key words (e.g., from notes or graphic organizers). **11. Supporting opinions** a. Support opinions or persuade others by expressing appropriate/accurate reasons using some textual evidence (e.g., paraphrasing facts from a text) or relevant background knowledge about content, with moderate support. b. Express attitude and opinions or temper statements with familiar modal expressions (e.g., *maybe/probably, can/must*).	**9. Presenting** Plan and deliver oral presentations on a variety of topics in a variety of content areas (e.g., providing an opinion speech on a current event, reciting a poem, recounting an experience, explaining a science process), with light support. **10. Writing** a. Write longer and more detailed literary and informational texts (e.g., an explanation of how camels survive without water for a long time) collaboratively (e.g., joint construction of texts with an adult or with peers) and independently by using appropriate text organization and growing understanding of register. b. Write clear and coherent summaries of texts and experiences using complete and concise sentences and key words (e.g., from notes or graphic organizers). **11. Supporting opinions** a. Support opinions or persuade others by expressing appropriate/accurate reasons using detailed textual evidence (e.g., quoting the text directly or specific events from text) or relevant background knowledge about content, with mild support. b. Express attitude and opinions or temper statements with nuanced modal expressions (e.g., *probably/certainly, should/would*) and phrasing (e.g., *In my opinion . . .*).

Texts and Discourse in Context		ELD Proficiency Level Continuum		
		→ Emerging →	→ Expanding →	→ Bridging →
Part I, strands 9–12, corresponding to the CA CCSS for ELA/Literacy 9. SL.5.4–6; L.5.1, 3, 6 10. W.5.1–10; L.5.1–3, 6 11. W.5.1, 4, 9–10; SL.5.4, 6; L.5.1–3, 6 12. W.5.4–5; SL.5.4, 6; L.5.1, 3, 5–6 **Purposes for using language include but are not limited to:** Describing, entertaining, informing, interpreting, analyzing, recounting, explaining, persuading, negotiating, justifying, evaluating, and so on. **Informational text types include but are not limited to:** Description (e.g., science log entry), procedure (e.g., how to solve a mathematics problem), recount (e.g., autobiography, science experiment results), information report (e.g., science or history report), explanation (e.g., how or why something happened), exposition (e.g., opinion), response (e.g., literary analysis), and so on. **Literary text types include but are not limited to:** Stories (e.g., fantasy, legends, fables), drama (e.g., readers' theater), poetry, retelling a story, and so on. **Audiences include but are not limited to:** Peers (one to one) Small group (one to a group) Whole group (one to many)	**C. Productive**	*12. Selecting language resources* a. Use a select number of general academic and domain-specific words to create precision while speaking and writing. b. Select a few frequently used affixes for accuracy and precision (e.g., She walks, I'm *un*happy).	*12. Selecting language resources* a. Use a growing number of general academic and domain-specific words, synonyms, and antonyms to create precision and shades of meaning while speaking and writing. b. Select a growing number of frequently used affixes for accuracy and precision (e.g., She walk*ed*. He likes . . . , I'm *un*happy).	*12. Selecting language resources* a. Use a wide variety of general academic and domain-specific words, synonyms, antonyms, and figurative language to create precision and shades of meaning while speaking and writing. b. Select a variety of appropriate affixes for accuracy and precision (e.g., She's walk*ing*. I'm *un*comfortable. They left reluctant*ly*).

Texts and Discourse in Context		ELD Proficiency Level Continuum		
		→ Emerging →	→ Expanding →	→ Bridging →
Part II, strands 1–2, corresponding to the CA CCSS for ELA/Literacy 1. RL.5.5; RI.5.5; W.5.1–5; SL.5.4 2. RL.5.5; RI.5.5; W.5.1–4; SL.5.4; L.5.1, 3 **Purposes for using language include but are not limited to:** Describing, entertaining, informing, interpreting, analyzing, recounting, explaining, persuading, negotiating, justifying, evaluating, and so on. **Informational text types include but are not limited to:** Description (e.g., science log entry), procedure (e.g., how to solve a mathematics problem), recount (e.g., autobiography, science experiment results), information report (e.g., science or history report), explanation (e.g., how or why something happened), exposition (e.g., opinion), response (e.g., literary analysis), and so on. **Literary text types include but are not limited to:** Stories (e.g., fantasy, legends, fables), drama (e.g., readers' theater), poetry, retelling a story, and so on. **Audiences include but are not limited to:** Peers (one to one) Small group (one to a group) Whole group (one to many)	**A. Structuring Cohesive Texts**	*1. Understanding text structure* Apply basic understanding of how different text types are organized to express ideas (e.g., how a narrative is organized sequentially with predictable stages versus how opinions/arguments are organized around ideas) to comprehending texts and writing basic texts. *2. Understanding cohesion* a. Apply basic understanding of language resources for referring the reader back or forward in text (e.g., how pronouns refer back to nouns in text) to comprehending texts and writing basic texts. b. Apply basic understanding of how ideas, events, or reasons are linked throughout a text using a select set of everyday connecting words or phrases (e.g., *first/next, at the beginning*) to comprehending texts and writing basic texts.	*1. Understanding text structure* Apply growing understanding of how different text types are organized to express ideas (e.g., how a narrative is organized sequentially with predictable stages versus how opinions/arguments are structured logically around reasons and evidence) to comprehending texts and writing texts with increasing cohesion. *2. Understanding cohesion* a. Apply growing understanding of language resources for referring the reader back or forward in text (e.g., how pronouns or synonyms refer back to nouns in text) to comprehending texts and writing texts with increasing cohesion. b. Apply growing understanding of how ideas, events, or reasons are linked throughout a text using a variety of connecting words or phrases (e.g., *for example, in the first place, as a result*) to comprehending texts and writing texts with increasing cohesion.	*1. Understanding text structure* Apply increasing understanding of how different text types are organized to express ideas (e.g., how a historical account is organized chronologically versus how opinions/arguments are structured logically around reasons and evidence) to comprehending texts and writing cohesive texts. *2. Understanding cohesion* a. Apply increasing understanding of language resources for referring the reader back or forward in text (e.g., how pronouns, synonyms, or nominalizations refer back to nouns in text) to comprehending texts and writing cohesive texts. b. Apply increasing understanding of how ideas, events, or reasons are linked throughout a text using an increasing variety of academic connecting and transitional words or phrases (e.g., *consequently, specifically, however*) to comprehending texts and writing cohesive texts.

Texts and Discourse in Context		ELD Proficiency Level Continuum		
		→ Emerging →	→ Expanding →	→ Bridging →
Part II, strands 3–5, corresponding to the CA CCSS for ELA/Literacy 3. W.5.5; SL.5.6; L.5.1, 3, 6 4. W.5.5; SL.5.6; L.5.1, 3, 6 5. W.5.5; SL.5.4,6; L.5.1, 3, 6 **Purposes for using language include but are not limited to:** Describing, entertaining, informing, interpreting, analyzing, recounting, explaining, persuading, negotiating, justifying, evaluating, and so on. **Informational text types include but are not limited to:** Description (e.g., science log entry), procedure (e.g., how to solve a mathematics problem), recount (e.g., autobiography, science experiment results), information report (e.g., science or history report), explanation (e.g., how or why something happened), exposition (e.g., opinion), response (e.g., literary analysis), and so on. **Literary text types include but are not limited to:** Stories (e.g., fantasy, legends, fables), drama (e.g., readers' theater), poetry, retelling a story, and so on. **Audiences include but are not limited to:** Peers (one to one) Small group (one to a group) Whole group (one to many)	**B. Expanding and Enriching Ideas**	*3. Using verbs and verb phrases* Use frequently used verbs (e.g., take, like, eat) and various verb types (e.g., doing, saying, being/having, thinking/feeling) and tenses appropriate to the text type and discipline (e.g., simple past for recounting an experience) on familiar topics. *4. Using nouns and noun phrases* Expand noun phrases in simple ways (e.g., adding an adjective to a noun) in order to enrich the meaning of sentences and add details about ideas, people, things, and the like. *5. Modifying to add details* Expand and enrich sentences with adverbials (e.g., adverbs, adverb phrases, prepositional phrases) to provide details (e.g., time, manner, place, cause, and the like) about a familiar activity or process.	*3. Using verbs and verb phrases* Use various verb types (e.g., doing, saying, being/having, thinking/feeling) and tenses appropriate to the task, text type, and discipline (e.g., simple past for recounting an experience, timeless present for a science description) on an increasing variety of topics. *4. Using nouns and noun phrases* Expand noun phrases in a variety of ways (e.g., adding comparative/ superlative adjectives to noun phrases or simple clause embedding) in order to enrich the meaning of sentences and add details about ideas, people, things, and the like. *5. Modifying to add details* Expand and enrich sentences with adverbials (e.g., adverbs, adverb phrases, prepositional phrases) to provide details (e.g., time, manner, place, cause, and the like) about a familiar or new activity or process.	*3. Using verbs and verb phrases* Use various verb types (e.g., doing, saying, being/having, thinking/feeling) and tenses appropriate to the task and text type (e.g., timeless present for science description, mixture of past and present for narrative or history explanation) on a variety of topics. *4. Using nouns and noun phrases* Expand noun phrases in an increasing variety of ways (e.g., adding comparative/ superlative and general academic adjectives to noun phrases or more complex clause embedding) in order to enrich the meaning of sentences and add details about ideas, people, things, and the like. *5. Modifying to add details* Expand and enrich sentences with adverbials (e.g., adverbs, adverb phrases, prepositional phrases) to provide details (e.g., time, manner, place, cause, and the like) about a variety of familiar and new activities and processes.

Texts and Discourse in Context		ELD Proficiency Level Continuum		
		→ Emerging →	→ Expanding →	→ Bridging →
Part II, strands 6–7, corresponding to the CA CCSS for ELA/Literacy 6. W.5.1–3, 5; SL.5.4, 6; L.5.1, 3, 6 7. W.5.1–3, 5; SL.5.4, 6; L.5.1, 3, 6 **Purposes for using language include but are not limited to:** Describing, entertaining, informing, interpreting, analyzing, recounting, explaining, persuading, negotiating, justifying, evaluating, and so on. **Informational text types include but are not limited to:** Description (e.g., science log entry), procedure (e.g., how to solve a mathematics problem), recount (e.g., autobiography, science experiment results), information report (e.g., science or history report), explanation (e.g., how or why something happened), exposition (e.g., opinion), response (e.g., literary analysis), and so on. **Literary text types include but are not limited to:** Stories (e.g., fantasy, legends, fables), drama (e.g., readers' theater), poetry, retelling a story, and so on. **Audiences include but are not limited to:** Peers (one to one) Small group (one to a group) Whole group (one to many)	**C. Connecting and Condensing Ideas**	*6. Connecting ideas* Combine clauses in a few basic ways to make connections between and join ideas (e.g., You must X because X) or to provide evidence to support ideas or opinions (e.g., creating compound sentences using *and, but, so*). *7. Condensing ideas* Condense clauses in simple ways (e.g., through simple embedded clauses as in, *The book is on the desk. The book is mine.* → *The book that is on the desk is mine*) to create precise and detailed sentences.	*6. Connecting ideas* Combine clauses in an increasing variety of ways (e.g., creating compound and complex sentences) to make connections between and join ideas, for example, to express cause/effect (e.g., *The deer ran because the mountain lion came*), to make a concession (e.g., *She studied all night even though she wasn't feeling well*), or to provide reasons to support ideas (e.g., *X is an extremely good book because _____*). *7. Condensing ideas* Condense clauses in an increasing variety of ways (e.g., through a growing number of types of embedded clauses and other condensing as in, *The book is mine. The book is about science. The book is on the desk.* → *The science book that's on the desk is mine*) to create precise and detailed sentences.	*6. Connecting ideas* Combine clauses in a wide variety of ways (e.g., creating compound and complex sentences) to make connections between and join ideas, for example, to express cause/effect (e.g., *The deer ran because the mountain lion approached them*), to make a concession (e.g., *She studied all night even though she wasn't feeling well*), to link two ideas that happen at the same time (e.g., *The cubs played while their mother hunted*), or to provide reasons to support ideas (e.g., *The author persuades the reader by _____*). *7. Condensing ideas* Condense clauses in a variety of ways (e.g., through various types of embedded clauses and some nominalizations as in, *They were a very strong army. They had a lot of enemies. They crushed their enemies because they were strong.* → *Their strength helped them crush their numerous enemies*) to create precise and detailed sentences.

Foundational literacy skills in an alphabetic writing system ● Print concepts ● Phonological awareness ● Phonics and word recognition ● Fluency	See chapter 6 for information on teaching foundational reading skills to English learners of various profiles based on age, native language, native language writing system, schooling experience, and literacy experience and proficiency. Some considerations are as follows: ● Native language and literacy (e.g., phoneme awareness or print concept skills in native language) should be assessed for potential transference to English language and literacy. ● Similarities between the native language and English should be highlighted (e.g., phonemes or letters that are the same in both languages). ● Differences between the native language and English should be highlighted (e.g., some phonemes in English may not exist in the student's native language; native language syntax may be different from English syntax).

Grade 6

Section 1: Overview

Goal: English learners read, analyze, interpret, and create a variety of literary and informational text types. They develop an understanding of how language is a complex, dynamic, and social resource for making meaning, as well as how content is organized in different text types and across disciplines using text structure, language features, and vocabulary depending on purpose and audience. They are aware that different languages and variations of English exist, and they recognize their home languages and cultures as resources to value in their own right and also to draw upon in order to build proficiency in English. English learners contribute actively to class and group discussions, asking questions, responding appropriately, and providing useful feedback. They demonstrate knowledge of content through oral presentations, writing tasks, collaborative conversations, and multimedia. They develop proficiency in shifting language use based on task, purpose, audience, and text type.

Critical Principles for Developing Language and Cognition in Academic Contexts: While advancing along the continuum of English language development levels, English learners at all levels engage in intellectually challenging literacy, disciplinary, and disciplinary literacy tasks. They use language in meaningful and relevant ways appropriate to grade level, content area, topic, purpose, audience, and text type in English language arts, mathematics, science, social studies, and the arts. Specifically, they use language to gain and exchange information and ideas in three communicative modes (collaborative, interpretive, and productive), and they apply knowledge of language to academic tasks via three cross-mode language processes (structuring cohesive texts, expanding and enriching ideas, and connecting and condensing ideas) using various linguistic resources.

Part I: Interacting in Meaningful Ways	Corresponding CA CCSS for ELA/Literacy*
A. Collaborative	
1. Exchanging information and ideas with others through oral collaborative discussions on a range of social and academic topics	• SL.6.1, 6; L.6.3, 6
2. Interacting with others in written English in various communicative forms (print, communicative technology, and multimedia)	• W.6.6; WHST.6.6; SL.6.2; L.6.3, 6
3. Offering and justifying opinions, negotiating with and persuading others in communicative exchanges	• W.6.1; WHST.6.1; SL.6.1, 4, 6; L.6.3, 6
4. Adapting language choices to various contexts (based on task, purpose, audience, and text type)	• W.6.4–5; WHST.6.4–5; SL.6.6; L.6.1, 3, 6

---

*The California English Language Development Standards correspond to the California Common Core State Standards for English Language Arts and Literacy in History/Social Science and Technical Subjects (CA CCSS for ELA/Literacy). English learners should have full access to opportunities to learn ELA, mathematics, science, history/social studies, and other content at the same time they are progressing toward full proficiency in English.

Part I: Interacting in Meaningful Ways	Corresponding CA CCSS for ELA/Literacy
B. Interpretive	
5. Listening actively to spoken English in a range of social and academic contexts	• SL.6.1, 3, 6; L.6.1, 3, 6
6. Reading closely literary and informational texts and viewing multimedia to determine how meaning is conveyed explicitly and implicitly through language	• RL.6.1–7, 9–10; RI.6.1–10; RH.6.1–10; RST.6.1–10; SL.6.2; L.6.1, 3, 6
7. Evaluating how well writers and speakers use language to support ideas and arguments with details or evidence depending on modality, text type, purpose, audience, topic, and content area	• RL.6.4–5; RI.6.4, 6, 8; RH.6.4–6, 8; RST.6.4–6, 8; SL.6.3; L.6.3, 5–6
8. Analyzing how writers and speakers use vocabulary and other language resources for specific purposes (to explain, persuade, entertain, etc.) depending on modality, text type, purpose, audience, topic, and content area	• RL.6.4–5; RI.6.4–5; RH.6.4–5; RST.6.4–5; SL.6.3; L.6.3, 5–6
C. Productive	
9. Expressing information and ideas in formal oral presentations on academic topics	• SL.6.4–6; L.6.1, 3
10. Writing literary and informational texts to present, describe, and explain ideas and information, using appropriate technology	• W.6.1–10; WHST.6.1–2, 4–10; L.6.1–6
11. Justifying own arguments and evaluating others' arguments in writing	• W.6.1, 8–9; WHST.6.1, 8–9; L.6.13, 6
12. Selecting and applying varied and precise vocabulary and language structures to effectively convey ideas	• W.6.4–5; WHST.6.4–5; SL.6.4, 6; L.6.1, 3, 5–6
Part II: Learning About How English Works	**Corresponding CA CCSS for ELA/Literacy**
A. Structuring Cohesive Texts	• RL.6.5; RI.6.5; RH.6.5; RST.6.5; W.6.1–5, 10; WHST.6.1–2, 4–5, 10; SL.6.4
1. Understanding text structure	
2. Understanding cohesion	• RI.6.5; RH.6.5; RST.6.5; W.6.1–5, 10; WHST.6.1–2, 4–5, 10; L.6.1, 3–6
B. Expanding and Enriching Ideas	
3. Using verbs and verb phrases	• W.6.5; WHST.6.5; SL.6.6; L.6.1, 3–6
4. Using nouns and noun phrases	• W.6.5; WHST.6.5; SL.6.6; L.6.1, 3–6
5. Modifying to add details	• W.6.4–5; WHST.6.4–5; SL.6.6; L.6.1, 3–6
C. Connecting and Condensing Ideas	
6. Connecting ideas	• W.6.1–5; WHST.6.1–2, 4–5; SL.6.4, 6; L.6.1, 3–6
7. Condensing ideas	• W.6.1–5; WHST.6.1–2, 4–5; SL.6.4, 6; L.6.1, 3–6
Part III: Using Foundational Literacy Skills	• RF.K–1.1–4; RF.2–5.3–4 (as appropriate)

Note: **Examples** provided in specific standards are offered *only as illustrative possibilities* and should not be misinterpreted as the only objectives of instruction or as the only types of language that English learners might or should be able to understand or produce.

Section 2: Elaboration on Critical Principles for Developing Language and Cognition in Academic Contexts
Part I: Interacting in Meaningful Ways

Texts and Discourse in Context		ELD Proficiency Level Continuum		
		→ Emerging →	→ Expanding →	→ Bridging →
Part I, strands 1–4, corresponding to the CA CCSS for ELA/Literacy 1. SL.6.1,6; L.6.3, 6 2. W.6.6; WHST.6.6; SL.6.2; L.6.3, 6 3. W.6.1; WHST.6.1; SL.6.1, 4, 6; L.6.3, 6 4. W.6.4–5; WHST.6.4–5; SL.6.6; L.6.1, 3, 6 **Purposes for using language include but are not limited to:** Describing, entertaining, informing, interpreting, analyzing, recounting, explaining, persuading, negotiating, justifying, evaluating, and so on. **Informational text types include but are not limited to:** Descriptions or accounts (e.g., scientific, historical, economic, technical), recounts (e.g., biography, memoir), information reports, explanations (e.g., causal, factual), expositions (e.g., speeches, opinion pieces, argument, debate), responses (e.g., literary analysis), and so on. **Literary text types include but are not limited to:** Stories (e.g., historical fiction, myths, graphic novels), poetry, drama, and so on. **Audiences include but are not limited to:** Peers (one to one) Small group (one to a group) Whole group (one to many)	**A. Collaborative**	*1. Exchanging information/ideas* Engage in conversational exchanges and express ideas on familiar topics by asking and answering *yes-no* and *wh-* questions and responding using simple phrases. *2. Interacting via written English* Engage in short written exchanges with peers and collaborate on simple written texts on familiar topics, using technology when appropriate. *3. Supporting opinions and persuading others* Negotiate with or persuade others in conversations (e.g., to gain and hold the floor or ask for clarification) using basic learned phrases (e.g., *I think . . . , Would you please repeat that?*), as well as open responses. *4. Adapting language choices* Adjust language choices according to social setting (e.g., classroom, break time) and audience (e.g., peers, teacher).	*1. Exchanging information/ideas* Contribute to class, group, and partner discussions by following turn-taking rules, asking relevant questions, affirming others, adding relevant information, and paraphrasing key ideas. *2. Interacting via written English* Engage in longer written exchanges with peers and collaborate on more detailed written texts on a variety of topics, using technology when appropriate. *3. Supporting opinions and persuading others* Negotiate with or persuade others in conversations (e.g., to provide counterarguments) using an expanded set of learned phrases (*I agree with X, but . . .*), as well as open responses. *4. Adapting language choices* Adjust language choices according to purpose (e.g., explaining, persuading, entertaining), task, and audience.	*1. Exchanging information/ideas* Contribute to class, group, and partner discussions by following turn-taking rules, asking relevant questions, affirming others, adding relevant information and evidence, paraphrasing key ideas, building on responses, and providing useful feedback. *2. Interacting via written English* Engage in extended written exchanges with peers and collaborate on complex written texts on a variety of topics, using technology when appropriate. *3. Supporting opinions and persuading others* Negotiate with or persuade others in conversations using appropriate register (e.g., to reflect on multiple perspectives) using a variety of learned phrases, indirect reported speech (e.g., *I heard you say X, and Gabriel just pointed out Y*), as well as open responses. *4. Adapting language choices* Adjust language choices according to task (e.g., facilitating a science experiment, providing peer feedback on a writing assignment), purpose, task, and audience.

Texts and Discourse in Context		ELD Proficiency Level Continuum		
		→ Emerging →	→ Expanding →	→ Bridging →
Part I, strands 5–8 corresponding to the CA CCSS for ELA/Literacy 5. SL.6.1, 3, 6; L.6.1, 3, 6 6. RL.6.1–7, 9–10; RI.6.1–10; RH.6.1–10; RST.6.1–10; SL.6.2; L.6.1, 3, 6 7. RL.6.4–5; RI.6.4, 6, 8; RH.6.4–6, 8; RST.6.4–6, 8; SL.6.3; L.6.3, 5–6 8. RL.6.4–5; RI.6.4–5; RH.6.4–5; RST.6.4–5; SL.6.3; L.6.3, 5–6 **Purposes for using language include but are not limited to:** Describing, entertaining, informing, interpreting, analyzing, recounting, explaining, persuading, negotiating, justifying, evaluating, and so on. **Informational text types include but are not limited to:** Descriptions or accounts (e.g., scientific, historical, economic, technical), recounts (e.g., biography, memoir), information reports, explanations (e.g., causal, factual), expositions (e.g., speeches, opinion pieces, argument, debate), responses (e.g., literary analysis), and so on. **Literary text types include but are not limited to:** Stories (e.g., historical fiction, myths, graphic novels), poetry, drama, and so on. **Audiences include but are not limited to:** Peers (one to one) Small group (one to a group) Whole group (one to many)	B. Interpretive	**5. Listening actively** Demonstrate active listening in oral presentation activities by asking and answering basic questions, with prompting and substantial support. **6. Reading/viewing closely** a. Explain ideas, phenomena, processes, and text relationships (e.g., compare/contrast, cause/effect, problem/solution) based on close reading of a variety of grade-level texts and viewing of multimedia, with substantial support. b. Express inferences and conclusions drawn based on close reading of grade-level texts and viewing of multimedia using some frequently used verbs (e.g., *shows that, based on*). c. Use knowledge of morphology (e.g., affixes, roots, and base words), context, reference materials, and visual cues to determine the meaning of unknown and multiple-meaning words on familiar topics. **7. Evaluating language choices** Explain how well writers and speakers use language to support ideas and arguments with detailed evidence (e.g., identifying the precise vocabulary used to present evidence, or the phrasing used to signal a shift in meaning) with substantial support.	**5. Listening actively** Demonstrate active listening in oral presentation activities by asking and answering detailed questions, with occasional prompting and moderate support. **6. Reading/viewing closely** a. Explain ideas, phenomena, processes, and text relationships (e.g., compare/contrast, cause/effect, problem/solution) based on close reading of a variety of grade-level texts and viewing of multimedia, with moderate support. b. Express inferences and conclusions drawn based on close reading of grade-level texts and viewing of multimedia using a variety of verbs (e.g., *suggests that, leads to*). c. Use knowledge of morphology (e.g., affixes, roots, and base words), context, reference materials, and visual cues to determine the meaning of unknown and multiple-meaning words on familiar and new topics. **7. Evaluating language choices** Explain how well writers and speakers use specific language to present ideas or support arguments and provide detailed evidence (e.g., showing the clarity of the phrasing used to present an argument) with moderate support.	**5. Listening actively** Demonstrate active listening in oral presentation activities by asking and answering detailed questions, with minimal prompting and support. **6. Reading/viewing closely** a. Explain ideas, phenomena, processes, and text relationships (e.g., compare/contrast, cause/effect, problem/solution) based on close reading of a variety of grade-level texts and viewing of multimedia, with light support. b. Express inferences and conclusions drawn based on close reading of grade-level texts and viewing of multimedia using a variety of precise academic verbs (e.g., *indicates that, influences*). c. Use knowledge of morphology (e.g., affixes, roots, and base words), context, reference materials, and visual cues to determine the meaning, including figurative and connotative meanings, of unknown and multiple-meaning words on a variety of new topics. **7. Evaluating language choices** Explain how well writers and speakers use specific language resources to present ideas or support arguments and provide detailed evidence (e.g., identifying the specific language used to present ideas and claims that are well supported and distinguishing them from those that are not) with light support.

Section 2: Elaboration on Critical Principles for Developing Language and Cognition in Academic Contexts
Part I: Interacting in Meaningful Ways

Texts and Discourse in Context		ELD Proficiency Level Continuum		
		→ Emerging →	→ Expanding →	→ Bridging →
Part I, strands 5–8 corresponding to the CA CCSS for ELA/Literacy 5. SL.6.1, 3, 6; L.6.1, 3, 6 6. RL.6.1–7, 9–10; RI.6.1–10; RH.6.1–10; RST.6.1–10; SL.6.2; L.6.1, 3, 6 7. RL.6.4–5; RI.6.4, 6, 8; RH.6.4–6, 8; RST.6.4–6, 8; SL.6.3; L.6.3, 5–6 8. RL.6.4–5; RI.6.4–5; RH.6.4–5; RST.6.4–5; SL.6.3; L.6.3, 5–6 **Purposes for using language include but are not limited to:** Describing, entertaining, informing, interpreting, analyzing, recounting, explaining, persuading, negotiating, justifying, evaluating, and so on. **Informational text types include but are not limited to:** Descriptions or accounts (e.g., scientific, historical, economic, technical), recounts (e.g., biography, memoir), information reports, explanations (e.g., causal, factual), expositions (e.g., speeches, opinion pieces, argument, debate), responses (e.g., literary analysis), and so on. **Literary text types include but are not limited to:** Stories (e.g., historical fiction, myths, graphic novels), poetry, drama, and so on. **Audiences include but are not limited to:** Peers (one to one) Small group (one to a group) Whole group (one to many)	B. Interpretive	**8. Analyzing language choices** Explain how phrasing or different common words with similar meaning (e.g., choosing to use the word *cheap* versus the phrase *a good saver*) produce different effects on the audience.	**8. Analyzing language choices** Explain how phrasing, different words with similar meaning (e.g., describing a character as *stingy* versus *economical*), or figurative language (e.g., *The room was like a dank cave, littered with food wrappers, soda cans, and piles of laundry*) produce shades of meaning and different effects on the audience.	**8. Analyzing language choices** Explain how phrasing, different words with similar meaning (e.g., *stingy, economical, frugal, thrifty*), or figurative language (e.g., *The room was depressed and gloomy. The room was like a dank cave, littered with food wrappers, soda cans, and piles of laundry*) produce shades of meaning, nuances, and different effects on the audience.

Section 2: Elaboration on Critical Principles for Developing Language and Cognition in Academic Contexts
Part I: Interacting in Meaningful Ways

Texts and Discourse in Context		ELD Proficiency Level Continuum		
		→ Emerging →	→ Expanding →	→ Bridging →
Part I, strands 9–12, corresponding to the CA CCSS for ELA/Literacy 9. SL.6.4–6; L.6.1, 3, 5, 6 10. W.6.1–10; WHST.6.1–10; L.6.1–3, 6 11. W.6.1, 4, 8–10; WHST.6.1, 4, 8–10; SL.6.3, 6; L.6.1–3, 6 12. RL.6.1–4; RI.6.1, 2, 4; W.6.1–10; WHST.6.1–10; SL.6.1, 2, 4, 6; L.6.3–6 **Purposes for using language include but are not limited to:** Describing, entertaining, informing, interpreting, analyzing, recounting, explaining, persuading, negotiating, justifying, evaluating, and so on. **Informational text types include but are not limited to:** Descriptions or accounts (e.g., scientific, historical, economic, technical), recounts (e.g., biography, memoir), information reports, explanations (e.g., causal, factual), expositions (e.g., speeches, opinion pieces, argument, debate), responses (e.g., literary analysis), and so on. **Literary text types include but are not limited to:** Stories (e.g., historical fiction, myths, graphic novels), poetry, drama, and so on. **Audiences include but are not limited to:** Peers (one to one) Small group (one to a group) Whole group (one to many)	**C. Productive**	*9. Presenting* Plan and deliver brief oral presentations on a variety of topics and content areas. *10. Writing* a. Write short literary and informational texts (e.g., an argument for protecting the rain forests) collaboratively (e.g., with peers) and independently. b. Write brief summaries of texts and experiences using complete sentences and key words (e.g., from notes or graphic organizers). *11. Justifying/arguing* a. Justify opinions by providing some textual evidence (e.g., quoting from the text) or relevant background knowledge, with substantial support. b Express attitude and opinions or temper statements with some basic modal expressions (e.g., *can, has to*).	*9. Presenting* Plan and deliver longer oral presentations on a variety of topics and content areas, using details and evidence to support ideas. *10. Writing* a. Write longer literary and informational texts (e.g., an argument for protecting the rain forests) collaboratively (e.g., with peers) and independently using appropriate text organization. b. Write increasingly concise summaries of texts and experiences using complete sentences and key words (e.g., from notes or graphic organizers). *11. Justifying/arguing* a. Justify opinions or persuade others by providing relevant textual evidence (e.g., quoting from the text or referring to what the text says) or relevant background knowledge, with moderate support. b. Express attitude and opinions or temper statements with a variety of familiar modal expressions (e.g., *maybe/probably, can/could, must*).	*9. Presenting* Plan and deliver longer oral presentations on a variety of topics and content areas, using reasoning and evidence to support ideas, as well as growing understanding of register. *10. Writing* a. Write longer and more detailed literary and informational texts (e.g., an argument for protecting the rain forests) collaboratively (e.g., with peers) and independently using appropriate text organization and growing understanding of register. b. Write clear and coherent summaries of texts and experiences using complete and concise sentences and key words (e.g., from notes or graphic organizers). *11. Justifying/arguing* a. Justify opinions or persuade others by providing detailed and relevant textual evidence (e.g., quoting from the text directly or referring to specific textual evidence) or relevant background knowledge, with light support. b. Express attitude and opinions or temper statements with nuanced modal expressions (e.g., *probably/certainly/definitely, should/would, might*) and phrasing (e.g., *In my opinion . . .*).

Section 2: Elaboration on Critical Principles for Developing Language and Cognition in Academic Contexts
Part I: Interacting in Meaningful Ways

Texts and Discourse in Context		ELD Proficiency Level Continuum		
		→ Emerging →	→ Expanding →	→ Bridging →
Part I, strands 9–12, corresponding to the CA CCSS for ELA/Literacy 9. SL.6.4–6; L.6.1, 3, 5, 6 10. W.6.1–10; WHST.6.1–10; L.6.1–3, 6 11. W.6.1, 4, 8–10; WHST.6.1, 4, 8–10; SL.6.3, 6; L.6.1–3, 6 12. RL.6.1–4; RI.6.1, 2, 4; W.6.1–10; WHST.6.1–10; SL.6.1, 2, 4, 6; L.6.3–6 **Purposes for using language include but are not limited to:** Describing, entertaining, informing, interpreting, analyzing, recounting, explaining, persuading, negotiating, justifying, evaluating, and so on. **Informational text types include but are not limited to:** Descriptions or accounts (e.g., scientific, historical, economic, technical), recounts (e.g., biography, memoir), information reports, explanations (e.g., causal, factual), expositions (e.g., speeches, opinion pieces, argument, debate), responses (e.g., literary analysis), and so on. **Literary text types include but are not limited to:** Stories (e.g., historical fiction, myths, graphic novels), poetry, drama, and so on. **Audiences include but are not limited to:** Peers (one to one) Small group (one to a group) Whole group (one to many)	**C. Productive**	*12. Selecting language resources* a. Use a select number of general academic words (e.g., *author, chart*) and domain-specific words (e.g., *scene, cell, fraction*) to create some precision while speaking and writing. b. Use knowledge of morphology to appropriately select affixes in basic ways (e.g., *She likes X*).	*12. Selecting language resources* a. Use a growing set of academic words (e.g., *author, chart, global, affect*), domain-specific words (e.g., *scene, setting, plot, point of view, fraction, cell membrane, democracy*), synonyms, and antonyms to create precision and shades of meaning while speaking and writing. b. Use knowledge of morphology to appropriately select affixes in a growing number of ways to manipulate language (e.g., *She likes X. That's impossible*).	*12. Selecting language resources* a. Use an expanded set of general academic words (e.g., *affect, evidence, demonstrate, reluctantly*), domain-specific words (e.g., *scene, setting, plot, point of view, fraction, cell membrane, democracy*), synonyms, antonyms, and figurative language to create precision and shades of meaning while speaking and writing. b. Use knowledge of morphology to appropriately select affixes in a variety of ways to manipulate language (e.g., changing *observe* → *observation, reluctant* → *reluctantly, produce* → *production*, and so on).

Texts and Discourse in Context		ELD Proficiency Level Continuum		
		→ Emerging →	→ Expanding →	→ Bridging →
Part II, strands 1–2, corresponding to the CA CCSS for ELA/Literacy 1. RL.6.5; RI.6.5; RH.6.5; RST.6.5; W.6.1–5, 10; WHST.6.1–2, 4–5,10; SL.6.4 2. RI.6.5; RH.6.5; RST.6.5; W.6.1–5, 10; WHST.6.1–2, 4–5, 10; L.6.1, 3–6 **Purposes for using language include but are not limited to:** Describing, entertaining, informing, interpreting, analyzing, recounting, explaining, persuading, negotiating, justifying, evaluating, and so on. **Informational text types include but are not limited to:** Descriptions or accounts (e.g., scientific, historical, economic, technical), recounts (e.g., biography, memoir), information reports, explanations (e.g., causal, factual), expositions (e.g., speeches, opinion pieces, argument, debate), responses (e.g., literary analysis), and so on. **Literary text types include but are not limited to:** Stories (e.g., historical fiction, myths, graphic novels), poetry, drama, and so on. **Audiences include but are not limited to:** Peers (one to one) Small group (one to a group) Whole group (one to many)	**A. Structuring Cohesive Texts**	**1. Understanding text structure** Apply basic understanding of how different text types are organized to express ideas (e.g., how a narrative is organized sequentially with predictable stages versus how arguments are organized around ideas) to comprehending texts and writing basic texts. **2. Understanding cohesion** a. Apply basic understanding of language resources for referring the reader back or forward in text (e.g., how pronouns refer back to nouns in text) to comprehending texts and writing basic texts. b. Apply basic understanding of how ideas, events, or reasons are linked throughout a text using a select set of everyday connecting words or phrases (e.g., *first/next, at the beginning*) to comprehending texts and writing basic texts.	**1. Understanding text structure** Apply growing understanding of how different text types are organized to express ideas (e.g., how a narrative is organized sequentially with predictable stages versus how arguments are structured logically around reasons and evidence) to comprehending texts and writing texts with increasing cohesion. **2. Understanding cohesion** a. Apply growing understanding of language resources for referring the reader back or forward in text (e.g., how pronouns or synonyms refer back to nouns in text) to comprehending texts and writing texts with increasing cohesion. b. Apply growing understanding of how ideas, events, or reasons are linked throughout a text using a variety of connecting words or phrases (e.g., *for example, in the first place, as a result, on the other hand*) to comprehending texts and writing texts with increasing cohesion.	**1. Understanding text structure** Apply increasing understanding of how different text types are organized to express ideas (e.g., how a historical account is organized chronologically versus how arguments are structured logically around reasons and evidence) to comprehending texts and writing cohesive texts. **2. Understanding cohesion** a. Apply increasing understanding of language resources for referring the reader back or forward in text (e.g., how pronouns, synonyms, or nominalizations refer back to nouns in text) to comprehending texts and writing cohesive texts. b. Apply increasing understanding of how ideas, events, or reasons are linked throughout a text using an increasing variety of academic connecting and transitional words or phrases (e.g., *consequently, specifically, however, moreover*) to comprehending texts and writing cohesive texts.

Section 2: Elaboration on Critical Principles for Developing Language and Cognition in Academic Contexts
Part II: Learning About How English Works

Texts and Discourse in Context		ELD Proficiency Level Continuum		
		→ Emerging →	→ Expanding →	→ Bridging →
Part II, strands 3–5, corresponding to the CA CCSS for ELA/Literacy 3. W.6.5; WHST.6.5; SL.6.6; L.6.1, 3–6 4. W.6.5; WHST.6.5; SL.6.6; L.6.1, 3–6 5. W.6.4–5; WHST.6.4–5; SL.6.6; L.6.1, 3–6 **Purposes for using language include but are not limited to:** Describing, entertaining, informing, interpreting, analyzing, recounting, explaining, persuading, negotiating, justifying, evaluating, and so on. **Informational text types include but are not limited to:** Descriptions or accounts (e.g., scientific, historical, economic, technical), recounts (e.g., biography, memoir), information reports, explanations (e.g., causal, factual), expositions (e.g., speeches, opinion pieces, argument, debate), responses (e.g., literary analysis), and so on. **Literary text types include but are not limited to:** Stories (e.g., historical fiction, myths, graphic novels), poetry, drama, and so on. **Audiences include but are not limited to:** Peers (one to one) Small group (one to a group) Whole group (one to many)	**B. Expanding and Enriching Ideas**	*3. Using verbs and verb phrases* Use a variety of verb types (e.g., doing, saying, being/having, thinking/feeling), tenses (e.g., present, past, future, simple, progressive) appropriate to the text type and discipline (e.g., simple past and past progressive for recounting an experience) on familiar topics. *4. Using nouns and noun phrases* Expand noun phrases in simple ways (e.g., adding a sensory adjective to a noun) in order to enrich the meaning of sentences and add details about ideas, people, things, and the like. *5. Modifying to add details* Expand sentences with simple adverbials (e.g., adverbs, adverb phrases, prepositional phrases) to provide details (e.g., time, manner, place, cause) about a familiar activity or process.	*3. Using verbs and verb phrases* Use various verb types (e.g., doing, saying, being/having, thinking/feeling, reporting), tenses (e.g., present, past, future, simple, progressive, perfect) appropriate to the task, text type, and discipline (e.g., simple present for literary analysis) on an increasing variety of topics. *4. Using nouns and noun phrases* Expand noun phrases in a variety of ways (e.g., adding comparative/ superlative adjectives to noun phrases or simple clause embedding) in order to enrich the meaning of sentences and add details about ideas, people, things, and the like. *5. Modifying to add details* Expand sentences with an increasing variety of adverbials (e.g., adverbs, adverb phrases, prepositional phrases) to provide details (e.g., time, manner, place, cause) about a familiar or new activity or process.	*3. Using verbs and verb phrases* Use various verb types (e.g., doing, saying, being/having, thinking/feeling, reporting), tenses (e.g., present, past, future, simple, progressive, perfect) appropriate to the task, text type, and discipline (e.g., the present perfect to describe previously made claims or conclusions) on a variety of topics. *4. Using nouns and noun phrases* Expand noun phrases in an increasing variety of ways (e.g., adding comparative/ superlative and general academic adjectives to noun phrases or more complex clause embedding) in order to enrich the meaning of sentences and add details about ideas, people, things, and the like. *5. Modifying to add details* Expand sentences with a variety of adverbials (e.g., adverbs, adverb phrases and clauses, prepositional phrases) to provide details (e.g., time, manner, place, cause) about a variety of familiar and new activities and processes.

Texts and Discourse in Context	ELD Proficiency Level Continuum		
	→ Emerging →	→ Expanding →	→ Bridging →
Part II, strands 6–7, corresponding to the CA CCSS for ELA/Literacy 6. W.6.1–5; WHST.6.1–2, 4–5; SL.6.4, 6; L.6.1, 3–6 7. W.6.1–5; WHST.6.1–2, 4–5; SL.6.4, 6; L.6.1, 3–6 **Purposes for using language include but are not limited to:** Describing, entertaining, informing, interpreting, analyzing, recounting, explaining, persuading, negotiating, justifying, evaluating, and so on. **Informational text types include but are not limited to:** Descriptions or accounts (e.g., scientific, historical, economic, technical), recounts (e.g., biography, memoir), information reports, explanations (e.g., causal, factual), expositions (e.g., speeches, opinion pieces, argument, debate), responses (e.g., literary analysis), and so on. **Literary text types include but are not limited to:** Stories (e.g., historical fiction, myths, graphic novels), poetry, drama, and so on. **Audiences include but are not limited to:** Peers (one to one) Small group (one to a group) Whole group (one to many)	**C. Connecting and Condensing Ideas** *6. Connecting ideas* Combine clauses in a few basic ways to make connections between and join ideas (e.g., creating compound sentences using *and, but, so*). *7. Condensing ideas* Condense ideas in simple ways (e.g., by compounding verbs, adding prepositional phrases, or through simple embedded clauses or other ways of condensing as in, This is a story about a girl. The girl changed the world. → This is a story about a girl *who changed the world*) to create precise and detailed sentences.	*6. Connecting ideas* Combine clauses in an increasing variety of ways (e.g., creating compound and complex sentences) to make connections between and join ideas, for example, to express a reason (e.g., *He stayed at home on Sunday to study for Monday's exam*) or to make a concession (e.g., *She studied all night even though she wasn't feeling well*). *7. Condensing ideas* Condense ideas in an increasing variety of ways (e.g., through various types of embedded clauses and other ways of condensing, as in, Organic vegetables are food. They're made without chemical fertilizers. They're made without chemical insecticides) → Organic vegetables are foods *that are made without chemical fertilizers or insecticides*) to create precise and detailed sentences.	*6. Connecting ideas* Combine clauses in a wide variety of ways (e.g., creating compound and complex sentences) to make connections between and join ideas, for example, to express a reason (e.g., *He stayed at home on Sunday because he had an exam on Monday*), to make a concession (e.g., *She studied all night even though she wasn't feeling well*), or to link two ideas that happen at the same time (e.g., *The students worked in groups while their teacher walked around the room*). *7. Condensing ideas* Condense ideas in a variety of ways (e.g., through various types of embedded clauses, ways of condensing, and nominalization as in, They *destroyed* the rain forest. Lots of animals *died* → The *destruction* of the rain forest led to *the death* of many animals) to create precise and detailed sentences.

Section 2: Elaboration on Critical Principles for Developing Language and Cognition in Academic Contexts **Part III: Using Foundational Literacy Skills**	
Foundational literacy skills in an alphabetic writing system • Print concepts • Phonological awareness • Phonics and word recognition • Fluency	See chapter 6 for information on teaching foundational reading skills to English learners of various profiles based on age, native language, native language writing system, schooling experience, and literacy experience and proficiency. Some considerations are as follows: • Native language and literacy (e.g., phoneme awareness or print concept skills in native language) should be assessed for potential transference to English language and literacy. • Similarities between native language and English should be highlighted (e.g., phonemes or letters that are the same in both languages). • Differences between native language and English should be highlighted (e.g., some phonemes in English may not exist in the student's native language; native language syntax may be different from English syntax).

Grade 7

Section 1: Overview

Goal: English learners read, analyze, interpret, and create a variety of literary and informational text types. They develop an understanding of how language is a complex, dynamic, and social resource for making meaning, as well as how content is organized in different text types and across disciplines using text structure, language features, and vocabulary depending on purpose and audience. They are aware that different languages and variations of English exist, and they recognize their home languages and cultures as resources to value in their own right and also to draw upon in order to build proficiency in English. English learners contribute actively to class and group discussions, asking questions, responding appropriately, and providing useful feedback. They demonstrate knowledge of content through oral presentations, writing tasks, collaborative conversations, and multimedia. They develop proficiency in shifting language use based on task, purpose, audience, and text type.

Critical Principles for Developing Language and Cognition in Academic Contexts: While advancing along the continuum of English language development levels, English learners at all levels engage in intellectually challenging literacy, disciplinary, and disciplinary literacy tasks. They use language in meaningful and relevant ways appropriate to grade level, content area, topic, purpose, audience, and text type in English language arts, mathematics, science, social studies, and the arts. Specifically, they use language to gain and exchange information and ideas in three communicative modes (collaborative, interpretive, and productive), and they apply knowledge of language to academic tasks via three cross-mode language processes (structuring cohesive texts, expanding and enriching ideas, and connecting and condensing ideas) using various linguistic resources.

Part I: Interacting in Meaningful Ways	Corresponding CA CCSS for ELA/Literacy*
A. Collaborative	
1. Exchanging information and ideas with others through oral collaborative discussions on a range of social and academic topics	• SL.7.1, 6; L.7.3, 6
2. Interacting with others in written English in various communicative forms (print, communicative technology and multimedia)	• W.7.6; WHST.7.6; SL.7.2; L.7.3, 6
3. Offering and justifying opinions, negotiating with and persuading others in communicative exchanges	• W.7.1; WHST.7.1; SL.7.1, 4, 6; L.7.3, 6
4. Adapting language choices to various contexts (based on task, purpose, audience, and text type)	• W.7.4–5; WHST.7.4–5; SL.7.6; L.7.1, 3, 6

*The California English Language Development Standards correspond to the California Common Core State Standards for English Language Arts and Literacy in History/Social Science and Technical Subjects (CA CCSS for ELA/Literacy). English learners should have full access to opportunities to learn ELA, mathematics, science, history/social studies, and other content at the same time they are progressing toward full proficiency in English.

Part I: Interacting in Meaningful Ways	Corresponding CA CCSS for ELA/Literacy
B. Interpretive	
5. Listening actively to spoken English in a range of social and academic contexts	• SL.7.1, 3, 6; L.7.1, 3, 6
6. Reading closely literary and informational texts and viewing multimedia to determine how meaning is conveyed explicitly and implicitly through language	• RL.7.1–7, 9–10; RI.7.1–10; RH.7.1–10; RST.7.1–10; SL.7.2; L.7.1, 3, 6
7. Evaluating how well writers and speakers use language to support ideas and arguments with details or evidence depending on modality, text type, purpose, audience, topic, and content area	• RL.7.4–5; RI.7.4, 6, 8; RH.7.4–6, 8; RST.7.4–6, 8; SL.7.3; L.7.3, 5–6
8. Analyzing how writers and speakers use vocabulary and other language resources for specific purposes (to explain, persuade, entertain, etc.) depending on modality, text type, purpose, audience, topic, and content area	• RL.7.4–5; RI.7.4–5; RH.7.4–5; RST.7.4–5; SL.7.3; L.7.3, 5–6
C. Productive	
9. Expressing information and ideas in formal oral presentations on academic topics	• SL.7.4–6; L.7.1, 3
10. Writing literary and informational texts to present, describe, and explain ideas and information, using appropriate technology	• W.7.1–10; WHST.7.1–2,4–10; L.7.1–6
11. Justifying own arguments and evaluating others' arguments in writing	• W.7.1, 8–9; WHST.7.1 ,8–9; L.7.1–3, 6
12. Selecting and applying varied and precise vocabulary and other language resources to effectively convey ideas	• W.7.4–5; WHST.7.4–5; SL.7.4, 6; L.7.1,3, 5–6
Part II: Learning About How English Works	Corresponding CA CCSS for ELA/Literacy
A. Structuring Cohesive Texts	• RL.7.5; RI.7.5; RH.7.5; RST.7.5; W.7.1–5, 10; WHST.7.1-2, 4–5,10; SL.7.4
1. Understanding text structure	
2. Understanding cohesion	• RI.7.5; RH.7.5; RST.7.5; W.7.1–5,10; WHST.7.1-2, 4–5, 10; L.7.1, 3–6
B. Expanding and Enriching Ideas	
3. Using verbs and verb phrases	• W.7.5; WHST.7.5; SL.7.6; L.7.1, 3–6
4. Using nouns and noun phrases	• W.7.5; WHST.7.5; SL.7.6; L.7.1, 3–6
5. Modifying to add details	• W.7.4–5; WHST.7.4–5; SL.7.6; L.7.1, 3–6
C. Connecting and Condensing Ideas	
6. Connecting ideas	• W.7.1–5; WHST.7.1–2, 4–5; SL.7.4, 6; L.7.1, 3–6
7. Condensing ideas	• W.7.1–5; WHST.7.1–2, 4–5; SL.7.4, 6; L.7.1, 3–6
Part III: Using Foundational Literacy Skills	• RF.K–1.1–4; RF.2–5.3–4 (as appropriate)

Note: **Examples** provided in specific standards are offered *only as illustrative possibilities* and should not be misinterpreted as the only objectives of instruction or as the only types of language that English learners might or should be able to understand or produce.

Section 2: Elaboration on Critical Principles for Developing Language and Cognition in Academic Contexts
Part I: Interacting in Meaningful Ways

Texts and Discourse in Context		ELD Proficiency Level Continuum		
		→ Emerging →	→ Expanding →	→ Bridging →
Part I, strands 1–4, corresponding to the CA CCSS for ELA/Literacy 1. SL.7.1,6; L.7.3, 6 2. W.7.6; WHST.7.6; SL.7.2; L.7.3, 6 3. W.7.1; WHST.7.1; SL.7.1,4, 6; L.7.3, 6 4. W.7.4–5; WHST.7.4-5; SL.7.6; L.7.1, 3, 6 **Purposes for using language include but are not limited to:** Describing, entertaining, informing, interpreting, analyzing, recounting, explaining, persuading, negotiating, justifying, evaluating, and so on. **Informational text types include but are not limited to:** Descriptions or accounts (e.g., scientific, historical, economic, technical), recounts (e.g., biography, memoir), information reports, explanations (e.g., causal, factual), expositions (e.g., speeches, opinion pieces, argument, debate), responses (e.g., literary analysis), and so on. **Literary text types include but are not limited to:** Stories (e.g., historical fiction, myths, graphic novels), poetry, drama, and so on. **Audiences include but are not limited to:** Peers (one to one) Small group (one to a group) Whole group (one to many)	**A. Collaborative**	***1. Exchanging information/ideas*** Engage in conversational exchanges and express ideas on familiar topics by asking and answering *yes-no* and *wh-* questions and responding using simple phrases. ***2. Interacting via written English*** Engage in short written exchanges with peers and collaborate on simple written texts on familiar topics, using technology when appropriate. ***3. Supporting opinions and persuading others*** Negotiate with or persuade others in conversations (e.g., to gain and hold the floor or ask for clarification) using learned phrases (e.g., *I think . . . , Would you please repeat that?*) and open responses. ***4. Adapting language choices*** Adjust language choices according to social setting (e.g., classroom, break time) and audience (e.g., peers, teacher).	***1. Exchanging information/ideas*** Contribute to class, group, and partner discussions by following turn-taking rules, asking relevant questions, affirming others, adding relevant information, and paraphrasing key ideas. ***2. Interacting via written English*** Engage in longer written exchanges with peers and collaborate on more detailed written texts on a variety of topics, using technology when appropriate. ***3. Supporting opinions and persuading others*** Negotiate with or persuade others in conversations (e.g., to provide counterarguments) using learned phrases (*I agree with X, but . . .*), and open responses. ***4. Adapting language choices*** Adjust language choices according to purpose (e.g., explaining, persuading, entertaining), task, and audience.	***1. Exchanging information/ideas*** Contribute to class, group, and partner discussions by following turn-taking rules, asking relevant questions, affirming others, adding relevant information and evidence, paraphrasing key ideas, building on responses, and providing useful feedback. ***2. Interacting via written English*** Engage in extended written exchanges with peers and collaborate on complex written texts on a variety of topics, using technology when appropriate. ***3. Supporting opinions and persuading others*** Negotiate with or persuade others in conversations using appropriate register (e.g., to acknowledge new information) using a variety of learned phrases, indirect reported speech (e.g., *I heard you say X, and I haven't thought about that before*), and open responses. ***4. Adapting language choices*** Adjust language choices according to task (e.g., facilitating a science experiment, providing peer feedback on a writing assignment), purpose, task, and audience.

Part I: Interacting in Meaningful Ways

Texts and Discourse in Context		ELD Proficiency Level Continuum		
		→ Emerging →	→ Expanding →	→ Bridging →
Part I, strands 5–8, corresponding to the CA CCSS for ELA/Literacy 5. SL.7.1,3, 6; L.7.1, 3, 6 6. RL.7.1–7, 9–10; RI.7.1–10; RH.7.1–10; RST.7.1–10; SL.7.2; L.7.1, 3, 6 7. RL.7.4–5; RI.7.4, 6, 8; RH.7.4–6, 8; RST.7.4–6, 8; SL.7.3; L.7.3, 5–6 8. RL.7.4–5; RI.7.4–5; RH.7.4–5; RST.7.4–5; SL.7.3; L.7.3, 5–6 **Purposes for using language include but are not limited to:** Describing, entertaining, informing, interpreting, analyzing, recounting, explaining, persuading, negotiating, justifying, evaluating, and so on. **Informational text types include but are not limited to:** Descriptions or accounts (e.g., scientific, historical, economic, technical), recounts (e.g., biography, memoir), information reports, explanations (e.g., causal, factual), expositions (e.g., speeches, opinion pieces, argument, debate), responses (e.g., literary analysis), and so on. **Literary text types include but are not limited to:** Stories (e.g., historical fiction, myths, graphic novels), poetry, drama, and so on. **Audiences include but are not limited to:** Peers (one to one) Small group (one to a group) Whole group (one to many)	B. Interpretive	**5. *Listening actively*** Demonstrate active listening in oral presentation activities by asking and answering basic questions, with prompting and substantial support. **6. *Reading/viewing closely*** a. Explain ideas, phenomena, processes, and text relationships (e.g., compare/contrast, cause/effect, problem/solution) based on close reading of a variety of grade-appropriate texts and viewing of multimedia, with substantial support. b. Express inferences and conclusions drawn based on close reading of grade-appropriate texts and viewing of multimedia using some frequently used verbs (e.g., *shows that, based on*). c. Use knowledge of morphology (e.g., affixes, roots, and base words), context, reference materials, and visual cues to determine the meaning of unknown and multiple-meaning words on familiar topics. **7. *Evaluating language choices*** Explain how well writers and speakers use language to support ideas and arguments with detailed evidence (e.g., identifying the precise vocabulary used to present evidence, or the phrasing used to signal a shift in meaning) when provided with substantial support.	**5. *Listening actively*** Demonstrate active listening in oral presentation activities by asking and answering detailed questions, with occasional prompting and moderate support. **6. *Reading/viewing closely*** a. Explain ideas, phenomena, processes, and text relationships (e.g., compare/contrast, cause/effect, problem/solution) based on close reading of a variety of grade-level texts and viewing of multimedia, with moderate support. b. Express inferences and conclusions drawn based on close reading of grade-appropriate texts and viewing of multimedia using a variety of verbs (e.g., *suggests that, leads to*). c. Use knowledge of morphology (e.g., affixes, roots, and base words), context, reference materials, and visual cues to determine the meaning of unknown and multiple-meaning words on familiar and new topics. **7. *Evaluating language choices*** Explain how well writers and speakers use specific language to present ideas of support arguments and provide detailed evidence (e.g., showing the clarity of the phrasing used to present an argument) when provided with moderate support.	**5. *Listening actively*** Demonstrate active listening in oral presentation activities by asking and answering detailed questions, with minimal prompting and support. **6. *Reading/viewing closely*** a. Explain ideas, phenomena, processes, and text relationships (e.g., compare/contrast, cause/effect, problem/solution) based on close reading of a variety of grade-level texts and viewing of multimedia, with light support. b. Express inferences and conclusions drawn based on close reading of grade-level texts and viewing of multimedia using a variety of precise academic verbs (e.g., *indicates that, influences*). c. Use knowledge of morphology (e.g., affixes, roots, and base words), context, reference materials, and visual cues to determine the meaning, including figurative and connotative meanings, of unknown and multiple-meaning words on a variety of new topics. **7. *Evaluating language choices*** Explain how well writers and speakers use specific language resources to present ideas or support arguments and provide detailed evidence (e.g., identifying the specific language used to present ideas and claims that are well supported and distinguishing them from those that are not) when provided with light support.

Section 2: Elaboration on Critical Principles for Developing Language and Cognition in Academic Contexts
Part I: Interacting in Meaningful Ways

Texts and Discourse in Context		ELD Proficiency Level Continuum		
		→ Emerging →	→ Expanding →	→ Bridging →
Part I, strands 5–8, corresponding to the CA CCSS for ELA/Literacy 5. SL.7.1,3, 6; L.7.1, 3, 6 6. RL.7.1–7, 9–10; RI.7.1–10; RH.7.1–10; RST.7.1–10; SL.7.2; L.7.1, 3, 6 7. RL.7.4–5; RI.7.4, 6, 8; RH.7.4–6, 8; RST.7.4–6, 8; SL.7.3; L.7.3, 5–6 8. RL.7.4–5; RI.7.4–5; RH.7.4–5; RST.7.4–5; SL.7.3; L.7.3, 5–6 **Purposes for using language include but are not limited to:** Describing, entertaining, informing, interpreting, analyzing, recounting, explaining, persuading, negotiating, justifying, evaluating, and so on. **Informational text types include but are not limited to:** Descriptions or accounts (e.g., scientific, historical, economic, technical), recounts (e.g., biography, memoir), information reports, explanations (e.g., causal, factual), expositions (e.g., speeches, opinion pieces, argument, debate), responses (e.g., literary analysis), and so on. **Literary text types include but are not limited to:** Stories (e.g., historical fiction, myths, graphic novels), poetry, drama, and so on. **Audiences include but are not limited to:** Peers (one to one) Small group (one to a group) Whole group (one to many)	B. Interpretive	*8. Analyzing language choices* Explain how phrasing or different common words with similar meaning (e.g., choosing to use the word *polite* versus *good*) produce different effects on the audience.	*8. Analyzing language choices* Explain how phrasing, different words with similar meaning (e.g., describing a character as *diplomatic* versus *respectful*) or figurative language (e.g., *The wind blew through the valley like a furnace*) produce shades of meaning and different effects on the audience.	*8. Analyzing language choices* Explain how phrasing, different words with similar meaning (e.g., *refined-respectful-polite-diplomatic*), or figurative language (e.g., *The wind whispered through the night*) produce shades of meaning, nuances, and different effects on the audience.

Texts and Discourse in Context		ELD Proficiency Level Continuum		
		→ Emerging →	→ Expanding →	→ Bridging →
Part I, strands 9–12, corresponding to the CA CCSS for ELA/Literacy 9. SL.7.4–6; L.7.1, 3 10. W.7.1–10; WHST.7.1–2, 4–10; L.7.1–6 11. W.7.1, 8–9; WHST.7.1, 8–9; L.7.1–3, 6 12. W.7.4–5; WHST.7.4–5; SL.7.4, 6; L.7.1, 3, 5–6 **Purposes for using language include but are not limited to:** Describing, entertaining, informing, interpreting, analyzing, recounting, explaining, persuading, negotiating, justifying, evaluating, and so on. **Informational text types include but are not limited to:** Descriptions or accounts (e.g., scientific, historical, economic, technical), recounts (e.g., biography, memoir), information reports, explanations (e.g., causal, factual), expositions (e.g., speeches, opinion pieces, argument, debate), responses (e.g., literary analysis), and so on. **Literary text types include but are not limited to:** Stories (e.g., historical fiction, myths, graphic novels), poetry, drama, and so on. **Audiences include but are not limited to:** Peers (one to one) Small group (one to a group) Whole group (one to many)	**C. Productive**	*9. Presenting* Plan and deliver brief informative oral presentations on familiar topics. *10. Writing* a. Write short literary and informational texts (e.g., an argument for wearing school uniforms) collaboratively (e.g., with peers) and independently. b. Write brief summaries of texts and experiences using complete sentences and key words (e.g., from notes or graphic organizers). *11. Justifying/arguing* a. Justify opinions by providing some textual evidence or relevant background knowledge, with substantial support. b. Express attitude and opinions or temper statements with familiar modal expressions (e.g., *can, may*).	*9. Presenting* Plan and deliver longer oral presentations on a variety of topics, using details and evidence to support ideas. *10. Writing* a. Write longer literary and informational texts (e.g., an argument for wearing school uniforms) collaboratively (e.g., with peers) and independently using appropriate text organization. b. Write increasingly concise summaries of texts and experiences using complete sentences and key words (e.g., from notes or graphic organizers). *11. Justifying/arguing* a. Justify opinions or persuade others by providing relevant textual evidence or relevant background knowledge, with moderate support. b. Express attitude and opinions or temper statements with a variety of familiar modal expressions (e.g., *possibly/likely, could/ would/should*).	*9. Presenting* Plan and deliver longer oral presentations on a variety of topics in a variety of disciplines, using reasoning and evidence to support ideas, as well as growing understanding of register. *10. Writing* a. Write longer and more detailed literary and informational texts (e.g., an argument for wearing school uniforms) collaboratively (e.g., with peers) and independently using appropriate text organization and growing understanding of register. b. Write clear and coherent summaries of texts and experiences using complete and concise sentences and key words (e.g., from notes or graphic organizers). *11. Justifying/arguing* a. Justify opinions or persuade others by providing detailed and relevant textual evidence or relevant background knowledge, with light support. b. Express attitude and opinions or temper statements with nuanced modal expressions (e.g., *possibly/potentially/absolutely, should/might*).

Texts and Discourse in Context		ELD Proficiency Level Continuum		
		→ Emerging →	→ Expanding →	→ Bridging →
Part I, strands 9–12, corresponding to the CA CCSS for ELA/Literacy 9. SL.7.4–6; L.7.1, 3 10. W.7.1–10; WHST.7.1–2, 4–10; L.7.1–6 11. W.7.1, 8–9; WHST.7.1, 8–9; L.7.1–3, 6 12. W.7.4–5; WHST.7.4–5; SL.7.4, 6; L.7.1, 3, 5–6 **Purposes for using language include but are not limited to:** Describing, entertaining, informing, interpreting, analyzing, recounting, explaining, persuading, negotiating, justifying, evaluating, and so on. **Informational text types include but are not limited to:** Descriptions or accounts (e.g., scientific, historical, economic, technical), recounts (e.g., biography, memoir), information reports, explanations (e.g., causal, factual), expositions (e.g., speeches, opinion pieces, argument, debate), responses (e.g., literary analysis), and so on. **Literary text types include but are not limited to:** Stories (e.g., historical fiction, myths, graphic novels), poetry, drama, and so on. **Audiences include but are not limited to:** Peers (one to one) Small group (one to a group) Whole group (one to many)	**C. Productive**	*12. Selecting language resources* a. Use a select number of general academic words (e.g., *cycle, alternative*) and domain-specific words (e.g., *scene, chapter, paragraph, cell*) to create some precision while speaking and writing. b. Use knowledge of morphology to appropriately select affixes in basic ways (e.g., She likes X. He walk*ed* to school).	*12. Selecting language resources* a. Use a growing set of academic words (e.g., *cycle, alternative, indicate, process*), domain-specific words (e.g., *scene, soliloquy, sonnet, friction, monarchy, fraction*), synonyms, and antonyms to create precision and shades of meaning while speaking and writing. b. Use knowledge of morphology to appropriately select affixes in a growing number of ways to manipulate language (e.g., She likes *walking* to school. That's *impossible*).	*12. Selecting language resources* a. Use an expanded set of general academic words (e.g., *cycle, alternative, indicate, process, emphasize, illustrate*), domain-specific words (e.g., *scene, soliloquy, sonnet, friction, monarchy, fraction*), synonyms, antonyms, and figurative language to create precision and shades of meaning while speaking and writing. b. Use knowledge of morphology to appropriately select affixes in a variety of ways to manipulate language (e.g., changing destroy → *destruction*, probably → *probability*, reluctant → *reluctantly*).

Section 2: Elaboration on Critical Principles for Developing Language and Cognition in Academic Contexts
Part II: Learning About How English Works

Texts and Discourse in Context		ELD Proficiency Level Continuum		
		→ Emerging →	→ Expanding →	→ Bridging →
Part II, strands 1–2 corresponding to the CA CCSS for ELA/Literacy 1. RL.7.5; RI.7.5; RH.7.5; RST.7.5; W.7.1–5, 10; WHST.7.1–2, 4–5, 10; SL.7.4 2. RI.7.5; RH.7.5; RST.7.5; W.7.1–5, 10; WHST.7.1–2, 4–5, 10; L.7.1, 3–6 **Purposes for using language include but are not limited to:** Describing, entertaining, informing, interpreting, analyzing, recounting, explaining, persuading, negotiating, justifying, evaluating, and so. **Informational text types include but are not limited to:** Descriptions or accounts (e.g., scientific, historical, economic, technical), recounts (e.g., biography, memoir), information reports, explanations (e.g., causal, factual), expositions (e.g., speeches, opinion pieces, argument, debate), responses (e.g., literary analysis), and so on. **Literary text types include but are not limited to:** Stories (e.g., historical fiction, myths, graphic novels), poetry, drama, and so on. **Audiences include but are not limited to:** Peers (one to one) Small group (one to a group) Whole group (one to many)	**A. Structuring Cohesive Texts**	***1. Understanding text structure*** Apply understanding of how different text types are organized to express ideas (e.g., how narratives are organized sequentially) to comprehending texts and to writing brief arguments, informative/explanatory texts and narratives. ***2. Understanding cohesion*** a. Apply knowledge of familiar language resources for referring to make texts more cohesive (e.g., how pronouns refer back to nouns in text) to comprehending texts and writing brief texts. b. Apply basic understanding of how ideas, events, or reasons are linked throughout a text using everyday connecting words or phrases (e.g., *at the end, next*) to comprehending texts and writing brief texts.	***1. Understanding text structure*** Apply understanding of the organizational features of different text types (e.g., how narratives are organized by an event sequence that unfolds naturally versus how arguments are organized around reasons and evidence) to comprehending texts and to writing increasingly clear and coherent arguments, informative/explanatory texts and narratives. ***2. Understanding cohesion*** a. Apply knowledge of familiar language resources for referring to make texts more cohesive (e.g., how pronouns refer back to nouns in text, how using synonyms helps avoid repetition) to comprehending texts and writing texts with increasing cohesion. b. Apply growing understanding of how ideas, events, or reasons are linked throughout a text using a variety of connecting words or phrases (e.g., *for example, as a result, on the other hand*) to comprehending texts and writing texts with increasing cohesion.	***1. Understanding text structure*** Apply understanding of the organizational structure of different text types (e.g., how narratives are organized by an event sequence that unfolds naturally versus how arguments are organized around reasons and evidence) to comprehending texts and to writing clear and cohesive arguments, informative/explanatory texts and narratives. ***2. Understanding cohesion*** a. Apply knowledge of familiar language resources for referring to make texts more cohesive (e.g., how pronouns, synonyms, or nominalizations are used to refer backward in a text) to comprehending texts and writing cohesive texts. b. Apply increasing understanding of how ideas, events, or reasons are linked throughout a text using an increasing variety of academic connecting and transitional words or phrases (e.g., *for instance, in addition, consequently*) to comprehending texts and writing texts with increasing cohesion.

Section 2: Elaboration on Critical Principles for Developing Language and Cognition in Academic Contexts
Part II: Learning About How English Works

Texts and Discourse in Context	ELD Proficiency Level Continuum		
	→ Emerging →	→ Expanding →	→ Bridging →
Part II, strands 3–5, corresponding to the CA CCSS for ELA/Literacy 3. W.7.5; WHST.7.5; SL.7.6; L.7.1, 3–6 4. W.7.5; WHST.7.5; SL.7.6; L.7.1, 3–6 5. W.7.4–5; WHST.7.4-5; SL.7.6; L.7.1, 3–6 **Purposes for using language include but are not limited to:** Describing, entertaining, informing, interpreting, analyzing, recounting, explaining, persuading, negotiating, justifying, evaluating, and so on. **Informational text types include but are not limited to:** Descriptions or accounts (e.g., scientific, historical, economic, technical), recounts (e.g., biography, memoir), information reports, explanations (e.g., causal, factual), expositions (e.g., speeches, opinion pieces, argument, debate), responses (e.g., literary analysis), and so on. **Literary text types include but are not limited to:** Stories (e.g., historical fiction, myths, graphic novels), poetry, drama, and so on. **Audiences include but are not limited to:** Peers (one to one) Small group (one to a group) Whole group (one to many)	**B. Expanding and Enriching Ideas**		
	3. Using verbs and verb phrases Use a variety of verbs in different tenses (e.g., present, past, future, simple, progressive) appropriate to the text type and discipline (e.g., simple past and past progressive for recounting an experience) on familiar topics. **4. Using nouns and noun phrases** Expand noun phrases in basic ways (e.g., adding a sensory adjective to a noun) in order to enrich the meaning of sentences and add details about ideas, people, and things. **5. Modifying to add details** Expand sentences with simple adverbials (e.g., adverbs, adverb phrases, prepositional phrases) to provide details (e.g., time, manner, place, cause) about a familiar activity or process.	**3. Using verbs and verb phrases** Use a variety of verbs in different tenses (e.g., present, past, future, simple, progressive, perfect) appropriate to the task, text type, and discipline (e.g., simple present for literary analysis) on an increasing variety of topics. **4. Using nouns and noun phrases** Expand noun phrases in a growing number of ways (e.g., adding adjectives to nouns or simple clause embedding) in order to enrich the meaning of sentences and add details about ideas, people, and things. **5. Modifying to add details** Expand sentences with adverbials (e.g., adverbs, adverb phrases, prepositional phrases) to provide details (e.g., time, manner, place, cause) about a familiar or new activity or process.	**3. Using verbs and verb phrases** Use a variety of verbs in different tenses (e.g., present, past, future, simple, progressive, perfect) appropriate to the task, text type, and discipline (e.g., the present perfect to describe previously made claims or conclusions) on a variety of topics. **4. Using nouns and noun phrases** Expand noun phrases in an increasing variety of ways (e.g., more complex clause embedding) in order to enrich the meaning of sentences and add details about ideas, people, and things. **5. Modifying to add details** Expand sentences with a variety of adverbials (e.g., adverbs, adverb phrases and clauses, prepositional phrases) to provide details (e.g., time, manner, place, cause) about a variety of familiar and new activities and processes.

Section 2: Elaboration on Critical Principles for Developing Language and Cognition in Academic Contexts
Part II: Learning About How English Works

Texts and Discourse in Context		ELD Proficiency Level Continuum		
		→ Emerging →	→ Expanding →	→ Bridging →
Part II, strands 6–7, corresponding to the CA CCSS for ELA/Literacy 6. W.7.1–5; WHST.7.1–2, 4–5; SL.7.4, 6; L.7.1, 3–6 7. W.7.1–5; WHST.7.1–2, 4–5; SL.7.4, 6; L.7.1, 3–6 **Purposes for using language include but are not limited to:** Describing, entertaining, informing, interpreting, analyzing, recounting, explaining, persuading, negotiating, justifying, evaluating, and so on. **Informational text types include but are not limited to:** Descriptions or accounts (e.g., scientific, historical, economic, technical), recounts (e.g., biography, memoir), information reports, explanations (e.g., causal, factual), expositions (e.g., speeches, opinion pieces, argument, debate), responses (e.g., literary analysis), and so on. **Literary text types include but are not limited to:** Stories (e.g., historical fiction, myths, graphic novels), poetry, drama, and so on. **Audiences include but are not limited to:** Peers (one to one) Small group (one to a group) Whole group (one to many)	**C. Connecting and Condensing Ideas**	*6. Connecting ideas* Combine clauses in a few basic ways to make connections between and join ideas (e.g., creating compound sentences using *and, but, so*; creating complex sentences using *because*). *7. Condensing ideas* Condense ideas in simple ways (e.g., by compounding verbs, adding prepositional phrases, or through simple embedded clauses or other ways of condensing as in, This is a story about a girl. The girl changed the world → This is a story about a girl *who changed the world*) to create precise and detailed sentences.	*6. Connecting ideas* Combine clauses in an increasing variety of ways (e.g., creating compound and complex sentences) to make connections between and join ideas, for example, to express a reason (e.g., *He stayed at home on Sunday in order to study for Monday's exam*) or to make a concession (e.g., *She studied all night even though she wasn't feeling well*). *7. Condensing ideas* Condense ideas in an increasing variety of ways (e.g., through various types of embedded clauses and other ways of condensing, as in, Organic vegetables are food. They're made without chemical fertilizers. They're made without chemical insecticides. → Organic vegetables are foods that are made without chemical fertilizers or insecticides) to create precise and detailed sentences.	*6. Connecting ideas* Combine clauses in a wide variety of ways (e.g., creating compound, complex, and compound–complex sentences) to make connections between and join ideas, for example, to show the relationship between multiple events or ideas (e.g., *After eating lunch, the students worked in groups while their teacher walked around the room*) or to evaluate an argument (e.g., *The author claims X, although there is a lack of evidence to support this claim*). *7. Condensing ideas* Condense ideas in a variety of ways (e.g., through various types of embedded clauses, ways of condensing, and nominalization as in, They *destroyed* the rain forest. Lots of animals *died* → The *destruction* of the rainforest led to *the death* of many animals) to create precise and detailed sentences.

Section 2: Elaboration on Critical Principles for Developing Language and Cognition in Academic Contexts
Part III: Using Foundational Literacy Skills

Foundational literacy skills in an alphabetic writing system • Print concepts • Phonological awareness • Phonics and word recognition • Fluency	See chapter 6 for information on teaching foundational reading skills to English learners of various profiles based on age, native language, native language writing system, schooling experience, and literacy experience and proficiency. Some considerations are as follows: Native language and literacy (e.g., phoneme awareness or print concept skills in native language) should be assessed for potential transference to English language and literacy. • Similarities between the native language and English should be highlighted (e.g., phonemes or letters that are the same in both languages). • Differences between the native language and English should be highlighted (e.g., some phonemes in English may not exist in the student's native language; native language syntax may be different from English syntax).

Grade 8

Section 1: Overview

Goal: English learners read, analyze, interpret, and create a variety of literary and informational text types. They develop an understanding of how language is a complex, dynamic, and social resource for making meaning, as well as how content is organized in different text types and across disciplines using text structure, language features, and vocabulary depending on purpose and audience. They are aware that different languages and variations of English exist, and they recognize their home languages and cultures as resources to value in their own right and also to draw upon in order to build proficiency in English. English learners contribute actively to class and group discussions, asking questions, responding appropriately, and providing useful feedback. They demonstrate knowledge of content through oral presentations, writing tasks, collaborative conversations, and multimedia. They develop proficiency in shifting language use based on task, purpose, audience, and text type.

Critical Principles for Developing Language and Cognition in Academic Contexts: While advancing along the continuum of English language development levels, English learners at all levels engage in intellectually challenging literacy, disciplinary, and disciplinary literacy tasks. They use language in meaningful and relevant ways appropriate to grade level, content area, topic, purpose, audience, and text type in English language arts, mathematics, science, social studies, and the arts. Specifically, they use language to gain and exchange information and ideas in three communicative modes (collaborative, interpretive, and productive), and they apply knowledge of language to academic tasks via three cross-mode language processes (structuring cohesive texts, expanding and enriching ideas, and connecting and condensing ideas) using various linguistic resources.

Part I: Interacting in Meaningful Ways	Corresponding CA CCSS for ELA/Literacy*
A. Collaborative	
1. Exchanging information and ideas with others through oral collaborative discussions on a range of social and academic topics	• SL.8.1, 6; L.8.3, 6
2. Interacting with others in written English in various communicative forms (print, communicative technology and multimedia)	• W.8.6; WHST.8.6; SL.8.2; L.8.3, 6
3. Offering and justifying opinions, negotiating with and persuading others in communicative exchanges	• W.8.1; WHST.8.1; SL.8.1, 4, 6; L.8.3, 6
4. Adapting language choices to various contexts (based on task, purpose, audience, and text type)	• W.8.4–5; WHST.8.4–5; SL.8.6; L.8.1, 3, 6

*The California English Language Development Standards correspond to the California Common Core State Standards for English Language Arts and Literacy in History/Social Science and Technical Subjects (CA CCSS for ELA/Literacy). English learners should have full access to opportunities to learn ELA, mathematics, science, history/social studies, and other content at the same time they are progressing toward full proficiency in English.

Part I: Interacting in Meaningful Ways	Corresponding CA CCSS for ELA/Literacy
B. Interpretive	
5. Listening actively to spoken English in a range of social and academic contexts	• SL.8.1, 3, 6; L.8.1, 3, 6
6. Reading closely literary and informational texts and viewing multimedia to determine how meaning is conveyed explicitly and implicitly through language	• RL.8.1–7,9–10; RI.8.1–10; RH.8.1–10; RST.8.1–10; SL.8.2; L.8.1, 3, 6
7. Evaluating how well writers and speakers use language to support ideas and arguments with details or evidence depending on modality, text type, purpose, audience, topic, and content area	• RL.8.4–5; RI.8.4, 6, 8; RH.8.4–6, 8; RST.8.4–6, 8; SL.8.3; L.8.3, 5–6
8. Analyzing how writers and speakers use vocabulary and other language resources for specific purposes (to explain, persuade, entertain, etc.) depending on modality, text type, purpose, audience, topic, and content area	• RL.8.4–5; RI.8.4–5; RH.8.4–5; RST.8.4–5; SL.8.3; L.8.3, 5–6
C. Productive	
9. Expressing information and ideas in formal oral presentations on academic topics	• SL.8.4–6; L.8.1, 3
10. Writing literary and informational texts to present, describe, and explain ideas and information, using appropriate technology	• W.8.1–10; WHST.8.1–2, 4–10; L.8.1–6
11. Justifying own arguments and evaluating others' arguments in writing	• W.8.1, 8–9; WHST.8.1, 8–9; L.8.1–3, 6
12. Selecting and applying varied and precise vocabulary and other language resources to effectively convey ideas.	• W.8.4–5; WHST.8.4–5; SL.8.4, 6; L.8.1, 3, 5–6
Part II: Learning About How English Works	**Corresponding CA CCSS for ELA/Literacy**
A. Structuring Cohesive Texts	
1. Understanding text structure	• RL.8.5; RI.8.5; RH.8.5; RST.8.5; W.8.1–5, 10; WHST.8.1–2, 4–5, 10; SL.8.4
2. Understanding cohesion	• RI.8.5; RH.8.5; RST.8.5; W.8.1–5, 10; WHST.8.1–2, 4–5,10; L.8.1, 3–6
B. Expanding and Enriching Ideas	
3. Using verbs and verb phrases	• W.8.5; WHST.8.5; SL.8.6; L.8.1, 3–6
4. Using nouns and noun phrases	• W.8.5; WHST.8.5; SL.8.6; L.8.1, 3–6
5. Modifying to add details	• W.8.4–5; WHST.8.4–5; SL.8.6; L.8.1, 3–6
C. Connecting and Condensing Ideas	
6. Connecting ideas	• W.8.1–5; WHST.8.1–2, 4–5; SL.8. 4, 6; L.8.1, 3–6
7. Condensing ideas	• W.8.1–5; WHST.8.1–2, 4–5; SL.8.4, 6; L.8.1, 3–6
Part III: Using Foundational Literacy Skills	• RF.K–1.1–4; RF.2–5.3–4 (as appropriate)

Note: **Examples** provided in specific standards are offered *only as illustrative possibilities* and should not be misinterpreted as the only objectives of instruction or as the only types of language that English learners might or should be able to understand or produce.

Section 2: Elaboration on Critical Principles for Developing Language and Cognition in Academic Contexts
Part I: Interacting in Meaningful Ways

Texts and Discourse in Context		ELD Proficiency Level Continuum		
		→ Emerging →	→ Expanding →	→ Bridging →
Part I, strands 1–4, corresponding to the CA CCSS for ELA/Literacy: 1. SL.8.1, 6; L.8.3, 6 2. W.8.6; WHST.8.6; SL.8.2; L.8.3, 6 3. W.8.1; WHST.8.1; SL.8.1, 4, 6; L.8.3, 6 4. W.8.4–5; WHST.8.4–5; SL.8.6; L.8.1, 3, 6 **Purposes for using language include but are not limited to:** Describing, entertaining, informing, interpreting, analyzing, recounting, explaining, persuading, negotiating, justifying, evaluating, and so on. **Informational text types include but are not limited to:** Descriptions or accounts (e.g., scientific, historical, economic, technical), recounts (e.g., biography, memoir), information reports, explanations (e.g., causal, factual, expositions (e.g., speeches, opinion pieces, argument, debate), responses (e.g., literary analysis), and so on. **Literary text types include but are not limited to:** Stories (e.g., historical fiction, myths, graphic novels), poetry, drama, and so on. **Audiences include but are not limited to:** Peers (one to one) Small group (one to a group) Whole group (one to many)	**A. Collaborative**	*1. Exchanging information/ideas* Engage in conversational exchanges and express ideas on familiar topics by asking and answering *yes-no* and *wh-* questions and responding using simple phrases. *2. Interacting via written English* Engage in short written exchanges with peers and collaborate on simple written texts on familiar topics, using technology when appropriate. *3. Supporting opinions and persuading others* Negotiate with or persuade others in conversations (e.g., to gain and hold the floor or to ask for clarification) using learned phrases (e.g., *I think . . . Would you please repeat that?*) and open responses. *4. Adapting language choices* Adjust language choices according to social setting (e.g., classroom, break time) and audience (e.g., peers, teacher).	*1. Exchanging information/ideas* Contribute to class, group, and partner discussions by following turn-taking rules, asking relevant questions, affirming others, adding relevant information, and paraphrasing key ideas. *2. Interacting via written English* Engage in longer written exchanges with peers and collaborate on more detailed written texts on a variety of topics, using technology when appropriate. *3. Supporting opinions and persuading others* Negotiate with or persuade others in conversations (e.g., to provide counter-arguments) using learned phrases (*I agree with X, but . . .*) and open responses. *4. Adapting language choices* Adjust language choices according to purpose (e.g., explaining, persuading, entertaining), task, and audience.	*1. Exchanging information/ideas* Contribute to class, group, and partner discussions by following turn-taking rules, asking relevant questions, affirming others, adding relevant information and evidence, paraphrasing key ideas, building on responses, and providing useful feedback. *2. Interacting via written English* Engage in extended written exchanges with peers and collaborate on complex written texts on a variety of topics, using technology when appropriate. *3. Supporting opinions and persuading others* Negotiate with or persuade others in conversations using an appropriate register (e.g., to acknowledge new information and justify views) using a variety of learned phrases, indirect reported speech (e.g., *I heard you say X, and that's a good point. I still think Y, though, because . . .*) and open responses. *4. Adapting language choices* Adjust language choices according to task (e.g., facilitating a science experiment, providing peer feedback on a writing assignment), purpose, and audience.

Texts and Discourse in Context		ELD Proficiency Level Continuum		
		→ Emerging →	→ Expanding →	→ Bridging →
Part I, strands 5–8, corresponding to the CA CCSS for ELA/Literacy: 5. SL.8.1, 3, 6; L.8.1, 3, 6 6. RL.8.1–7,9–10; RI.8.1–10; RH.8.1–10; RST.8.1–10; SL.8.2; L.8.1, 3, 6 7. RL.8.4–5; RI.8.4, 6, 8; RH.8.4–6, 8; RST.8.4–6, 8; SL.8.3; L.8.3, 5–6 8. RL.8.4–5; RI.8.4–5; RH.8.4–5; RST.8.4–5; SL.8.3; L.8.3, 5–6 **Purposes for using language include but are not limited to:** Describing, entertaining, informing, interpreting, analyzing, recounting, explaining, persuading, negotiating, justifying, evaluating, and so on. **Informational text types include but are not limited to:** Descriptions or accounts (e.g., scientific, historical, economic, technical), recounts (e.g., biography, memoir), information reports, explanations (e.g., causal, factual), expositions (e.g., speeches, opinion pieces, argument, debate), responses (e.g., literary analysis), and so on. **Literary text types include but are not limited to:** Stories (e.g., historical fiction, myths, graphic novels), poetry, drama, and so on. **Audiences include but are not limited to:** Peers (one to one) Small group (one to a group) Whole group (one to many)	**B. Interpretive**	*5. Listening actively* Demonstrate active listening in oral presentation activities by asking and answering basic questions, with prompting and substantial support. *6. Reading/viewing closely* a. Explain ideas, phenomena, processes, and text relationships (e.g., compare/contrast, cause/effect, problem/solution) based on close reading of a variety of grade-appropriate texts and viewing of multimedia, with substantial support. b. Express inferences and conclusions drawn based on close reading of grade-appropriate texts and viewing of multimedia using some frequently used verbs (e.g., *shows that, based on*). c. Use knowledge of morphology (e.g., affixes, roots, and base words), context, reference materials, and visual cues to determine the meanings of unknown and multiple-meaning words on familiar topics.	*5. Listening actively* Demonstrate active listening in oral presentation activities by asking and answering detailed questions, with occasional prompting and moderate support. *6. Reading/viewing closely* a. Explain ideas, phenomena, processes, and text relationships (e.g., compare/contrast, cause/effect, problem/solution) based on close reading of a variety of grade-appropriate texts and viewing of multimedia, with moderate support. b. Express inferences and conclusions drawn based on close reading grade-appropriate texts and viewing of multimedia using a variety of verbs (e.g., *suggests that, leads to*). c. Use knowledge of morphology (e.g., affixes, roots, and base words), context, reference materials, and visual cues to determine the meanings of unknown and multiple-meaning words on familiar and new topics.	*5. Listening actively* Demonstrate active listening in oral presentation activities by asking and answering detailed questions, with minimal prompting and support. *6. Reading/viewing closely* a. Explain ideas, phenomena, processes, and text relationships (e.g., compare/contrast, cause/effect, problem/solution) based on close reading of a variety of grade-level texts and viewing of multimedia, with light support. b. Express inferences and conclusions drawn based on close reading of grade-level texts and viewing of multimedia using a variety of precise academic verbs (e.g., *indicates that, influences*). c. Use knowledge of morphology (e.g., affixes, roots, and base words), context, reference materials, and visual cues to determine the meanings, including figurative and connotative meanings, of unknown and multiple-meaning words on a variety of new topics.

Section 2: Elaboration on Critical Principles for Developing Language and Cognition in Academic Contexts
Part I: Interacting in Meaningful Ways

Texts and Discourse in Context		ELD Proficiency Level Continuum		
		→ Emerging →	→ Expanding →	→ Bridging →
Part I, strands 5–8, corresponding to the CA CCSS for ELA/Literacy 5. SL.8.1, 3, 6; L.8.1, 3, 6 6. RL.8.1–7,9–10; RI.8.1–10; RH.8.1–10; RST.8.1–10; SL.8.2; L.8.1, 3, 6 7. RL.8.4–5; RI.8.4, 6, 8; RH.8.4–6, 8; RST.8.4–6, 8; SL.8.3; L.8.3, 5–6 8. RL.8.4–5; RI.8.4–5; RH.8.4–5; RST.8.4–5; SL.8.3; L.8.3, 5–6 **Purposes for using language include but are not limited to:** Describing, entertaining, informing, interpreting, analyzing, recounting, explaining, persuading, negotiating, justifying, evaluating, and so on. **Informational text types include but are not limited to:** Descriptions or accounts (e.g., scientific, historical, economic, technical), recounts (e.g., biography, memoir), information reports, explanations (e.g., causal, factual), expositions (e.g., speeches, opinion pieces, argument, debate), responses (e.g., literary analysis), and so on. **Literary text types include but are not limited to:** Stories (e.g., historical fiction, myths, graphic novels), poetry, drama, and so on. **Audiences include but are not limited to:** Peers (one to one) Small group (one to a group) Whole group (one to many)	B. Interpretive	*7. Evaluating language choices* Explain how well writers and speakers use language to support ideas and arguments with detailed evidence (e.g., identifying the precise vocabulary used to present evidence, or the phrasing used to signal a shift in meaning) when provided with substantial support. *8. Analyzing language choices* Explain how phrasing or different common words with similar meanings (e.g., choosing to use the word persistent versus the term *hard worker*) produce different effects on the audience.	*7. Evaluating language choices* Explain how well writers and speakers use specific language to present ideas or support arguments and provide detailed evidence (e.g., showing the clarity of the phrasing used to present an argument) when provided with moderate support. *8. Analyzing language choices* Explain how phrasing or different words with similar meanings (e.g., describing a character as *stubborn* versus *persistent*) or figurative language (e.g., *Let me throw some light onto the topic*) produce shades of meaning and different effects on the audience.	*7. Evaluating language choices* Explain how well writers and speakers use specific language resources to present ideas or support arguments and provide detailed evidence (e.g., identifying the specific language used to present ideas and claims that are well supported and distinguishing them from those that are not) when provided with light support. *8. Analyzing language choices* Explain how phrasing or different words with similar meanings (e.g., *cunning* versus *smart, stammer* versus say) or figurative language (e.g., *Let me throw some light onto the topic*) produce shades of meaning, nuances, and different effects on the audience.

Section 2: Elaboration on Critical Principles for Developing Language and Cognition in Academic Contexts
Part I: Interacting in Meaningful Ways

Texts and Discourse in Context		ELD Proficiency Level Continuum		
		→ Emerging →	→ Expanding →	→ Bridging →
Part I, strands 9–12 corresponding to the CA CCSS for ELA/Literacy 9. SL.8.4–6; L.8.1, 3 10. W.8.1–10; WHST.8.1–2,4–10; L.8.1–6 11. W.8.1, 8–9; WHST.8.1, 8–9; L.8.1–3, 6 12. W.8.4–5; WHST.8.4–5; SL.8.4, 6; L.8.1,3, 5–6 **Purposes for using language include but are not limited to:** Describing, entertaining, informing, interpreting, analyzing, recounting, explaining, persuading, negotiating, justifying, evaluating, and so on. **Informational text types include but are not limited to:** Descriptions or accounts (e.g., scientific, historical, economic, technical), recounts (e.g., biography, memoir), information reports, explanations (e.g., causal, factual), expositions (e.g., speeches, opinion pieces, argument, debate), responses (e.g., literary analysis), and so on. **Literary text types include but are not limited to:** Stories (e.g., historical fiction, myths, graphic novels), poetry, drama, and so on. **Audiences include but are not limited to:** Peers (one to one) Small group (one to a group) Whole group (one to many)	**C. Productive**	*9. Presenting* Plan and deliver brief informative oral presentations on concrete topics. *10. Writing* a. Write short literary and informational texts (e.g., an argument about whether the government should fund research using stem cells) collaboratively (e.g., with peers) and independently. b. Write brief summaries of texts and experiences using complete sentences and key words (e.g., from notes or graphic organizers). *11. Justifying/arguing* a. Justify opinions by providing some textual evidence or relevant background knowledge, with substantial support. b. Express attitude and opinions or temper statements with familiar modal expressions (e.g., *can, may*).	*9. Presenting* Plan and deliver longer oral presentations on a variety of topics using details and evidence to support ideas. *10. Writing* a. Write longer literary and informational texts (e.g., an argument about whether the government should fund research using stem cells) collaboratively (e.g., with peers) and independently using appropriate text organization. b. Write increasingly concise summaries of texts and experiences using complete sentences and key words (e.g., from notes or graphic organizers). *11. Justifying/arguing* a. Justify opinions or persuade others by providing relevant textual evidence or relevant background knowledge, with moderate support. b. Express attitude and opinions or temper statements with a variety of familiar modal expressions (e.g., *possibly/likely, could/would*).	*9. Presenting* Plan and deliver longer oral presentations on a variety of concrete and abstract topics using reasoning and evidence to support ideas and using a growing understanding of register. *10. Writing* a. Write longer and more detailed literary and informational texts (e.g., an argument about whether the government should fund research using stem cells) collaboratively (e.g., with peers) and independently using appropriate text organization and growing understanding of register. b. Write clear and coherent summaries of texts and experiences using complete and concise sentences and key words (e.g., from notes or graphic organizers). *11. Justifying/arguing* a. Justify opinions or persuade others by providing detailed and relevant textual evidence or relevant background knowledge, with light support. b. Express attitude and opinions or temper statements with nuanced modal expressions (e.g., *potentially/certainly/absolutely, should/might*).

Texts and Discourse in Context		ELD Proficiency Level Continuum		
		→ Emerging →	→ Expanding →	→ Bridging →
Part I, strands 9–12, corresponding to the CA CCSS for ELA/Literacy 9. SL.8.4–6; L.8.1, 3 10. W.8.1–10; WHST.8.1-2, 4–10; L.8.1–6 11. W.8.1, 8–9; WHST.8.1, 8–9; L.8.1–3, 6 12. W.8.4–5; WHST.8.4-5; SL.8.4, 6; L.8.1, 3, 5–6 **Purposes for using language include but are not limited to:** Describing, entertaining, informing, interpreting, analyzing, recounting, explaining, persuading, negotiating, justifying, evaluating, and so on. **Informational text types include but are not limited to:** Descriptions or accounts (e.g., scientific, historical, economic, technical), recounts (e.g., biography, memoir), information reports, explanations (e.g., causal, factual), expositions (e.g., speeches, opinion pieces, argument, debate), responses (e.g., literary analysis), and so on. **Literary text types include but are not limited to:** Stories (e.g., historical fiction, myths, graphic novels), poetry, drama, and so on. **Audiences include but are not limited to:** Peers (one to one) Small group (one to a group) Whole group (one to many)	**C. Productive**	*12. Selecting language resources* a. Use a select number of general academic words (e.g., *specific, contrast*) and domain-specific words (e.g., *scene, cell, fraction*) to create some precision while speaking and writing. b. Use knowledge of morphology to appropriately select affixes in basic ways (e.g., She likes X. He walk*ed* to school).	*12. Selecting language resources* a. Use a growing set of academic words (e.g., *specific, contrast, significant, function*), domain-specific words (e.g., *scene, irony, suspense, analogy, cell membrane, fraction*), synonyms, and antonyms to create precision and shades of meaning while speaking and writing. b. Use knowledge of morphology to appropriately select affixes in a growing number of ways to manipulate language (e.g., She likes walk*ing* to school. That's *impossible*).	*12. Selecting language resources* a. Use an expanded set of general academic words (e.g., *specific, contrast, significant, function, adequate, analysis*), domain-specific words (e.g., *scene, irony, suspense, analogy, cell membrane, fraction*), synonyms, antonyms, and figurative language to create precision and shades of meaning while speaking and writing. b. Use knowledge of morphology to appropriately select affixes in a variety of ways to manipulate language (e.g., changing *destroy → destruction, probably → probability, reluctant → reluctantly*).

Section 2: Elaboration on Critical Principles for Developing Language and Cognition in Academic Contexts
Part II: Learning About How English Works

Texts and Discourse in Context		ELD Proficiency Level Continuum		
		→ Emerging →	→ Expanding →	→ Bridging →
Part II, strands 1–2, corresponding to the CA CCSS for ELA/Literacy 1. RL.8.5; RI.8.5; RH.8.5; RST.8.5; W.8.1–5, 10; WHST.8.1–2, 4–5, 10; SL.8.4 2. RI.8.5; RH.8.5; RST.8.5; W.8.1–5, 10; WHST.8.1–2, 4–5, 10; L.8.1, 3–6 **Purposes for using language include but are not limited to:** Describing, entertaining, informing, interpreting, analyzing, recounting, explaining, persuading, negotiating, justifying, evaluating, and so on. **Informational text types include but are not limited to:** Descriptions or accounts (e.g., scientific, historical, economic, technical), recounts (e.g., biography, memoir), information reports, explanations (e.g., causal, factual), expositions (e.g., speeches, opinion pieces, argument, debate), responses (e.g., literary analysis), and so on. **Literary text types include but are not limited to:** Stories (e.g., historical fiction, myths, graphic novels), poetry, drama, and so on. **Audiences include but are not limited to:** Peers (one to one) Small group (one to a group) Whole group (one to many)	**A. Structuring Cohesive Texts**	***1. Understanding text structure*** Apply understanding of how different text types are organized to express ideas (e.g., how narratives are organized sequentially) to comprehending texts and to writing brief arguments, informative/explanatory texts and narratives. ***2. Understanding cohesion*** a. Apply knowledge of familiar language resources for referring to make texts more cohesive (e.g., how pronouns refer back to nouns in text) to comprehending and writing brief texts. b. Apply basic understanding of how ideas, events, or reasons are linked throughout a text using everyday connecting words or phrases (e.g., *at the end, next*) to comprehending and writing brief texts.	***1. Understanding text structure*** Apply understanding of the organizational features of different text types (e.g., how narratives are organized by an event sequence that unfolds naturally versus how arguments are organized around reasons and evidence) to comprehending texts and to writing increasingly clear and coherent arguments, informative/explanatory texts and narratives. ***2. Understanding cohesion*** a. Apply knowledge of familiar language resources for referring to make texts more cohesive (e.g., how pronouns refer back to nouns in text, how using synonyms helps avoid repetition) to comprehending and writing texts with increasing cohesion. b. Apply growing understanding of how ideas, events, or reasons are linked throughout a text using a variety of connecting words or phrases (e.g., *for example, as a result, on the other hand*) to comprehending and writing texts with increasing cohesion.	***1. Understanding text structure*** Apply understanding of the organizational structure of different text types (e.g., how narratives are organized by an event sequence that unfolds naturally versus how arguments are organized around reasons and evidence) to comprehending texts and to writing clear and cohesive arguments, informative/explanatory texts and narratives. ***2. Understanding cohesion*** a. Apply knowledge of familiar language resources for referring to make texts more cohesive (e.g., how pronouns, synonyms, or nominalizations are used to refer backward in a text) to comprehending texts and writing cohesive texts. b. Apply increasing understanding of how ideas, events, or reasons are linked throughout a text using an increasing variety of academic connecting and transitional words or phrases (e.g., *for instance, in addition, consequently*) to comprehending and writing texts with increasing cohesion.

Section 2: Elaboration on Critical Principles for Developing Language and Cognition in Academic Contexts
Part II: Learning About How English Works

Texts and Discourse in Context		ELD Proficiency Level Continuum		
		→ Emerging →	→ Expanding →	→ Bridging →
Part II, strands 3–5, corresponding to the CA CCSS for ELA/Literacy 3. W.8.5; WHST.8.5; SL.8.6; L.8.1, 3–6 4. W.8.5; WHST.8.5; SL.8.6; L.8.1, 3–6 5. W.8.4–5; WHST.8.4–5; SL.8.6; L.8.1, 3–6 **Purposes for using language include but are not limited to:** Describing, entertaining, informing, interpreting, analyzing, recounting, explaining, persuading, negotiating, justifying, evaluating, and so on. **Informational text types include but are not limited to:** Descriptions or accounts (e.g., scientific, historical, economic, technical), recounts (e.g., biography, memoir), information reports, explanations (e.g., causal, factual), expositions (e.g., speeches, opinion pieces, argument, debate), responses (e.g., literary analysis), and so on. **Literary text types include but are not limited to:** Stories (e.g., historical fiction, myths, graphic novels), poetry, drama, and so on. **Audiences include but are not limited to:** Peers (one to one) Small group (one to a group) Whole group (one to many)	**B. Expanding and Enriching Ideas**	***3. Using verbs and verb phrases*** Use a variety of verbs in different tenses (e.g., past, present, future, simple, progressive) appropriate to the text type and discipline (e.g., simple past and past progressive for recounting an experience) on familiar topics. ***4. Using nouns and noun phrases*** Expand noun phrases in basic ways (e.g., adding a sensory adjective to a noun) in order to enrich the meaning of sentences and add details about ideas, people, things, and so on. ***5. Modifying to add details*** Expand sentences with simple adverbials (e.g., adverbs, adverb phrases, prepositional phrases) to provide details (e.g., time, manner, place, cause) about a familiar activity or process.	***3. Using verbs and verb phrases*** Use a variety of verbs in different tenses (e.g., past, present, future, simple, progressive, perfect) appropriate to the task, text type, and discipline (e.g., the present perfect to describe previously made claims or conclusions) on an increasing variety of topics. ***4. Using nouns and noun phrases*** Expand noun phrases in a growing number of ways (e.g., adding prepositional or adjective phrases) in order to enrich the meaning of sentences and add details about ideas, people, things, and so on. ***5. Modifying to add details*** Expand sentences with adverbials (e.g., adverbs, adverb phrases, prepositional phrases) to provide details (e.g., time, manner, place, cause) about a familiar or new activity or process.	***3. Using verbs and verb phrases*** Use a variety of verbs in different tenses (e.g., past, present, future, simple, progressive, perfect), voices (active and passive), and moods (e.g., declarative, interrogative, subjunctive) appropriate to the task, text type, and discipline (e.g., the passive voice in simple past to describe the methods of a scientific experiment) on a variety of topics. ***4. Using nouns and noun phrases*** Expand noun phrases in an increasing variety of ways (e.g., embedding relative or complement clauses) in order to enrich the meaning of sentences and add details about ideas, people, things, and so on. ***5. Modifying to add details*** Expand sentences with increasingly complex adverbials (e.g., adverbs, adverb phrases and clauses, prepositional phrases) to provide details (e.g., time, manner, place, cause) about a variety of familiar and new activities and processes.

Texts and Discourse in Context		ELD Proficiency Level Continuum		
		→ Emerging →	→ Expanding →	→ Bridging →
Part II, strands 6–7, corresponding to the CA CCSS for ELA/Literacy 6. W.8.1–5; WHST.8.1–2, 4–5; SL.8.4, 6; L.8.1, 3–6 7. W.8.1–5; WHST.8.1–2, 4–5; SL.8.4, 6; L.8.1, 3–6 **Purposes for using language include but are not limited to:** Describing, entertaining, informing, interpreting, analyzing, recounting, explaining, persuading, negotiating, justifying, evaluating, and so on. **Informational text types include but are not limited to:** Descriptions or accounts (e.g., scientific, historical, economic, technical), recounts (e.g., biography, memoir), information reports, explanations (e.g., causal, factual), expositions (e.g., speeches, opinion pieces, argument, debate), responses (e.g., literary analysis), and so on. **Literary text types include but are not limited to:** Stories (e.g., historical fiction, myths, graphic novels), poetry, drama, and so on. **Audiences include but are not limited to:** Peers (one to one) Small group (one to a group) Whole group (one to many)	**C. Connecting and Condensing Ideas**	*6. Connecting ideas* Combine clauses in a few basic ways to make connections between and join ideas (e.g., creating compound sentences using *and, but, so;* creating complex sentences using because). *7. Condensing ideas* Condense ideas in simple ways (e.g., by compounding verbs, adding prepositional phrases, or through simple embedded clauses or other ways of condensing as in, This is a story about a girl. The girl changed the world. → This is a story about a girl *who changed the world*) to create precise and detailed sentences.	*6. Connecting ideas* Combine clauses in an increasing variety of ways (e.g., creating compound and complex sentences) to make connections between and join ideas, for example, to express a reason (e.g., *He stayed at home on Sunday to study for Monday's exam*) or to make a concession (e.g., *She studied all night even though she wasn't feeling well*). *7. Condensing ideas* Condense ideas in an increasing variety of ways (e.g., through various types of embedded clauses and other ways of condensing, as in, Organic vegetables are food. They're made without chemical fertilizers. They're made without chemical insecticides. → Organic vegetables are foods *that are made without chemical fertilizers or insecticides*) to create precise and detailed sentences.	*6. Connecting ideas* Combine clauses in a wide variety of ways (e.g., creating compound and complex sentences, and compound-complex sentences) to make connections between and join ideas, for example, to show the relationship between multiple events or ideas (e.g., *After eating lunch, the students worked in groups while their teacher walked around the room*) or to evaluate an argument (e.g., *The author claims X, although there is a lack of evidence to support this claim*). *7. Condensing ideas* Condense ideas in a variety of ways (e.g., through various types of embedded clauses, ways of condensing, and nominalization as in, They *destroyed* the rain forest. Lots of animals *died*. → The *destruction* of the rain forest led to *the death* of many animals) to create precise and detailed sentences.

Section 2: Elaboration on Critical Principles for Developing Language and Cognition in Academic Contexts	
Part III: Using Foundational Literacy Skills	
Foundational literacy skills in an alphabetic writing system • Print concepts • Phonological awareness • Phonics and word recognition • Fluency	See chapter 6 for information on teaching foundational reading skills to English learners of various profiles based on age, native language, native language writing system, schooling experience, and literacy experience and proficiency. Some considerations are as follows: • Native language and literacy (e.g., phoneme awareness or print concept skills in native language) should be assessed for potential transference to English language and literacy. • Similarities between the native language and English should be highlighted (e.g., phonemes or letters that are the same in both languages). • Differences between the native language and English should be highlighted (e.g., some phonemes in English may not exist in the student's native language; native language syntax may be different from English syntax).

Section 1: Overview

Goal: English learners read, analyze, interpret, and create a variety of literary and informational text types. They develop an understanding of how language is a complex, dynamic, and social resource for making meaning, as well as how content is organized in different text types and across disciplines using text structure, language features, and vocabulary depending on purpose and audience. They are aware that different languages and variations of English exist, and they recognize their home languages and cultures as resources to value in their own right and also to draw upon in order to build proficiency in English. English learners contribute actively to class and group discussions, asking questions, responding appropriately, and providing useful feedback. They demonstrate knowledge of content through oral presentations, writing tasks, collaborative conversations, and multimedia. They develop proficiency in shifting language use based on task, purpose, audience, and text type.

Critical Principles for Developing Language and Cognition in Academic Contexts: While advancing along the continuum of English language development levels, English learners at all levels engage in intellectually challenging literacy, disciplinary, and disciplinary literacy tasks. They use language in meaningful and relevant ways appropriate to grade level, content area, topic, purpose, audience, and text type in English language arts, mathematics, science, social studies, and the arts. Specifically, they use language to gain and exchange information and ideas in three communicative modes (collaborative, interpretive, and productive), and they apply knowledge of language to academic tasks via three cross-mode language processes (structuring cohesive texts, expanding and enriching ideas, and connecting and condensing ideas) using various linguistic resources.

Part I: Interacting in Meaningful Ways	Corresponding CA CCSS for ELA/Literacy*
A. Collaborative	
1. Exchanging information and ideas with others through oral collaborative discussions on a range of social and academic topics	• SL.9–10.1, 6; L.9–10.3, 6
2. Interacting with others in written English in various communicative forms (print, communicative technology and multimedia)	• W.9–10.6; WHST.9–10.6; SL.9–10.2; L.9–10.3, 6
3. Offering and justifying opinions, negotiating with and persuading others in communicative exchanges	• W.9–10.1; WHST.9–10.1; SL.9–10.1, 4, 6; L.9–10.3, 6
4. Adapting language choices to various contexts (based on task, purpose, audience, and text type)	• W.9–10.4-5; WHST. 9–10.4-5; SL.9–10.6; L.9–10.1, 3, 6

*The California English Language Development Standards correspond to the California Common Core State Standards for English Language Arts and Literacy in History/Social Science and Technical Subjects (CA CCSS for ELA/Literacy). English learners should have full access to opportunities to learn ELA, mathematics, science, history/social studies, and other content at the same time they are progressing toward full proficiency in English.

Part I: Interacting in Meaningful Ways	Corresponding CA CCSS for ELA/Literacy
B. Interpretive	
5. Listening actively to spoken English in a range of social and academic contexts	• SL.9–10.1, 3, 6; L.9–10.1, 3, 6
6. Reading closely literary and informational texts and viewing multimedia to determine how meaning is conveyed explicitly and implicitly through language	• RL.9–10.1–7, 9–10; RI.9–10.1–10; RH.9–10.1–10; RST.9–10.1–10; SL.9–10.2; L.9–10.1, 3, 6
7. Evaluating how well writers and speakers use language to support ideas and arguments with details or evidence depending on modality, text type, purpose, audience, topic, and content area	• RL.9–10.4–5; RI.9–10.4, 6, 8; RH.9–10.4–6, 8; RST.9–10.4–6, 8; SL.9–10.3; L.9–10.3, 5–6
8. Analyzing how writers and speakers use vocabulary and other language resources for specific purposes (to explain, persuade, entertain, etc.) depending on modality, text type, purpose, audience, topic, and content area	• RL.9–10.4–5; RI.9–10.4–5; RH.9–10.4–5; RST.9–10.4–5; SL.9–10.3; L.9–10.3, 5–6
C. Productive	
9. Expressing information and ideas in formal oral presentations on academic topics	• SL.9–10.4–6; L.9–10.1, 3
10. Writing literary and informational texts to present, describe, and explain ideas and information, using appropriate technology	• W.9–10.1–10; WHST.9–10.1–2, 4–10; L.9–10.1–6
11. Justifying own arguments and evaluating others' arguments in writing	• W.9–10.1, 8–9; WHST.9–10.1, 8–9; L.9–10.1–3, 6
12. Selecting and applying varied and precise vocabulary and other language resources to effectively convey ideas	• W.9–10.4–5; WHST.9–10.4–5; SL.9–10.4, 6; L.9–10.1, 3, 5–6
Part II: Learning About How English Works	**Corresponding CA CCSS for ELA/Literacy**
A. Structuring Cohesive Texts	• RL.9–10.5; RI.9–10.5; RH.9–10.5; RST.9–10.5; W.9–10.1–5, 10; WHST.9–10.1–2, 4–5, 10; SL.9–10.4
1. Understanding text structure	
2. Understanding cohesion	• RI.9–10.5; RH.9–10.5; RST.9–10.5; W.9–10.1–5, 10; WHST.9–10.1–2, 4–5, 10; L.9–10.1, 3–6
B. Expanding and Enriching Ideas	• W.9–10.5; WHST.9–10.5; SL.9–10.6; L.9–10.1, 3–6
3. Using verbs and verb phrases	• W.9–10.5; WHST.9–10.5; SL.9–10.6; L.9–10.1, 3–6
4. Using nouns and noun phrases	• W.9–10.4–5; WHST.9–10.4–5; SL.9–10.6; L.9–10.1, 3–6
5. Modifying to add details	
C. Connecting and Condensing Ideas	• W.9–10.1-5; WHST.9–10.1–2, 4–5; SL.9–10.4, 6; L.9–10.1, 3–6
6. Connecting ideas	
7. Condensing ideas	• W.9–10.1-5; WHST.9–10.1–2, 4–5; SL.9–10.4, 6; L.9–10.1, 3–6
Part III: Using Foundational Literacy Skills	• RF.K–1.1–4; RF.2–5.3–4 (as appropriate)

Note: **Examples** provided in specific standards are offered *only as illustrative possibilities* and should not be misinterpreted as the only objectives of instruction or as the only types of language that English learners might or should be able to understand or produce.

Section 2: Elaboration on Critical Principles for Developing Language and Cognition in Academic Contexts
Part I: Interacting in Meaningful Ways

Texts and Discourse in Context		ELD Proficiency Level Continuum		
		→ Emerging →	→ Expanding →	→ Bridging →
Part I, strands 1–4, corresponding to the CA CCSS for ELA/Literacy 1. SL.9–10.1,6; L.9–10.3, 6 2. W.9–10.6; WHST.9–10.6; SL.9–10.2; L.9–10.3, 6 3. W.9–10.1; WHST.9–10.1; SL.9–10.1, 4, 6; L.9–10.3, 6 4. W.9–10.4-5; WHST.9–10.4-5; SL.9–10.6; L.9–10.1, 3, 6 **Purposes for using language include but are not limited to:** Describing, entertaining, informing, interpreting, analyzing, recounting, explaining, persuading, negotiating, justifying, evaluating, and so on. **Informational text types include but are not limited to:** Descriptions or accounts (e.g., scientific, historical, economic, technical), recounts (e.g., biography, memoir), information reports, explanations (e.g., causal, factual), expositions (e.g., speeches, opinion pieces, argument, debate), responses (e.g., literary analysis), and so on. **Literary text types include but are not limited to:** Stories (e.g., historical fiction, myths, graphic novels), poetry, drama, and so on. **Audiences include but are not limited to:** Peers (one to one) Small group (one to a group) Whole group (one to many)	**A. Collaborative**	*1. Exchanging information/ideas* Engage in conversational exchanges and express ideas on familiar current events and academic topics by asking and answering *yes-no* questions and *wh-* questions and responding using phrases and short sentences. *2. Interacting via written English* Collaborate with peers to engage in short, grade-appropriate written exchanges and writing projects, using technology as appropriate. *3. Supporting opinions and persuading others* Negotiate with or persuade others in conversations using learned phrases (e.g., *Would you say that again? I think . . .*), as well as open responses to express and defend opinions. *4. Adapting language choices* Adjust language choices according to the context (e.g., classroom, community) and audience (e.g., peers, teachers).	*1. Exchanging information/ideas* Contribute to class, group, and partner discussions, sustaining conversations on a variety of age and grade-appropriate academic topics by following turn-taking rules, asking and answering relevant, on-topic questions, affirming others, providing additional, relevant information, and paraphrasing key ideas. *2. Interacting via written English* Collaborate with peers to engage in increasingly complex grade-appropriate written exchanges and writing projects, using technology as appropriate. *3. Supporting opinions and persuading others* Negotiate with or persuade others in conversations (e.g., to provide counter-arguments) using a growing number of learned phrases (*I see your point, but . . .*) and open responses to express and defend nuanced opinions. *4. Adapting language choices* Adjust language choices according to the context (e.g., classroom, community), purpose (e.g., to persuade, to provide arguments or counterarguments), task, and audience (e.g., peers, teachers, guest lecturer).	*1. Exchanging information/ideas* Contribute to class, group, and partner discussions, sustaining conversations on a variety of age and grade-appropriate academic topics by following turn-taking rules, asking and answering relevant, on-topic questions, affirming others, and providing coherent and well-articulated comments and additional information. *2. Interacting via written English* Collaborate with peers to engage in a variety of extended written exchanges and complex grade-appropriate writing projects, using technology as appropriate. *3. Supporting opinions and persuading others* Negotiate with or persuade others in conversations in appropriate registers (e.g., to acknowledge new information in an academic conversation but then politely offer a counterpoint) using a variety of learned phrases, indirect reported speech (e.g., *I heard you say X, and I haven't thought about that before. However . . .*), and open responses to express and defend nuanced opinions. *4. Adapting language choices* Adjust language choices according to the task (e.g., group presentation of research project), context (e.g., classroom, community), purpose (e.g., to persuade, to provide arguments or counterarguments), and audience (e.g., peers, teachers, college recruiter).

Section 2: Elaboration on Critical Principles for Developing Language and Cognition in Academic Contexts
Part I: Interacting in Meaningful Ways

Texts and Discourse in Context		ELD Proficiency Level Continuum		
		→ Emerging →	→ Expanding →	→ Bridging →
Part I, strands 5–8, corresponding to the CA CCSS for ELA/Literacy 5. SL.9–10.1, 3, 6; L.9–10.1, 3, 6 6. RL.9–10.1–7,9–10; RI.9–10.1–10; RH.9–10.1–10; RST.9–10.1–10; SL.9–10.2; L.9–10.1, 3, 6 7. RL.9–10.4–5; RI.9–10.4, 6, 8; RH.9–10.4–6, 8; RST.9–10.4–6, 8; SL.9–10.3; L.9–10.3, 5–6 8. RL.9–10.4–5; RI.9–10.4–5; RH.9–10.4–5; RST.9–10.4–5; SL.9–10.3; L.9–10.3, 5–6 **Purposes for using language include but are not limited to:** Describing, entertaining, informing, interpreting, analyzing, recounting, explaining, persuading, negotiating, justifying, evaluating, and so on. **Informational text types include but are not limited to:** Descriptions or accounts (e.g., scientific, historical, economic, technical), recounts (e.g., biography, memoir), information reports, explanations (e.g., causal, factual), expositions (e.g., speeches, opinion pieces, argument, debate), responses (e.g., literary analysis), and so on. **Literary text types include but are not limited to:** Stories (e.g., historical fiction, myths, graphic novels), poetry, drama, and so on. **Audiences include but are not limited to:** Peers (one to one) Small group (one to a group) Whole group (one to many)	**B. Interpretive**	*5. Listening actively* Demonstrate comprehension of oral presentations and discussions on familiar social and academic topics by asking and answering questions, with prompting and substantial support. *6. Reading/viewing closely* a. Explain ideas, phenomena, processes, and text relationships (e.g., compare/contrast, cause/effect, evidence-based argument) based on close reading of a variety of grade-appropriate texts, presented in various print and multimedia formats, using short sentences and a select set of general academic and domain-specific words. b. Explain inferences and conclusions drawn from close reading of grade-appropriate texts and viewing of multimedia using familiar verbs (e.g., *seems that*). c. Use knowledge of morphology (e.g., common prefixes and suffixes), context, reference materials, and visual cues to determine the meaning of unknown and multiple-meaning words on familiar topics.	*5. Listening actively* Demonstrate comprehension of oral presentations and discussions on a variety of social and academic topics by asking and answering questions that show thoughtful consideration of the ideas or arguments, with moderate support. *6. Reading/viewing closely* a. Explain ideas, phenomena, processes, and relationships within and across texts (e.g., compare/contrast, cause/effect, themes, evidence-based argument) based on close reading of a variety of grade-appropriate texts, presented in various print and multimedia formats, using increasingly detailed sentences, and an increasing variety of general academic and domain-specific words. b. Explain inferences and conclusions drawn from close reading of grade-appropriate texts and viewing of multimedia using an increasing variety of verbs and adverbials (e.g., *indicates that, suggests, as a result*). c. Use knowledge of morphology (e.g., affixes, Greek and Latin roots), context, reference materials, and visual cues to determine the meaning of unknown and multiple-meaning words on familiar and new topics.	*5. Listening actively* Demonstrate comprehension of oral presentations and discussions on a variety of social and academic topics by asking and answering detailed and complex questions that show thoughtful consideration of the ideas or arguments, with light support. *6. Reading/viewing closely* a. Explain ideas, phenomena, processes, and relationships within and across texts (e.g., compare/contrast, cause/effect, themes, evidence-based argument) based on close reading of a variety of grade-level texts, presented in various print and multimedia formats, using a variety of detailed sentences and a range of general academic and domain-specific words. b. Explain inferences and conclusions drawn from close reading of grade-level texts and viewing of multimedia using a variety of verbs and adverbials (e.g., *creates the impression that, consequently*). c. Use knowledge of morphology (e.g., derivational suffixes), context, reference materials, and visual cues to determine the meaning, including figurative and connotative meanings, of unknown and multiple-meaning words on a variety of new topics.

Texts and Discourse in Context		ELD Proficiency Level Continuum		
		→ Emerging →	→ Expanding →	→ Bridging →
Part I, strands 5–8, corresponding to the CA CCSS for ELA/Literacy 5. SL.9–10.1, 3, 6; L.9–10.1, 3, 6 6. RL.9–10.1–7,9–10; RI.9–10.1–10; RH.9–10.1–10; RST.9–10.1–10; SL.9–10.2; L.9–10.1, 3, 6 7. RL.9–10.4–5; RI.9–10.4, 6, 8; RH.9–10.4–6, 8; RST.9–10.4–6, 8; SL.9–10.3; L.9–10.3, 5–6 8. RL.9–10.4–5; RI.9–10.4-5; RH.9–10.4–5; RST.9–10.4–5; SL.9–10.3; L.9–10.3, 5–6 **Purposes for using language include but are not limited to:** Describing, entertaining, informing, interpreting, analyzing, recounting, explaining, persuading, negotiating, justifying, evaluating, and so on. **Informational text types include but are not limited to:** Descriptions or accounts (e.g., scientific, historical, economic, technical), recounts (e.g., biography, memoir), information reports, explanations (e.g., causal, factual), expositions (e.g., speeches, opinion pieces, argument, debate), responses (e.g., literary analysis), and so on. **Literary text types include but are not limited to:** Stories (e.g., historical fiction, myths, graphic novels), poetry, drama, and so on. **Audiences include but are not limited to:** Peers (one to one) Small group (one to a group) Whole group (one to many)	**B. Interpretive**	*7. Evaluating language choices* Explain how successfully writers and speakers structure texts and use language (e.g., specific word or phrasing choices) to persuade the reader (e.g., by providing evidence to support claims or connecting points in an argument) or create other specific effects, with substantial support. *8. Analyzing language choices* Explain how a writer's or speaker's choice of phrasing or specific words (e.g., describing a character or action as *aggressive* versus *bold*) produces nuances and different effects on the audience.	*7. Evaluating language choices* Explain how successfully writers and speakers structure texts and use language (e.g., specific word or phrasing choices) to persuade the reader (e.g., by providing well-worded evidence to support claims or connecting points in an argument in specific ways) or create other specific effects, with moderate support. *8. Analyzing language choices* Explain how a writer's or speaker's choice of phrasing or specific words (e.g., using figurative language or words with multiple meanings to describe an event or character) produces nuances and different effects on the audience.	*7. Evaluating language choices* Explain how successfully writers and speakers structure texts and use language (e.g., specific word or phrasing choices) to persuade the reader (e.g., by providing well-worded evidence to support claims or connecting points in an argument in specific ways) or create other specific effects, with light support. *8. Analyzing language choices* Explain how a writer's or speaker's choice of a variety of different types of phrasing or words (e.g., hyperbole, varying connotations, the cumulative impact of word choices) produces nuances and different effects on the audience.

Section 2: Elaboration on Critical Principles for Developing Language and Cognition in Academic Contexts

Part I: Interacting in Meaningful Ways

Texts and Discourse in Context		ELD Proficiency Level Continuum: Emerging	Expanding	Bridging
Part I, strands 9–12, corresponding to the CA CCSS for ELA/Literacy 9. SL.9-10.4-6; L.9-10.1, 3 10. W.9-10.1-10; WHST.9-10.-1-2, 4-10; L.9-10.1-6 11. W.9-10.1, 8-9; WHST.9-10.1, 8-9; L.9-10.1-3, 6 12. W.9-10.4-5; WHST.9-10.4-5; SL.9-10.4, 6; L.9-10.1, 3, 5-6 **Purposes for using language include but are not limited to:** Describing, entertaining, informing, interpreting, analyzing, recounting, explaining, persuading, negotiating, justifying, evaluating, and so on. **Informational text types include but are not limited to:** Descriptions or accounts (e.g., scientific, historical, economic, technical), recounts (e.g., biography, memoir), information reports, explanations (e.g., causal, factual), expositions (e.g., speeches, opinion pieces, argument, debate), responses (e.g., literary analysis), and so on. **Literary text types include but are not limited to:** Stories (e.g., historical fiction, myths, graphic novels), poetry, drama, and so on. **Audiences include but are not limited to:** Peers (one to one) Small group (one to a group) Whole group (one to many)	**C. Productive**	***9. Presenting*** Plan and deliver brief oral presentations and reports on grade-appropriate topics that present evidence and facts to support ideas. ***10. Writing*** a. Write short literary and informational texts (e.g., an argument about water rights) collaboratively (e.g., with peers) and independently. b. Write brief summaries of texts and experiences by using complete sentences and key words (e.g., from notes or graphic organizers). ***11. Justifying/arguing*** a. Justify opinions by articulating some relevant textual evidence or background knowledge, with visual support. b. Express attitude and opinions or temper statements with familiar modal expressions (e.g., *can, may*).	***9. Presenting*** Plan and deliver a variety of oral presentations and reports on grade-appropriate topics that present evidence and facts to support ideas by using growing understanding of register. ***10. Writing*** a. Write longer literary and informational texts (e.g., an argument about water rights) collaboratively (e.g., with peers) and independently by using appropriate text organization and growing understanding of register. b. Write increasingly concise summaries of texts and experiences by using complete sentences and key words (e.g., from notes or graphic organizers). ***11. Justifying/arguing*** a. Justify opinions and positions or persuade others by making connections between ideas and articulating relevant textual evidence or background knowledge. b. Express attitude and opinions or temper statements with a variety of familiar modal expressions (e.g., *possibly/likely, could/would*).	***9. Presenting*** Plan and deliver a variety of oral presentations and reports on grade-appropriate topics that express complex and abstract ideas well supported by evidence and sound reasoning, and are delivered using an appropriate level of formality and understanding of register. ***10. Writing*** a. Write longer and more detailed literary and informational texts (e.g., an argument about water rights) collaboratively (e.g., with peers) and independently using appropriate text organization and register. b. Write clear and coherent summaries of texts and experiences by using complete and concise sentences and key words (e.g., from notes or graphic organizers). ***11. Justifying/arguing*** a. Justify opinions or persuade others by making connections and distinctions between ideas and texts and articulating sufficient, detailed, and relevant textual evidence or background knowledge, using appropriate register. b. Express attitude and opinions or temper statements with nuanced modal expressions (e.g., *possibly/ potentially/ certainly/ absolutely, should/might*).

Section 2: Elaboration on Critical Principles for Developing Language and Cognition in Academic Contexts
Part I: Interacting in Meaningful Ways

Texts and Discourse in Context		ELD Proficiency Level Continuum		
		→ Emerging →	→ Expanding →	→ Bridging →
Part I, strands 9–12, corresponding to the CA CCSS for ELA/Literacy 9. SL.9-10.4-6; L.9-10.1, 3 10. W.9-10.1-10; WHST.9-10.1-2, 4-10; L.9-10.1-6 11. W.9-10.1, 8-9; WHST.9-10.1, 8-9; L.9-10.1-3, 6 12. W.9-10.4-5; WHST.9-10.4-5; SL.9-10.4, 6; L.9-10.1, 3, 5-6 **Purposes for using language include but are not limited to:** Describing, entertaining, informing, interpreting, analyzing, recounting, explaining, persuading, negotiating, justifying, evaluating, and so on. **Informational text types include but are not limited to:** Descriptions or accounts (e.g., scientific, historical, economic, technical), recounts (e.g., biography, memoir), information reports, explanations (e.g., causal, factual), expositions (e.g., speeches, opinion pieces, argument, debate), responses (e.g., literary analysis), and so on. **Literary text types include but are not limited to:** Stories (e.g., historical fiction, myths, graphic novels), poetry, drama, and so on. **Audiences include but are not limited to:** Peers (one to one) Small group (one to a group) Whole group (one to many)	**C. Productive**	*12. Selecting language resources* a. Use familiar general academic (e.g., temperature, document) and domain-specific (e.g., *characterization, photosynthesis, society, quadratic functions*) words to create clear spoken and written texts. b. Use knowledge of morphology to appropriately select basic affixes (e.g., The skull protects the brain).	*12. Selecting language resources* a. Use an increasing variety of grade-appropriate general academic (e.g., *dominate, environment*) and domain-specific (e.g., *characterization, photosynthesis, society, quadratic functions*) academic words accurately and appropriately when producing increasingly complex written and spoken texts. b. Use knowledge of morphology to appropriately select affixes in a growing number of ways to manipulate language (e.g., diplomatic, stems are branched or unbranched).	*12. Selecting language resources* a. Use a variety of grade-appropriate general (e.g., *anticipate, transaction*) and domain-specific (e.g., *characterization, photosynthesis, society, quadratic functions*) academic words and phrases, including persuasive language, accurately and appropriately when producing complex written and spoken texts. b. Use knowledge of morphology to appropriately select affixes in a variety of ways to manipulate language (e.g., changing *humiliate* to *humiliation* or *incredible* to *incredibly*).

Section 2: Elaboration on Critical Principles for Developing Language and Cognition in Academic Contexts
Part II: Learning About How English Works

Texts and Discourse in Context		ELD Proficiency Level Continuum		
		→ Emerging →	→ Expanding →	→ Bridging →
Part II, strands 1–2, corresponding to the CA CCSS for ELA/Literacy 1. RL.9–10.5; RI.9–10.5; RH.9–10.5; RST.9–10.5; W.9–10.1–5, 10; WHST.9–10.1–2, 4–5, 10; SL.9–10.4 2. RI.9–10.5; RH.9–10.5; RST.9–10.5; W.9–10.1–5,10; WHST.9–10.1–2, 4–5, 10; L.9–10.1, 3–6 **Purposes for using language include but are not limited to:** Describing, entertaining, informing, interpreting, analyzing, recounting, explaining, persuading, negotiating, justifying, evaluating, and so on. **Informational text types include but are not limited to:** Descriptions or accounts (e.g., scientific, historical, economic, technical), recounts (e.g., biography, memoir), information reports, explanations (e.g., causal, factual), expositions (e.g., speeches, opinion pieces, argument, debate), responses (e.g., literary analysis), and so on. **Literary text types include but are not limited to:** Stories (e.g., historical fiction, myths, graphic novels), poetry, drama, and so on. **Audiences include but are not limited to:** Peers (one to one) Small group (one to a group) Whole group (one to many)	**A. Structuring Cohesive Texts**	*1. Understanding text structure* Apply analysis of the organizational structure of different text types (e.g., how arguments are organized by establishing clear relationships among claims, counterclaims, reasons, and evidence) to comprehending texts and to writing brief arguments, informative/explanatory texts and narratives. *2. Understanding cohesion* a. Apply knowledge of familiar language resources for referring to make texts more cohesive (e.g., using pronouns to refer back to nouns in text) to comprehending and writing brief texts. b. Apply knowledge of familiar language resources for linking ideas, events, or reasons throughout a text (e.g., using connecting/transition words and phrases, such as *first, second, third*) to comprehending and writing brief texts.	*1. Understanding text structure* Apply analysis of the organizational structure of different text types (e.g., how arguments are organized by establishing clear relationships among claims, counterclaims, reasons, and evidence) to comprehending texts and to writing increasingly clear and cohesive arguments, informative/explanatory texts and narratives. *2. Understanding cohesion* a. Apply knowledge of a growing number of language resources for referring to make texts more cohesive (e.g., using nominalizations to refer back to an action or activity described earlier) to comprehending texts and to writing increasingly cohesive texts for specific purposes and audiences. b. Apply knowledge of familiar language resources for linking ideas, events, or reasons throughout a text (e.g., using connecting/transition words and phrases, such as *meanwhile, however, on the other hand*) to comprehending texts and to writing increasingly cohesive texts for specific purposes and audiences.	*1. Understanding text structure* Apply analysis of the organizational structure of different text types (e.g., how arguments are organized by establishing clear relationships among claims, counterclaims, reasons, and evidence) to comprehending texts and to writing clear and cohesive arguments, informative/explanatory texts and narratives. *2. Understanding cohesion* a. Apply knowledge of a variety of language resources for referring to make texts more cohesive (e.g., using nominalization, paraphrasing, or summaries to reference or recap an idea or explanation provided earlier) to comprehending grade-level texts and to writing clear and cohesive grade-level texts for specific purposes and audiences. b. Apply knowledge of familiar language resources for linking ideas, events, or reasons throughout a text (e.g., using connecting/transition words and phrases, such as *on the contrary, in addition, moreover*) to comprehending grade-level texts and to writing cohesive texts for specific purposes and audiences.

Section 2: Elaboration on Critical Principles for Developing Language and Cognition in Academic Contexts
Part II: Learning About How English Works

Texts and Discourse in Context		ELD Proficiency Level Continuum		
		→ Emerging →	→ Expanding →	→ Bridging →
Part II, strands 3–5, corresponding to the CA CCSS for ELA/Literacy 3. W.9–10.5; WHST.9–10.5; SL.9–10.6; L.9–10.1, 3–6 4. W.9–10.5; WHST.9–10.5; SL.9–10.6; L.9–10.1, 3–6 5. W.9–10.4–5; WHST.9–10.4–5; SL.9–10.6; L.9–10.1, 3–6 **Purposes for using language include but are not limited to:** Describing, entertaining, informing, interpreting, analyzing, recounting, explaining, persuading, negotiating, justifying, evaluating, and so on. **Informational text types include but are not limited to:** Descriptions or accounts (e.g., scientific, historical, economic, technical), recounts (e.g., biography, memoir), information reports, explanations (e.g., causal, factual), expositions (e.g., speeches, opinion pieces, argument, debate), responses (e.g., literary analysis), and so on. **Literary text types include but are not limited to:** Stories (e.g., historical fiction, myths, graphic novels), poetry, drama, and so on. **Audiences include but are not limited to:** Peers (one to one) Small group (one to a group) Whole group (one to many)	**B. Expanding and Enriching Ideas**	***3. Using verbs and verb phrases*** Use a variety of verbs in different tenses (e.g., past, present, future, simple, progressive) appropriate to the text type and discipline to create short texts on familiar academic topics. ***4. Using nouns and noun phrases*** Expand noun phrases to create increasingly detailed sentences (e.g., adding adjectives for precision) about personal and familiar academic topics. ***5. Modifying to add details*** Expand sentences with simple adverbials (e.g., adverbs, adverb phrases, prepositional phrases) to provide details (e.g., time, manner, place, cause) about familiar activities or processes.	***3. Using verbs and verb phrases*** Use a variety of verbs in different tenses (e.g., past, present, future, simple, progressive, perfect) appropriate to the text type and discipline to create a variety of texts that explain, describe, and summarize concrete and abstract thoughts and ideas. ***4. Using nouns and noun phrases*** Expand noun phrases in a growing number of ways (e.g., adding adjectives to nouns; simple clause embedding) to create detailed sentences that accurately describe, explain, and summarize information and ideas on a variety of personal and academic topics. ***5. Modifying to add details*** Expand sentences with a growing variety of adverbials (e.g., adverbs, adverb phrases, prepositional phrases) to provide details (e.g., time, manner, place, cause) about familiar or new activities or processes.	***3. Using verbs and verb phrases*** Use a variety of verbs in different tenses (e.g., past, present, future, simple, progressive, perfect), and mood (e.g., subjunctive) appropriate to the text type and discipline to create a variety of texts that describe concrete and abstract ideas, explain procedures and sequences, summarize texts and ideas, and present and critique points of view. ***4. Using nouns and noun phrases*** Expand noun phrases in a variety of ways (e.g., more complex clause embedding) to create detailed sentences that accurately describe concrete and abstract ideas, explain procedures and sequences, summarize texts and ideas, and present and critique points of view on a variety of academic topics. ***5. Modifying to add details*** Expand sentences with a variety of adverbials (e.g., adverbs, adverb phrases and clauses, prepositional phrases) to provide details (e.g., time, manner, place, cause) about a variety of familiar and new activities and processes.

Texts and Discourse in Context		ELD Proficiency Level Continuum		
		→ Emerging →	→ Expanding →	→ Bridging →
Part II, strands 6–7, corresponding to the CA CCSS for ELA/Literacy 6. W.9-10.1-5; WHST.9-10.1-2, 4-5; SL.9-10.4,6; L.9-10.1,3-6 7. W.9-10.1-5; WHST.9-10.1-2, 4-5; SL.9-10.4, 6; L.9-10.1, 3-6 **Purposes for using language include but are not limited to:** Describing, entertaining, informing, interpreting, analyzing, recounting, explaining, persuading, negotiating, justifying, evaluating, and so on. **Informational text types include but are not limited to:** Descriptions or accounts (e.g., scientific, historical, economic, technical), recounts (e.g., biography, memoir), information reports, explanations (e.g., causal, factual), expositions (e.g., speeches, opinion pieces, argument, debate), responses (e.g., literary analysis), and so on. **Literary text types include but are not limited to:** Stories (e.g., historical fiction, myths, graphic novels), poetry, drama, and so on. **Audiences include but are not limited to:** Peers (one to one) Small group (one to a group) Whole group (one to many)	**C. Connecting and Condensing Ideas**	*6. Connecting ideas* Combine clauses in a few basic ways (e.g., creating compound sentences using *and, but, so;* creating complex sentences using *because*) to make connections between and to join ideas (e.g., *I want to read this book because it describes the solar system*). *7. Condensing ideas* Condense ideas in a few basic ways (e.g., by compounding verb or prepositional phrases) to create precise and detailed simple, compound, and complex sentences (e.g., *The students asked survey questions and recorded the responses*).	*6. Connecting ideas* Combine clauses in a growing number of ways to create compound and complex sentences that make connections between and link concrete and abstract ideas, for example, to express a reason (e.g., *He stayed at home on Sunday in order to study for Monday's exam*) or to make a concession (e.g., *She studied all night even though she wasn't feeling well*). *7. Condensing ideas* Condense ideas in a growing number of ways (e.g., through embedded clauses or by compounding verbs or prepositional phrases) to create more precise and detailed simple, compound, and complex sentences (e.g., *Species that could not adapt to the changing climate eventually disappeared*).	*6. Connecting ideas* Combine clauses in a variety of ways to create compound and complex sentences that make connections between and link concrete and abstract ideas, for example, to make a concession (e.g., *While both characters strive for success,* they each take different approaches through which to reach their goals.), or to establish cause (e.g., Women's lives were changed forever after World War II *as a result of joining the workforce*). *7. Condensing ideas* Condense ideas in a variety of ways (e.g., through a variety of embedded clauses, or by compounding verbs or prepositional phrases, nominalization) to create precise simple, compound, and complex sentences that condense concrete and abstract ideas (e.g., *Another issue that people may be concerned with* is the amount of money *that it will cost to construct the new building*).

Section 2: Elaboration on Critical Principles for Developing Language and Cognition in Academic Contexts
Part III: Using Foundational Literacy Skills

Foundational literacy skills in an alphabetic writing system • Print concepts • Phonological awareness • Phonics and word recognition • Fluency	See chapter 6 for information on teaching foundational reading skills to English learners of various profiles based on age, native language, native language writing system, schooling experience, and literacy experience and proficiency. Some considerations are as follows: ● Native language and literacy (e.g., phoneme awareness or print concept skills in native language) should be assessed for potential transference to English language and literacy. ● Similarities between the native language and English should be highlighted (e.g., phonemes or letters that are the same in both languages). ● Differences between the native language and English should be highlighted (e.g., some phonemes in English may not exist in the student's native language; native language syntax may be different from English syntax).

Section 1: Overview

Goal: English learners read, analyze, interpret, and create a variety of literary and informational text types. They develop an understanding of how language is a complex, dynamic, and social resource for making meaning, as well as how content is organized in different text types and across disciplines using text structure, language features, and vocabulary depending on purpose and audience. They are aware that different languages and variations of English exist, and they recognize their home languages and cultures as resources to value in their own right and also to draw upon in order to build proficiency in English. English learners contribute actively to class and group discussions, asking questions, responding appropriately, and providing useful feedback. They demonstrate knowledge of content through oral presentations, writing tasks, collaborative conversations, and multimedia. They develop proficiency in shifting language use based on task, purpose, audience, and text type.

Critical Principles for Developing Language and Cognition in Academic Contexts: While advancing along the continuum of English language development levels, English learners at all levels engage in intellectually challenging literacy, disciplinary, and disciplinary literacy tasks. They use language in meaningful and relevant ways appropriate to grade level, content area, topic, purpose, audience, and text type in English language arts, mathematics, science, social studies, and the arts. Specifically, they use language to gain and exchange information and ideas in three communicative modes (collaborative, interpretive, and productive), and they apply knowledge of language to academic tasks via three cross-mode language processes (structuring cohesive texts, expanding and enriching ideas, and connecting and condensing ideas) using various linguistic resources.

Part I: Interacting in Meaningful Ways	Corresponding CA CCSS for ELA/Literacy*
A. Collaborative	
1. Exchanging information and ideas with others through oral collaborative discussions on a range of social and academic topics	• SL.11–12.1, 6; L.11–12.3, 6
2. Interacting with others in written English in various communicative forms (print, communicative technology and multimedia)	• W.11–12.6; WHST.11–12.6; SL.11–12.2; L.11–12.3, 6
3. Offering and justifying opinions, negotiating with and persuading others in communicative exchanges	• W.11–12.1; WHST.11–12.1; SL.11–12.1, 4, 6; L.11–12.3, 6
4. Adapting language choices to various contexts (based on task, purpose, audience, and text type)	• W.11–12.4–5; WHST.11–12.4–5; SL.11–12.6; L.11–12.1, 3, 6

*The California English Language Development Standards correspond to the California Common Core State Standards for English Language Arts and Literacy in History/Social Science and Technical Subjects (CA CCSS for ELA/Literacy). English learners should have full access to opportunities to learn ELA, mathematics, science, history/social studies, and other content at the same time they are progressing toward full proficiency in English.

Part I: Interacting In Meaningful Ways	Corresponding CA CCSS for ELA/Literacy
B. Interpretive	
5. Listening actively to spoken English in a range of social and academic contexts	• SL.11–12.1, 3, 6; L.11–12.1, 3, 6
6. Reading closely literary and informational texts and viewing multimedia to determine how meaning is conveyed explicitly and implicitly through language	• RL.11–12.1–7, 9–10; RI.11–12.110;– RH.11–12.1–10; RST.11–12.1–10; SL.11–12.2; L.11–12.1, 3, 6
7. Evaluating how well writers and speakers use language to support ideas and arguments with details or evidence depending on modality, text type, purpose, audience, topic, and content area	• RL.11–12.4–5; RI.11–12.4, 6, 8; RH.11–12.4–6, 8; RST.11–12.4–6, 8; SL.11–12.3; L.11–12.3, 5–6
8. Analyzing how writers and speakers use vocabulary and other language resources for specific purposes (to explain, persuade, entertain, etc.) depending on modality, text type, purpose, audience, topic, and content area	• RL.11–12.4–5; RI.11–12.4–5; RH.11–12.4–5; RST.11–12.4–5; SL.11–12.3; L.11–12.3, 5–6
C. Productive	
9. Expressing information and ideas in formal oral presentations on academic topics	• SL.11–12.4–6; L.11–12.1, 3
10. Writing literary and informational texts to present, describe, and explain ideas and information, using appropriate technology	• W.11–12.1–10; WHST.11–12.1–2, 4–10; L.11–12.1–6
11. Justifying own arguments and evaluating others' arguments in writing	• W.11–12.1, 8–9; WHST.11–12.1, 8–9;L.11–12.1–3, 6
12. Selecting and applying varied and precise vocabulary and other language resources to effectively convey ideas	• W.11–12.4–5; WHST.11–12.4–5; SL.11–12.4, 6; L.11–12.1, 3, 5–6
Part II: Learning About How English Works	Corresponding CA CCSS for ELA/Literacy
A. Structuring Cohesive Texts	
1. Understanding text structure	• RL.11–12.5; RI.11–12.5; RH.11–12.5; RST.11–12.5; W.11–12.1–5, 10; WHST.11–12.1–2, 4–5, 10;SL.11–12.4
2. Understanding cohesion	• RI.11–12.5; RH.11–12.5; RST.11–12.5; W.11–12.1–5, 10; WHST.11–12.1–2, 4–5, 10; L.11–12.1, 3–6
B. Expanding and Enriching Ideas	
3. Using verbs and verb phrases	• W.11–12.5; WHST.11–12.5; SL.11–12.6; L.11–12.1, 3–6
4. Using nouns and noun phrases	• W.11–12.5; WHST.11–12.5; SL.11–12.6; L.11–12.1, 3–6
5. Modifying to add details	• W.11–12.4–5; WHST.11–12.4–5; SL.11–12.6; L.11–12.1, 3–6
C. Connecting and Condensing Ideas	• W.11–12.1–5; WHST.11–12.1–2, 4–5; SL.11–12.4, 6; L.11–12.1, 3–6
6. Connecting ideas	
7. Condensing ideas	• W.11–12.1–5; WHST.11–12.1–2, 4–5; SL.11–12.4, 6; L.11–12.1, 3–6
Part III: Using Foundational Literacy Skills	• RF.K–1.1–4; RF.2–5.3–4 (as appropriate)

Note: **Examples** provided in specific standards are offered *only as illustrative possibilities* and should not be misinterpreted as the only objectives of instruction or as the only types of language that English learners might or should be able to understand or produce.

Section 2: Elaboration on Critical Principles for Developing Language and Cognition in Academic Contexts
Part I: Interacting in Meaningful Ways

Texts and Discourse in Context	ELD Proficiency Level Continuum		
	→ Emerging →	→ Expanding →	→ Bridging →
Part I, strands 1–4, corresponding to the CA CCSS for ELA/Literacy 1. SL.11–12.1,6; L.11–12.3, 6 2. W.11–12.6; WHST.11–12.6; SL.11–12.2; L.11–12.3, 6 3. W.11–12.1; WHST.11–12.1; SL.11–12.1, 4, 6; L.11–12.3, 6 4. W.11–12.4–5; WHST.4–5; SL.11–12.6; L.11–12.1, 3, 6 **Purposes for using language include but are not limited to:** Describing, entertaining, informing, interpreting, analyzing, recounting, explaining, persuading, negotiating, justifying, evaluating, and so on. **Informational text types include but are not limited to:** Descriptions or accounts (e.g., scientific, historical, economic, technical), recounts (e.g., biography, memoir), information reports, explanations (e.g., causal, factual), expositions (e.g., speeches, opinion pieces, argument, debate), responses (e.g., literary analysis), and so on. **Literary text types include but are not limited to:** Stories (e.g., historical fiction, myths, graphic novels), poetry, drama, and so on. **Audiences include but are not limited to:** Peers (one to one) Small group (one to a group) Whole group (one to many)	**1. Exchanging information/ideas** Engage in conversational exchanges and express ideas on familiar current events and academic topics by asking and answering *yes-no* questions and *wh-* questions and responding using phrases and short sentences. **2. Interacting via written English** Collaborate with peers to engage in short, grade-appropriate written exchanges and writing projects, using technology as appropriate. **3. Supporting opinions and persuading others** Negotiate with or persuade others in conversations (e.g., ask for clarification or repetition) using learned phrases (e.g., *Could you repeat that please? I believe . . .*) and open responses to express and defend opinions. **4. Adapting language choices** Adjust language choices according to the context (e.g., classroom, community) and audience (e.g., peers, teachers).	**1. Exchanging information/ideas** Contribute to class, group, and partner discussions, sustaining conversations on a variety of age and grade-appropriate academic topics by following turn-taking rules, asking and answering relevant, on-topic questions, affirming others, providing additional, relevant information, and paraphrasing key ideas. **2. Interacting via written English** Collaborate with peers to engage in increasingly complex grade-appropriate written exchanges and writing projects, using technology as appropriate. **3. Supporting opinions and persuading others** Negotiate with and persuade others (e.g., by presenting counter-arguments) in discussions and conversations using learned phrases (e.g., *You make a valid point, but my view is . . .*) and open responses to express and defend nuanced opinions. **4. Adapting language choices** Adjust language choices according to the context (e.g., classroom, community), purpose (e.g., to persuade, to provide arguments or counterarguments), task, and audience (e.g., peers, teachers, guest lecturer).	**1. Exchanging information/ideas** Contribute to class, group, and partner discussions, sustaining conversations on a variety of age and grade-appropriate academic topics by following turn-taking rules, asking and answering relevant, on-topic questions, affirming others, and providing coherent and well-articulated comments and additional information. **2. Interacting via written English** Collaborate with peers to engage in a variety of extended written exchanges and complex grade-appropriate writing projects, using technology as appropriate. **3. Supporting opinions and persuading others** Negotiate with or persuade others in discussions and conversations in appropriate registers (e.g., to acknowledge new information and politely offer a counterpoint) using a variety of learned phrases (e.g., *You postulate that X. However, I've reached a different conclusion on this issue*) and open responses to express and defend nuanced opinions. **4. Adapting language choices** Adjust language choices according to the task (e.g., group presentation of research project), context (e.g., classroom, community), purpose (e.g., to persuade, to provide arguments or counterarguments), and audience (e.g., peers, teachers, college recruiter).

A. Collaborative

Section 2: Elaboration on Critical Principles for Developing Language and Cognition in Academic Contexts
Part I: Interacting in Meaningful Ways

Texts and Discourse in Context		ELD Proficiency Level Continuum		
		→ Emerging →	→ Expanding →	→ Bridging →
Part I, strands 5–8, corresponding to the CA CCSS for ELA/Literacy 5. SL.11–12.1, 3, 6; L.11–12.1, 3, 6 6. RL.11–12.1–7, 9–10; RI.11–12.1–10; RH.11–12.1–10; RST.11–12.1–10; SL.11–12.2; L.11–12.1, 3, 6 7. RL.11–12.4–5; RI.11–12.4, 6, 8; RH.11–12.4–6, 8; RST.11–12.4–6, 8; SL.11–12.3; L.11–12.3, 5–6 8. RL.11–12.4–5; RI.11–12.4–5; RH.11–12.4–5; RST.11–12.4–5; SL.11–12.3; L.11–12.3, 5–6 **Purposes for using language include but are not limited to:** Describing, entertaining, informing, interpreting, analyzing, recounting, explaining, persuading, negotiating, justifying, evaluating, and so on. **Informational text types include but are not limited to:** Descriptions or accounts (e.g., scientific, historical, economic, technical), recounts (e.g., biography, memoir), information reports, explanations (e.g., causal, factual), expositions (e.g., speeches, opinion pieces, argument, debate), responses (e.g., literary analysis), and so on. **Literary text types include but are not limited to:** Stories (e.g., historical fiction, myths, graphic novels), poetry, drama, and so on. **Audiences include but are not limited to:** Peers (one to one) Small group (one to a group) Whole group (one to many)	**B. Interpretive**	**5. *Listening actively*** Demonstrate comprehension of oral presentations and discussions on familiar social and academic topics by asking and answering questions with prompting and substantial support. **6. *Reading/viewing closely*** a. Explain ideas, phenomena, processes, and text relationships (e.g., compare/contrast, cause/effect, evidence-based argument) based on close reading of a variety of grade-appropriate texts, presented in various print and multimedia formats, using phrases, short sentences, and a select set of general academic and domain-specific words. b. Explain inferences and conclusions drawn from close reading of grade-appropriate texts and viewing of multimedia, using familiar verbs (e.g., *seems that*). c. Use knowledge of morphology (e.g., common prefixes and suffixes), context, reference materials, and visual cues to determine the meaning of unknown and multiple-meaning words on familiar topics.	**5. *Listening actively*** Demonstrate comprehension of oral presentations and discussions on a variety of social and academic topics by asking and answering questions that show thoughtful consideration of the ideas or arguments with moderate support. **6. *Reading/viewing closely*** a. Explain ideas, phenomena, processes, and relationships within and across texts (e.g., compare/contrast, cause/effect, themes, evidence-based argument) based on close reading of a variety of grade-appropriate texts, presented in various print and multimedia formats, using increasingly detailed sentences, and a range of general academic and domain-specific words. b. Explain inferences and conclusions drawn from close reading of grade-appropriate texts and viewing of multimedia using a variety of verbs and adverbials (e.g., *indicates that, suggests, as a result*). c. Use knowledge of morphology (e.g., affixes, Greek and Latin roots), context, reference materials, and visual cues to determine the meaning of unknown and multiple-meaning words on familiar and new topics.	**5. *Listening actively*** Demonstrate comprehension of oral presentations and discussions on a variety of social and academic topics by asking and answering detailed and complex questions that show thoughtful consideration of the ideas or arguments with light support. **6. *Reading/viewing closely*** a. Explain ideas, phenomena, processes, and relationships within and across texts (e.g., compare/contrast, cause/effect, themes, evidence-based argument) based on close reading of a variety of grade-level texts, presented in various print and multimedia formats, using a variety of detailed sentences and precise general academic and domain-specific words. b. Explain inferences and conclusions drawn from close reading of grade-level texts and viewing of multimedia using a variety of verbs and adverbials (e.g., *creates the impression that, consequently*). c. Use knowledge of morphology (e.g., derivational suffixes), context, reference materials, and visual cues to determine the meaning, including figurative and connotative meanings, of unknown and multiple-meaning words on a variety of new topics.

Texts and Discourse in Context		ELD Proficiency Level Continuum		
		→ Emerging →	→ Expanding →	→ Bridging →
Part I, strands 5–8, corresponding to the CA CCSS for ELA/Literacy 5. SL.11–12.1, 3, 6; L.11–12.1, 3, 6 6. RL.11–12.1–7,9–10; RI.11–12.1–10; RH.11–12.1 –10; RST.11–12.1–10; L.11–12.2; L.11–12.1, 3, 6 7. RL.11–12.4–5; RI.11–12.4, 6, 8; RH.11–12.4–6, 8; RST.11–12.4–6, 8; SL.11–12.3; L.11–12.3, 5–6 8. RL.11–12.4–5; RI.11–12.4–5; RH.11–12.4–5; RST.11–12.4–5; SL.11–12.3; L.11–12.3, 5–6 **Purposes for using language include but are not limited to:** Describing, entertaining, informing, interpreting, analyzing, recounting, explaining, persuading, negotiating, justifying, evaluating, and so on. **Informational text types include but are not limited to:** Descriptions or accounts (e.g., scientific, historical, economic, technical), recounts (e.g., biography, memoir), information reports, explanations (e.g., causal, factual), expositions (e.g., speeches, opinion pieces, argument, debate), responses (e.g., literary analysis), and so on. **Literary text types include but are not limited to:** Stories (e.g., historical fiction, myths, graphic novels), poetry, drama, and so on. **Audiences include but are not limited to:** Peers (one to one) Small group (one to a group) Whole group (one to many)	**B. Interpretive**	***7. Evaluating language choices*** Explain how successfully writers and speakers structure texts and use language (e.g., specific word or phrasing choices) to persuade the reader (e.g., by providing evidence to support claims or connecting points in an argument) or create other specific effects. ***8. Analyzing language choices*** Explain how a writer's or speaker's choice of phrasing or specific words (e.g., describing a character or action as *aggressive* versus *bold*) produces nuances or different effects on the audience.	***7. Evaluating language choices*** Explain how successfully writers and speakers structure texts and use language (e.g., specific word or phrasing choices) to persuade the reader (e.g., by providing well-worded evidence to support claims or connecting points in an argument in specific ways) or create other specific effects, with moderate support. ***8. Analyzing language choices*** Explain how a writer's or speaker's choice of phrasing or specific words (e.g., using figurative language or words with multiple meanings to describe an event or character) produces nuances and different effects on the audience.	***7. Evaluating language choices*** Explain how successfully writers and speakers structure texts and use language (e.g., specific word or phrasing choices) to persuade the reader (e.g., by providing well-worded evidence to support claims or connecting points in an argument in specific ways) or create other specific effects, with light support. ***8. Analyzing language choices*** Explain how a writer's or speaker's choice of a variety of different types of phrasing or words (e.g., hyperbole, varying connotations, the cumulative impact of word choices) produces nuances and different effects on the audience.

Section 2: Elaboration on Critical Principles for Developing Language and Cognition in Academic Contexts
Part I: Interacting in Meaningful Ways

Texts and Discourse in Context		ELD Proficiency Level Continuum		
		→ Emerging →	→ Expanding →	→ Bridging →
Part I, strands 9–12, corresponding to the CA CCSS for ELA/Literacy 9. SL.11–12.4–6; L.11–12.1, 3 10. W.11–12.1–10; WHST.11–12.1–2, 4–10; L.11–12.1–6 11. W.11–12.1, 8–9; WHST.11–12.1, 8–9; L.11–12.1–3, 6 12. W.11–12.4–5; WHST.11–12.4–5; SL.11–12.4, 6; L.11–12.1, 3, 5–6 **Purposes for using language include but are not limited to:** Describing, entertaining, informing, interpreting, analyzing, recounting, explaining, persuading, negotiating, justifying, evaluating, and so on. **Informational text types include but are not limited to:** Descriptions or accounts (e.g., scientific, historical, economic, technical), recounts (e.g., biography, memoir), information reports, explanations (e.g., causal, factual), expositions (e.g., speeches, opinion pieces, argument, debate), responses (e.g., literary analysis), and so on. **Literary text types include but are not limited to:** Stories (e.g., historical fiction, myths, graphic novels), poetry, drama, and so on. **Audiences include but are not limited to:** Peers (one to one) Small group (one to a group) Whole group (one to many)	**C. Productive**	*9. Presenting* Plan and deliver brief oral presentations and reports on grade-appropriate topics that present evidence and facts to support ideas. *10. Writing* a. Write short literary and informational texts (e.g., an argument about free speech) collaboratively (e.g., with peers) and independently. b. Write brief summaries of texts and experiences by using complete sentences and key words (e.g., from notes or graphic organizers). *11. Justifying/arguing* a. Justify opinions by articulating some textual evidence or background knowledge with visual support. b. Express attitude and opinions or temper statements with familiar modal expressions (e.g., *can, may*).	*9. Presenting* Plan and deliver a variety of oral presentations and reports on grade-appropriate topics that present evidence and facts to support ideas by using growing understanding of register. *10. Writing* a. Write longer literary and informational texts (e.g., an argument about free speech) collaboratively (e.g., with peers) and independently by using appropriate text organization and growing understanding of register. b. Write increasingly concise summaries of texts and experiences by using complete sentences and key words (e.g., from notes or graphic organizers). *11. Justifying/arguing* a. Justify opinions and positions or persuade others by making connections between ideas and articulating relevant textual evidence or background knowledge. b. Express attitude and opinions or temper statements with a variety of familiar modal expressions (e.g., *possibly/likely, could/would*).	*9. Presenting* Plan and deliver a variety of oral presentations and reports on grade-appropriate topics that express complex and abstract ideas, well supported by evidence and reasoning, and are delivered by using an appropriate level of formality and understanding of register. *10. Writing* a. Write longer and more detailed literary and informational texts (e.g., an argument about free speech) collaboratively (e.g., with peers) and independently by using appropriate text organization and register. b. Write clear and coherent summaries of texts and experiences by using complete and concise sentences and key words (e.g., from notes or graphic organizers). *11. Justifying/arguing* a. Justify opinions or persuade others by making connections and distinctions between ideas and texts and articulating sufficient, detailed, and relevant textual evidence or background knowledge by using appropriate register. b. Express attitude and opinions or temper statements with nuanced modal expressions (e.g., *possibly/potentially/certainly/absolutely, should/might*).

Section 2: Elaboration on Critical Principles for Developing Language and Cognition in Academic Contexts
Part I: Interacting in Meaningful Ways

Texts and Discourse in Context		ELD Proficiency Level Continuum		
		→ Emerging →	→ Expanding →	→ Bridging →
Part I, strands 9–12, corresponding to the CA CCSS for ELA/Literacy 9. SL.11–12.4–6; L.11–12.1, 3 10. W.11–12.1–10; WHST.11–12.1–2, 4–10; L.11–12.1–6 11. W.11–12.1, 8–9; WHST.11–12.1, 8–9; L.11–12.1–3, 6 12. W.11–12.4–5; WHST.11–12.4–5; SL.11–12.4, 6; L.11–12.1, 3, 5–6 **Purposes for using language include but are not limited to:** Describing, entertaining, informing, interpreting, analyzing, recounting, explaining, persuading, negotiating, justifying, evaluating, and so on. **Informational text types include but are not limited to:** Descriptions or accounts (e.g., scientific, historical, economic, technical), recounts (e.g., biography, memoir), information reports, explanations (e.g., causal, factual), expositions (e.g., speeches, opinion pieces, argument, debate), responses (e.g., literary analysis), and so on. **Literary text types include but are not limited to:** Stories (e.g., historical fiction, myths, graphic novels), poetry, drama, and so on. **Audiences include but are not limited to:** Peers (one to one) Small group (one to a group) Whole group (one to many)	**C. Productive**	*12. Selecting language resources* a. Use familiar general academic (e.g., *temperature, document*) and domain-specific (e.g., *cell, the Depression*) words to create clear spoken and written texts. b. Use knowledge of morphology to appropriately select basic affixes (e.g., The news media rel*ies* on official sources).	*12. Selecting language resources* a. Use an increasing variety of grade-appropriate general academic (e.g., *fallacy, dissuade*) and domain-specific (e.g., *chromosome, federalism*) academic words accurately and appropriately when producing increasingly complex written and spoken texts. b. Use knowledge of morphology to appropriately select affixes in a growing number of ways to manipulate language (e.g., The card*iac* muscle works continuous*ly*.).	*12. Selecting language resources* a. Use a variety of grade-appropriate general (e.g., *alleviate, salutary*) and domain-specific (e.g., *soliloquy, micro-organism*) academic words and phrases, including persuasive language, accurately and appropriately when producing complex written and spoken texts. b. Use knowledge of morphology to appropriately select affixes in a variety of ways to manipulate language (e.g., changing *inaugurate* to *inauguration*).

Section 2: Elaboration on Critical Principles for Developing Language and Cognition in Academic Contexts
Part II: Learning About How English Works

Texts and Discourse in Context		ELD Proficiency Level Continuum		
		→ Emerging →	→ Expanding →	→ Bridging →
Part II, strands 1–2, corresponding to the CA CCSS for ELA/Literacy 1. RL.11–12.5; RI.11–12.5; RH.11–12.5; RST.11–12.5; W.11–12.1–5, 10; WHST.11–12.1–2, 4–5, 10; SL.11–12.4 2. RI.11–12.5; RH.11–12.5; RST.11–12.5; W.11–12.1–5, 10; WHST.11–12.1–2, 4–5, 10; L.11–12.1, 3–6 **Purposes for using language include but are not limited to:** Describing, entertaining, informing, interpreting, analyzing, recounting, explaining, persuading, negotiating, justifying, evaluating, and so on. **Informational text types include but are not limited to:** Descriptions or accounts (e.g., scientific, historical, economic, technical), recounts (e.g., biography, memoir), information reports, explanations (e.g., causal, factual), expositions (e.g., speeches, opinion pieces, argument, debate), responses (e.g., literary analysis), and so on. **Literary text types include but are not limited to:** Stories (e.g., historical fiction, myths, graphic novels), poetry, drama, and so on. **Audiences include but are not limited to:** Peers (one to one) Small group (one to a group) Whole group (one to many)	**A. Structuring Cohesive Texts**	***1. Understanding text structure*** Apply analysis of the organizational structure of different text types (e.g., how arguments are organized by establishing clear relationships among claims, counterclaims, reasons, and evidence) to comprehending texts and to writing brief arguments, informative/explanatory texts, and narratives. ***2. Understanding cohesion*** a. Apply knowledge of familiar language resources for referring to make texts more cohesive (e.g., using pronouns or synonyms to refer back to characters or concepts introduced earlier) to comprehending and writing brief texts. b. Apply knowledge of familiar language resources for linking ideas, events, or reasons throughout a text (e.g., using connecting/transition words and phrases, such as *first, second, finally*) to comprehending and writing brief texts.	***1. Understanding text structure*** Apply analysis of the organizational structure of different text types (e.g., how arguments are organized by establishing clear relationships among claims, counterclaims, reasons, and evidence) to comprehending texts and to writing increasingly clear and cohesive arguments, informative/explanatory texts, and narratives. ***2. Understanding cohesion*** a. Apply knowledge of a growing number of language resources for referring to make texts more cohesive (e.g., using nominalizations to refer back to an action or activity described earlier) to comprehending texts and to writing increasingly cohesive texts for specific purposes and audiences. b. Apply knowledge of familiar language resources for linking ideas, events, or reasons throughout a text (e.g., using connecting/transition words and phrases, such as *meanwhile, however, on the other hand*) to comprehending texts and to writing increasingly cohesive texts for specific purposes and audiences.	***1. Understanding text structure*** Apply analysis of the organizational structure of different text types (e.g., how arguments are organized by establishing clear relationships among claims, counterclaims, reasons, and evidence) to comprehending texts and to writing clear and cohesive arguments, informative/explanatory texts, and narratives. ***2. Understanding cohesion*** a. Apply knowledge of a variety of resources for referring to make texts more cohesive (e.g., using nominalization, paraphrases, or summaries to reference or recap an idea or explanation provided earlier) to comprehending grade-level texts and to writing clear and cohesive texts for specific purposes and audiences. b. Apply knowledge of familiar language resources for linking ideas, events, or reasons throughout a text (e.g., using connecting/transition words and phrases, such as *on the contrary, in addition, moreover*) to comprehending grade-level texts and writing cohesive texts for specific purposes and audiences.

Section 2: Elaboration on Critical Principles for Developing Language and Cognition in Academic Contexts
Part II: Learning About How English Works

Texts and Discourse in Context		ELD Proficiency Level Continuum		
		→ Emerging →	→ Expanding →	→ Bridging →
Part II, strands 3–5, corresponding to the CA CCSS for ELA/Literacy 3. W.11–12.5; WHST.11–12.5; SL.11–12.6; L.11–12.1, 3–6 4. W.11–12.5; WHST.11–12.5; SL.11–12.6; L.11–12.1, 3–6 5. W.11–12.4–5; WHST.11–12.4–5; SL.11–12.6; L.11–12.1, 3–6 **Purposes for using language include but are not limited to:** Describing, entertaining, informing, interpreting, analyzing, recounting, explaining, persuading, negotiating, justifying, evaluating, and so on. **Informational text types include but are not limited to:** Descriptions or accounts (e.g., scientific, historical, economic, technical), recounts (e.g., biography, memoir), information reports, explanations (e.g., causal, factual), expositions (e.g., speeches, opinion pieces, argument, debate), responses (e.g., literary analysis), and so on. **Literary text types include but are not limited to:** Stories (e.g., historical fiction, myths, graphic novels), poetry, drama, and so on. **Audiences include but are not limited to:** Peers (one to one) Small group (one to a group) Whole group (one to many)	**B. Expanding and Enriching Ideas**	***3. Using verbs and verb phrases*** Use a variety of verbs in different tenses (e.g., past, present, future, simple, progressive) appropriate to the text type and discipline to create short texts on familiar academic topics. ***4. Using nouns and noun phrases*** Expand noun phrases to create increasingly detailed sentences (e.g., adding adjectives for precision) about personal and familiar academic topics. ***5. Modifying to add details*** Expand sentences with simple adverbials (e.g., adverbs, adverb phrases, prepositional phrases) to provide details (e.g., time, manner, place, cause) about familiar activities or processes.	***3. Using verbs and verb phrases*** Use a variety of verbs in different tenses (e.g., past, present, future, simple, progressive, perfect) appropriate to the text type and discipline to create a variety of texts that explain, describe, and summarize concrete and abstract thoughts and ideas. ***4. Using nouns and noun phrases*** Expand noun phrases in a growing number of ways (e.g., adding adjectives to nouns, simple clause embedding) to create detailed sentences that accurately describe, explain, and summarize information and ideas on a variety of personal and academic topics. ***5. Modifying to add details*** Expand sentences with a growing variety of adverbials (e.g., adverbs, adverb phrases, prepositional phrases) to provide details (e.g., time, manner, place, cause) about familiar or new activities or processes.	***3. Using verbs and verb phrases*** Use a variety of verbs in different tenses (e.g., past, present, future, simple, progressive, perfect), and mood (e.g., subjunctive) appropriate to the text type and discipline to create a variety of texts that describe concrete and abstract ideas, explain procedures and sequences, summarize texts and ideas, and present and critique points of view. ***4. Using nouns and noun phrases*** Expand noun phrases in a variety of ways (e.g., complex clause embedding) to create detailed sentences that accurately describe concrete and abstract ideas, explain procedures and sequences, summarize texts and ideas, and present and critique points of view on a variety of academic topics. ***5. Modifying to add details*** Expand sentences with a variety of adverbials (e.g., adverbs, adverb phrases and clauses, prepositional phrases) to provide details (e.g., time, manner, place, cause) about a variety of familiar and new activities and processes.

Texts and Discourse in Context	ELD Proficiency Level Continuum		
	→ Emerging →	→ Expanding →	→ Bridging →
Part II, strands 6–7, corresponding to the CA CCSS for ELA/Literacy 6. W.11–12.1–5; WHST.11–12.1–2, 4–5; SL.11–12.4, 6; L.11–12.1, 3–6 7. W.11–12.1–5; WHST.11–12.1–2, 4–5; SL.11–12.4, 6; L.11–12.1, 3–6 **Purposes for using language include but are not limited to:** Describing, entertaining, informing, interpreting, analyzing, recounting, explaining, persuading, negotiating, justifying, evaluating, and so on. **Informational text types include but are not limited to:** Descriptions or accounts (e.g., scientific, historical, economic, technical), recounts (e.g., biography, memoir), information reports, explanations (e.g., causal, factual), expositions (e.g., speeches, opinion pieces, argument, debate), responses (e.g., literary analysis), and so on. **Literary text types include but are not limited to:** Stories (e.g., historical fiction, myths, graphic novels), poetry, drama, and so on. **Audiences include but are not limited to:** Peers (one to one) Small group (one to a group) Whole group (one to many)	*6. Connecting ideas* Combine clauses in a few basic ways (e.g., creating compound sentences using *and, but, so;* creating complex sentences using *because*) to make connections between and join ideas (e.g., *I want to read this book because it tells the history of Pi*). *7. Condensing ideas* Condense ideas in a few basic ways (e.g., by compounding verb or prepositional phrases) to create precise and detailed simple, compound, and complex sentences (e.g., *The students asked survey questions and recorded the responses*).	*6. Connecting ideas* Combine clauses in a growing number of ways to create compound and complex sentences that make connections between and link concrete and abstract ideas, for example, to express a reason (e.g., *He stayed at home on Sunday in order to study for Monday's exam*) or to make a concession (e.g., *She studied all night even though she wasn't feeling well*). *7. Condensing ideas* Condense ideas in a growing number of ways (e.g., through embedded clauses or by compounding verb or prepositional phrases) to create more precise and detailed simple, compound, and complex sentences (e.g., *Species that could not adapt to the changing climate* eventually disappeared).	*6. Connecting ideas* Combine clauses in a variety of ways to create compound and complex sentences that make connections between and link concrete and abstract ideas, for example, to make a concession (e.g., *While both characters strive for success, they each take different approaches to reach their goals*), or to establish cause (e.g., *Women's lives were changed forever after World War II as a result of joining the workforce*). *7. Condensing ideas* Condense ideas in a variety of ways (e.g., through a variety of embedded clauses, or by compounding verb or prepositional phrases, nominalization) to create precise simple, compound, and complex sentences that condense concrete and abstract ideas (e.g., *The epidemic, which ultimately affected hundreds of thousands of people, did not subside for another year*).

C. Connecting and Condensing Ideas

Section 2: Elaboration on Critical Principles for Developing Language and Cognition in Academic Contexts
Part III: Using Foundational Literacy Skills

Foundational literacy skills in an alphabetic writing system • Print concepts • Phonological awareness • Phonics and word recognition • Fluency	See chapter 6 for information on teaching foundational reading skills to English learners of various profiles based on age, native language, native language writing system, schooling experience, and literacy experience and proficiency. Some considerations are as follows: • Native language and literacy (e.g., phoneme awareness or print concept skills in native language) should be assessed for potential transference to English language and literacy. • Similarities between the native language and English should be highlighted (e.g., phonemes or letters that are the same in both languages). • Differences between the native language and English should be highlighted (e.g., some phonemes in English may not exist in the student's native language; native language syntax may be different from English syntax).

Professional Learning for Successful Implementation of the California English Language Development Standards

Chapter 4

Theoretical Foundations and the Research Base of the California English Language Development Standards

California's 2012 English Language Development Standards (the CA ELD Standards) reflect an extensive review of established and emerging theories, research, and other relevant resources pertaining to the education of K–12 English learners (ELs). This wide body of scholarship and guidance was used to inform the development of the CA ELD Standards. The research base was relied upon to ensure that the CA ELD Standards highlight and amplify the language demands in the California Common Core State Standards for English Language Arts and Literacy in History/Social Studies, Science, and Technical Subjects (CA CCSS for ELA/Literacy) that are necessary for the development of advanced English and academic success across disciplines. The CA CCSS for ELA/Literacy served as the core foundation for developing the CA ELD Standards, which aim to guide teachers in supporting ELs' English language development while students learn rigorous academic content.

The development of the CA ELD Standards was informed by multiple theories and a large body of research pertaining to the linguistic and academic education of ELs. Sociolinguistic, sociocultural, and sociocognitive theories emphasize how learning is a social activity and how language is both a form of social action and a resource for accomplishing things in the world. Among other things, these theories highlight the importance of recognizing and leveraging students' prior knowledge in order to make connections to and foster new learning, helping them to build conceptual networks, and suppoting them to think about their thinking (metacognitive knowledge) and language use (metalinguistic knowledge). Teachers making use of the theories and research studies can help students to consciously apply particular cognitive strategies (e.g., inferring what the text means by examining textual evidence) and linguistic practices (e.g., intentionally selecting specific words or phrases to persuade others). These metacognitive and metalinguistic abilities support students' self-regulation, self-monitoring, intentional learning, and strategic use of language (Christie 2012; Duke et al. 2011; Halliday 1993; Hess et al. 2009;

Palinscar and Brown 1984; Pearson 2011; Schleppegrell 2004). From this perspective, language and interaction play a central role in mediating both linguistic and cognitive development, and learning occurs through social interaction that is carefully structured to intellectually and linguistically challenge learners while also providing appropriate levels of support (Bruner 1983; Cazden 1986; Vygotsky 1978; Walquí and van Lier 2010).

Reviews of the research, individual studies, and teacher practice guides synthesizing the research for classroom application demonstrate the effectiveness of enacting the theories outlined above for teaching ELs (see, for example, Anstrom et al. 2010; August and Shanahan 2006; Francis et al. 2006; Genesee et al. 2006; Short and Fitzsimmons 2007). One of the key findings from the research is that effective instructional experiences for ELs have the following features:

- They are interactive and engaging, meaningful and relevant, and intellectually rich and challenging.
- They are appropriately scaffolded in order to provide strategic support that moves learners toward independence.
- They value and build on home language and culture and other forms of prior knowledge.
- They build both academic English and content knowledge.

Interacting in Meaningful and Intellectually Challenging Ways

The importance of providing opportunities for English learners to interact in meaningful ways around intellectually challenging content has been demonstrated in multiple studies. Meaningful interaction in K–12 settings includes, among other tasks, engaging in collaborative oral discussions with a peer or a small group of peers about texts or content topics. Not all students come to school knowing how to engage in these interactive processes with other students. However, research in classrooms with ELs has demonstrated that teachers can successfully "apprentice" their students into engaging in more academic ways of interacting with one another, using the language of the specific content in question, acquiring the language of academic discourse, and developing content knowledge (Gibbons 2009; Walquí and van Lier 2010).

Teachers can carefully structure collaborative learning practices that promote small-group discussion among students about, for example, the science and history texts they read. Structured collaborative learning practices foster comprehension of the texts, the acquisition of vocabulary and grammatical structures associated with the texts, and more academic ways of engaging in conversations about the texts (Heller and Greenleaf 2007; Klingner et al. 2004; Kosanovich, Reed, and Miller 2010; Short, Echevarría, and Richards-Tutor 2011; Vaughn et al. 2011).

Teachers can provide structured and strategically supportive opportunities for students to develop more ways of interacting meaningfully. For example, the kinds of discourse skills expected in academic conversations can be fostered when teachers:

- establish routines and expectations for equitable and accountable conversations (e.g., specific roles in a conversation, such as "facilitator");

- carefully construct questions that promote extended discussions about academic content (e.g., questions that require students to infer or explain something for which they have sufficient background knowledge);

- provide appropriate linguistic support (e.g., a sentence stem, such as "I agree with _____ that_____. However, _____.").

  With strategic scaffolding, students can learn to adopt particular ways of organizing their discourse during group work and "practicing" aspects of academic English that approach the more "literate" ways of communicating that are highly valued in school (Dutro and Kinsella 2010; Gibbons 2009; Merino and Scarcella 2005; Schleppegrell 2010).

Scaffolding

Teachers play a central role in providing *temporary* supportive frameworks, adjusted to students' particular developmental needs, in order to improve access to meaning and ongoing linguistic and cognitive development. The metaphorical term *scaffolding* (Bruner 1983; Cazden 1986; Celce-Murcia 2001; Mariani 1997) refers to ways in which these temporary supportive frameworks can be applied. The term draws from Vygotsky's (1978) notion of the "zone of proximal development (ZPD)": the instructional space that exists between what the learner can do independently and that which is too difficult for the learner to do without strategic support, or scaffolding. Scaffolding is temporary help that is future-oriented. In other words, scaffolding supports students in how to do something today that they will be able to do independently in the future.

As Hammond (2006, 271) has emphasized, scaffolding "does not just spontaneously occur" but is, rather, intentionally designed for a learner's particular needs and then systematically and strategically carried out. The level of scaffolding that a student needs depends on a variety of factors, including the nature of the task and the learner's background knowledge of relevant content, as well as the learner's proficiency with the language required to engage in and complete the task. Scaffolding does not change the intellectual challenge of the task, but merely allows learners to build the knowledge and skills for independent performance of the task at some future point.

Scaffolding practices are selected in accordance with the standards-based goals of the lesson, the identified needs of the learner, and the anticipated challenge of the task. Gibbons (2009) has offered a way of conceptualizing the dual goal of engaging ELs in intellectually challenging instructional activities while also providing them with the appropriate level of support:

Figure 4.1 Optimizing Scaffolding for English Learners Engaged in Academic Tasks (Gibbons 2009, adapted from Mariani 1997)

The CA ELD Standards establish three overall levels of scaffolding that teachers can provide to ELs during instruction: *substantial, moderate,* and *light.* ELs at the emerging level of English language proficiency will generally require more substantial support to develop capacity for many academic tasks than will students at the bridging level. **This does not mean that these students will always require substantial, moderate, or light scaffolding for every task.** EL students at every level of English proficiency will engage in some academic tasks that require *light* or *no* scaffolding because they have already mastered the requisite skills for the given tasks, and students will engage in some academic tasks that require *moderate* or *substantial* scaffolding because they have not yet acquired the cognitive or linguistic skills required by the task. For example, when a challenging academic task requires students to extend their thinking and stretch their language, students at expanding and bridging levels of English proficiency may also require *substantial* support. Teachers need to provide the level of scaffolding appropriate to specific tasks and learners' cognitive and linguistic needs, and students will need more or less support depending on these and other variables.

Examples of planned *scaffolding*[1] that teachers prepare in advance, during lesson and curriculum planning, in order to support ELs' access to academic

content and linguistic development include, but are not limited to, the following:

- Taking into account what students already know, including their primary language and culture, and relating it to what they are to learn
- Selecting and sequencing tasks, such as modeling and explaining, and providing guided practice, in a logical order
- Frequently checking for understanding during instruction, as well as gauging progress at appropriate intervals throughout the year
- Choosing texts carefully for specific purposes (e.g., motivational, linguistic, content)
- Providing a variety of collaborative groups
- Constructing good questions that promote critical thinking and extended discourse
- Using a range of information systems, such as graphic organizers, diagrams, photographs, videos, or other multimedia, to enhance access to content
- Providing students with language models, such as sentence frames/starters, academic vocabulary walls, language frame charts, exemplary writing samples, or teacher language modeling (e.g., using academic vocabulary or phrasing)

This planned scaffolding allows teachers to provide *just-in-time* scaffolding during instruction, which flexibly attends to ELs' needs as they interact with content and language. Examples of this type of scaffolding include:

- prompting a student to elaborate on a response to extend his or her language use and thinking;
- paraphrasing a student's response and including target academic language as a model and, at the same time, accepting the student's response using everyday or "flawed" language;
- adjusting instruction on the spot based on frequent checking for understanding;
- linking what a student is saying to prior knowledge or to learning that will come (previewing).

For ELs, instruction and/or strategic support in the student's primary language can also serve as a powerful scaffold to English literacy (August and Shanahan

---

1. There are many ways to categorize scaffolding. The terms used here are adapted from Hammond and Gibbons (2005), who refer to "designed-in" and "interactional" scaffolding. *Designed-in* (or *planned*) *scaffolding* refers to the support teachers consciously plan in advance. *Interactional scaffolding* refers to the indirect support teachers provide spontaneously through dialogue during instruction or other interaction.

2006; CDE 2010; Genesee et al. 2006; Goldenberg 2008). The research evidence indicates that EL students in programs where biliteracy is the goal and bilingual instruction is used demonstrate stronger literacy performance in English, with the added metalinguistic and metacognitive benefits of bilingualism.

Developing Academic English

For K–12 settings, *academic English* broadly refers to the language used in school to help students develop content knowledge and the language students are expected to use to convey their understanding of this knowledge. Interpreting, discussing, analyzing, evaluating, and writing academic texts are complex literacy processes that involve the integration of multiple linguistic and cognitive skills, including word-level processing, such as decoding and spelling. Furthermore, these advanced English literacy tasks especially involve higher-order cognitive and linguistic processes, including applying prior knowledge, making inferences, recognizing the grammatical structures and linguistic features of texts, resolving ambiguities (e.g., semantic or syntactic), and selecting appropriate language resources for specific purposes, not to mention stamina and motivation.

The CA ELD Standards position English as a meaning-making resource with different language choices available based on discipline, topic, audience, task, and purpose. This notion of English as a meaning-making resource expands the notion of *academic language* from simplistic definitions (e.g., academic vocabulary or syntax) to a broader concept that encompasses discourse practices, text structures, grammatical structures, and vocabulary, and views them as inseparable from meaning (Bailey and Huang 2011; Wong Fillmore and Fillmore 2012; Snow and Uccelli 2009). Academic English shares characteristics across disciplines—it is densely packed with meaning, authoritatively presented, and highly structured—but is also highly dependent upon disciplinary content (Christie and Derewianka 2008; Moje 2010; Quinn, Lee, and Valdes 2012; Schleppegrell 2004). The CA CCSS for ELA/Literacy emphasize the need for all students to be able to comprehend and produce complex texts in a variety of disciplines so that they are college- and career-ready. Research suggests that teachers can foster, and even accelerate, the development of academic English for EL students through multilayered and multicomponent approaches that focus on the way English works in different contexts.

The Importance of Vocabulary

Over the past several decades, research has repeatedly identified vocabulary knowledge as a critical and powerful factor underlying language and literacy proficiency, including disciplinary literacy (e.g., Graves 1986; Chall, Jacobs, and Baldwin 1990; Beck and McKeown 1991; Hart and Risley 1995; Blachowicz and Fisher 2004; Baumann, Kame'enui, and Ash 2003; Bowers and Kirby 2010; Carlisle 2010; McCutchen and Logan 2011). Comprehensive and multi-faceted approaches to vocabulary instruction include a combination of several critical components: rich and varied language experiences (e.g., wide reading, teacher read-alouds), teaching individual academic words (both general academic and domain-specific), teaching word-learning strategies (including cognate awareness and morphology), and fostering word consciousness and language play (Graves 2000, 2006, 2009). The CA CCSS for ELA/Literacy draw particular attention to domain-specific and general academic vocabulary knowledge and usage due to the prevalence of these types of vocabulary in academic contexts. Research conducted over the past decade, in particular, has demonstrated the positive effects of focusing on domain-specific and general academic vocabulary with K–12 EL students (August et al. 2005; Calderón et al. 2005; Carlo et al. 2004; Collins 2005; Kieffer and Lesaux 2008, 2010; Silverman 2007; Snow, Lawrence, and White, 2009; Spycher 2009; Townsend and Collins 2009).

The Importance of Grammatical and Discourse-Level Understandings

Although academic vocabulary is a critical aspect of academic English, it is only one part. The CA ELD Standards were further informed by genre- and meaning-based theories of language, which view language as a social process and a meaning-making system and seek to understand how language choices construe meaning in oral and written texts. These theories have identified how networks of interrelated language resources—including grammatical, lexical, and discourse features—interact to form registers that vary depending upon context and situation (Halliday and Matthiessen 2004). Advanced English proficiency hinges on the mastery of a set of academic registers used in academic settings and texts that "construe multiple and complex meanings at all levels and in all subjects of schooling" (Schleppegrell 2009, 1).

Register refers to the ways in which grammatical and lexical resources are combined to meet the expectations of the context (i.e., the content area, topic, audience, and mode in which the message is conveyed). In this sense, "register variation" (Schleppegrell 2012) depends on what is happening (the content), who the communicators are and their relationship to one another (e.g., peer-to-peer, expert-to-peer), and how the message is conveyed (e.g., written, spoken, multimodal texts). Informal ("spoken-like") registers might include chatting with a friend about a movie or texting a relative. Formal ("written-like") registers might include writing an essay for history class, participating in a debate about a scientific topic, or making a formal presentation about a work of literature. The characteristics of these academic registers, which are critical for school success, include specialized and technical vocabulary, sentences and clauses that are densely packed with meaning and combined in purposeful ways, and whole texts that are highly structured and cohesive in ways that depend upon the disciplinary area and social purpose (Christie and Derewianka 2008; Halliday and Matthiessen 2004; O'Dowd 2010; Schleppegrell 2004).

Language is the medium through which teaching and learning take place in schools, the medium through which we transform and develop our thinking about concepts; and in this way, language and content are inextricably linked (Halliday 1993). For this and other reasons, language has been referred to as the "hidden curriculum" of schooling and accounts for why school success can be seen as largely a language matter (Christie 1999). EL students often find it challenging to move from everyday or informal registers of English to formal academic registers. Understanding and gaining proficiency with academic registers and the language resources that build them opens up possibilities for expressing ideas and understanding the world. From this perspective, teachers who understand the lexical, grammatical, and discourse features of academic English and how to make these features explicit to their students in purposeful ways that build both linguistic and content knowledge are in a better position to help their students fulfill their linguistic and academic potential.

Teaching about the grammatical patterns found in particular disciplines has been shown to help ELs' reading comprehension and writing proficiency. The main pedagogical aims of this research are to help students become more conscious of how language is used to construct meaning in different contexts and to provide students with a wider range of linguistic resources. Knowing how to make appropriate language choices will enable students to comprehend and construct meaning in oral and written texts. Accordingly, the instructional interventions studied in the applied research in this area have focused on identifying the language features of the academic texts that students read and are expected to write in school (e.g., narratives, explanations, arguments) and on developing students' awareness of and proficiency in using the language features of these academic registers (e.g., how ideas are condensed in science texts through nominalization, how arguments are constructed by connecting clauses in particular ways, or how agency is hidden in history texts by using the passive voice) so that they can better comprehend and create academic texts (Brisk 2012; Gebhard et al. 2010; Fang and Schleppegrell 2010; Gibbons 2008; Hammond 2006; Rose and Acevedo 2006; Schleppegrell and de Oliveira 2006).

Research on genre- and meaning-based approaches to literacy education with EL students in the United States and other countries has demonstrated the effectiveness of teaching EL students about how language works to achieve different purposes in a variety of contexts and disciplines (Achugar, Schleppegrell, and Oteíza 2007; Aguirre-Muñoz et al. 2008; Gebhard and Martin 2010; Schleppegrell, Achugar, and Oteíza 2004; Spycher 2007). This research has stressed the importance of positioning ELs as competent and capable of achieving academic literacies, providing them with an intellectually challenging curriculum with appropriate levels of support, apprenticing them into successful use of academic language, and making the features of academic language transparent in order to build proficiency with and critical awareness of the features of academic language (Christie 2012; Derewianka 2011; Gibbons 2009; Halliday 1993; Hyland 2004; Schleppegrell 2004).

The extensive body of theories and research drawn upon to inform and guide the development of the CA ELD Standards demonstrates that effective instruction for ELs focuses on critical principles for developing language and cognition in academic contexts. These principles emphasize meaningful interaction; the development of metalinguistic awareness in contexts that are intellectually rich and challenging, focused on content, strategically scaffolded, and respectful of the cultural and linguistic knowledge students bring to school; and the use of such knowledge as a resource.

Other Relevant Guidance Documents Consulted

Additional state, national, and international documents designed to inform and guide policy and practice for the education of ELs were consulted. These documents include the following:

- *Understanding Language: Language, Literacy, and Learning in the Content Areas*—Commissioned Papers on Language and Literacy Issues in the Common Core State Standards and Next Generation Science Standards (Stanford University)
- *The Framework for English Language Proficiency Development Standards Corresponding to the Common Core State Standards and the Next Generation Science Standards* (Council of Chief State School Officers 2012)
- *Improving Education for English Learners: Research-Based Approaches* (CDE 2010)
- *The Common European Framework of Reference for Languages: Learning, Teaching, Assessment* (Council of Europe, Language Policy Unit, n.d.)
- *Standards for Foreign Language Learning in the 21st Century* (National Standards in Foreign Language Education Project 2006)
- The *Framework for High-Quality English Language Proficiency Standards and Assessments* (Assessment and Accountability Comprehensive Center 2009)
- ELD/English Language Proficiency (ELP) standards from multiple states
- The Australian National Curriculum

Conclusion

The theoretical bases and body of research and resources that were consulted for the development of the California ELD Standards were complemented by the writing team's knowledge working in schools across California with both EL students (as teachers) and teachers of EL students (as professional developers, research partners, and consultants in various capacities). At every stage of the development and review process, this practical knowledge about what goes on in classrooms, paired with extensive knowledge of the theories and research pertaining to the education of EL students contributed to the development of a rigorous and balanced set of ELD standards.

References

Acevedo, C., and D. Rose. 2007. "Reading (and Writing) to Learn in the Middle Years of Schooling." *Primary English Teaching Association* 157:1–8.

Achugar, M., M. Schleppegrell, and T. Oteíza. 2007. "Engaging Teachers in Language Analysis: A Functional Linguistic Approach to Reflective Literacy." *English Teaching: Practice and Technique* 6 (2): 8–24.

Aguirre-Muñoz, Z., J. E. Park, A. Amabisca, and C. K. Boscardin. 2008. "Developing Teacher Capacity for Serving ELLs' Writing Instructional Needs: A Case for Systemic Functional Linguistics." *Bilingual Research Journal* 31 (1): 295–322.

Anstrom, K., P. DiCerbo, F. Butler, A. Katz, J. Millet, and C. Rivera. 2010. *A Review of the Literature on Academic English: Implications for K–12 English Language Learners.* Arlington, VA: The George Washington University Center for Equity and Excellence in Education.

Assessment and Accountability Comprehensive Center. 2009. *Framework for High-Quality English Language Proficiency Standards and Assessments.* San Francisco, CA: WestEd.

August, D., M. Carlo, C. Dressler, and C. Snow. 2005. "The Critical Role of Vocabulary Development for English Language Learners." *Learning Disabilities Research and Practice* 20 (1): 50–57.

August, D., and T. Shanahan, eds. 2006. Developing Literacy in Second-Language Learners: *Report of the National Literacy Panel on Language-Minority Children and Youth.* Mahwah, NJ: Lawrence Erlbaum Associates and the Center for Applied Linguistics.

Bailey, A. L., and B. H. Huang. 2011. "Do Current English Language Development/Proficiency Standards Reflect the English Needed for Success in School?" *Language Testing* 28: 343–65.

Baumann, J. F., E. J. Kame'enui, and G. E. Ash. 2003. "Research on Vocabulary Instruction: Voltaire Redux." In *Handbook of Research on Teaching the English Language Arts,* 2nd ed., edited by J. Flood, D. Lapp, J. R. Squire, and J. M. Jensen, 752–85. Mahwah, NJ: Erlbaum.

Beck, I. L., and M. G. McKeown. 1991. "Conditions of Vocabulary Acquisition." In *Handbook of Reading Research, Vol. II*, edited by R. Barr, M. Kamil, P. Mosenthal, and P. D. Pearson, 789–814. White Plains, NY: Longman.

Biemiller, A. 2003. "Oral Comprehension Sets the Ceiling on Reading Comprehension." *American Educator* 27 (1).

Blachowicz, C., and P. Fisher. 2004. "Vocabulary Lessons." *Educational Leadership* 61 (6): 66–69.

Bowers, P. N., and J. R. Kirby. 2010. "Effects of Morphological Instruction on Vocabulary Acquisition." *Reading and Writing: An Interdisciplinary Journal* 23 (5): 515–37.

Bravo, M. A., E. H. Hiebert, and P. D. Pearson. 2005. "Tapping the Linguistic Resources of Spanish/English Bilinguals: The Role of Cognates in Science." In *Vocabulary Acquisition: Implications for Reading Comprehension*, edited by R. K. Wagner, A. E. Muse, and K. R. Tannenbaum, 140–56. New York: Guilford Press.

Brisk, M. E. 2012. "Young Bilingual Writers' Control of Grammatical Person in Different Genres." *Elementary School Journal* 112 (3): 445–68.

Brown, A. L. 1980. "Metacognitive Development and Reading." In *Theoretical Issues in Reading Comprehension*, edited by R. S. Spiro, B. B. Bruce, and W. L. Brewer. Hillsdale, NJ: Erlbaum.

Brown, A. L., and J. C. Campione. 1996. "Psychological Theory and the Design of Innovative Learning Environments: On Procedures, Principles, and Systems." In *Innovations in Learning*, edited by L. Schauble and R. Glaser, 289–325. Mahwah, NJ: Erlbaum.

Bruner, J. S. 1983. *Child's Talk: Learning to Use Language.* New York: Norton.

Calderón, M., D. August, R. Slavin, D. Duran, N. Madden, and A. Cheung. 2005. "Bring Words to Life in Classrooms with English-Language Learners." In *Teaching and Learning Vocabulary: Bringing Research to Practice*, edited by E. H. Hiebert and M. L. Kamil. Mahwah, NJ: Erlbaum.

California Department of Education (CDE). 2010. *Improving Education for English Learners: Research-Based Approaches.* Sacramento: California Department of Education.

Carlisle, J. F. 2010. "Effects of Instruction in Morphological Awareness on Literacy Achievement: An Integrative Review." *Reading Research Quarterly* 45:464–87.

Carlo, M. S., D. August, B. McLaughlin, C. E. Snow, C. Dressler, D. Lippman, T. Lively, and C. White. 2004. "Closing the Gap: Addressing the Vocabulary Needs of English Language Learners in Bilingual and Mainstream Classrooms." *Reading Research Quarterly* 39 (2): 188–215.

Cazden, C. B. 1986. "Classroom Discourse." In *Handbook of Research on Teaching*, 3rd ed., edited by M C. Wittrock. New York: Macmillan.

Celce-Murcia, M., ed. 2001. *Teaching English as a Second or Foreign language.* 3rd ed. Boston: Heinle Thomson.

Chall, J. S., V. A. Jacobs, and L. E. Baldwin. 1990. *The Reading Crisis: Why Poor Children Fall Behind.* Cambridge, MA: Harvard University Press.

Christie, F., ed. 1999. *Pedagogy and the Shaping of Consciousness: Linguistic and Social Processes.* London, UK: Cassell Academic.

_____. 2005. *Language Education in the Primary Years.* Sydney, Australia: UNSW Press.

_____. 2012. *Language Education Throughout the School Years: A Functional Perspective.* West Sussex, UK: Wiley-Blackwell.

Christie, F., and B. Derewianka. 2008. *School Discourse: Learning to Write Across the Years of Schooling.* London, UK: Continuum.

Collins, M. F. 2005. "ESL Preschoolers' English Vocabulary Acquisition from Storybook Reading." *Reading Research Quarterly* 40 (4): 406–8.

Council of Chief State School Officers. 2012. *Framework for English Language Proficiency Development Standards Corresponding to the Common Core State Standards and the Next Generation Science Standards.* Washington, DC: CCSSO.

Council of Europe, Language Policy Unit. n.d. *Common European Framework of Reference for Languages: Learning, Teaching, Assessment.* Cambridge, UK: Cambridge University Press.

Culican, S. J. 2007. "Troubling Teacher Talk: The Challenge of Changing Class-room Discourse Patterns." *The Australian Educational Researcher* 34 (2): 7–28.

de Oliveira, L. C., and K. N. Dodds. 2010. "Beyond General Strategies for English Language Learners: Language Dissection in Science." *Electronic Journal of Literacy Through Science* 9. http://ejlts.ucdavis.edu/sites/ejlts.ucdavis.edu/files/articles/EJLTS%20Oliveria_Dodds%20Final.pdf (accessed October 14, 2013).

Derewianka, B. 2011. *A New Grammar Companion for Teachers.* Sydney, Australia: Primary English Teaching Association.

Dixon, L. Q., J. Zhao, J. Shin, S. Wu, J. Su, R. Burgess-Brigham, M. U. Gezer, and C. Snow. 2012. "Four Perspectives: What We Know About Second Language Acquisition: A Synthesis from Four Perspectives." *Review of Educational Research* 82 (1): 5–60.

Duke, N. K., P. D. Pearson, S. L. Strachan, and A. K. Billman. 2011. "Essential Elements of Fostering and Teaching Reading Comprehension." In *What Research Has to Say About Reading Instruction,* 4th ed., edited by S. J. Samuels and A. Farstrup, 51–93. Newark, DE: International Reading Association.

Dutro, S., and K. Kinsella. 2010. "English Language Development: Issues and Implementation at Grades Six Through Twelve." In *Improving Education for English Learners: Research-Based Approaches.* Sacramento: California Department of Education.

Fang, Z., and M. Schleppegrell. 2010. "Disciplinary Literacies Across Content Areas: Supporting Secondary Reading Through Functional Language Analysis." *Journal of Adolescent and Adult Literacy* 53 (7): 587–97.

Francis, D., M. Rivera, N. Lesaux, M. Kieffer, and H. Rivera. 2006. *Practical Guidelines for the Education of English Language Learners: Research-Based Recommendations for Instruction and Academic Interventions.* Portsmouth, NH: RMC Research Corporation, Center on Instruction.

Gebhard, M., and J. Martin. 2010. "Grammar and Literacy Learning." In *Handbook of Research on Teaching the English Language Arts,* edited by D. Fisher and D. Lapp. Mahwah, NJ: Erlbaum/Taylor and Francis.

Gebhard, M., J. Willett, J. Jimenez, and A. Piedra. 2010. "Systemic Functional Linguistics, Teachers' Professional Development, and ELLs' Academic Literacy Practices." In *Preparing All Teachers to Teach English Language Learners,* edited by T. Lucas, 91–110. Mahwah: NJ: Erlbaum.

Genesee, F., K. Lindholm-Leary, W. M. Saunders, and D. Christian. 2006. *Educating English Language Learners: A Synthesis of Research Evidence.* New York: Cambridge University Press.

Gersten, R., S. K. Baker, T. Shanahan, S. Linan-Thompson, P. Collins, and R. Scarcella. 2007. *Effective Literacy and English Language Instruction for English Learners in the Elementary Grades: A Practice Guide* (NCEE 2007-4011). Washington, DC: National Center for Education Evaluation and Regional Assistance, Institute of Education Sciences, U.S. Department of Education.

Gibbons, P. 2006. *Bridging Discourses in the ESL Classroom: Students, Teachers and Researchers.* London, UK: Continuum.

———. 2008. "'It Was Taught Good and I Learned a Lot': Intellectual Practices and ESL Learners in the Middle Years." *Australian Journal of Language and Literacy* 31 (2): 155–73.

———. 2009. *English Learners, Academic Literacy, and Thinking: Learning in the Challenge Zone.* Portsmouth, NH: Heinemann.

Goldenberg, C. 2008. "Teaching English Language Learners: What the Research Does—and Does Not—Say." *American Educator* 32 (2): 8–23, 42–44.

Graves, M. F. 1986. "Vocabulary Learning and Instruction." In *Review of Research in Education.* Vol. 13, 49–90. Washington, DC: American Educational Research Association.

———. 2000. "A Vocabulary Program to Complement and Bolster a Middle-Grade Comprehension Program." In *Reading for Meaning: Fostering Comprehension in the Middle Grades,* edited by B. M. Taylor, M. F. Graves, and P. Van Den Brock. New York: Teachers College Press.

———. 2006. *The Vocabulary Book: Learning and Instruction.* New York: Teachers College Press.

———. 2009. *Teaching Individual Words: One Size Does Not Fit All.* New York: Teachers College Press and International Reading Association.

Graves, M. F., D. August, and J. Mancilla-Martinez. Forthcoming. *Teaching Vocabulary to English Language Learners.* New York: Teachers College Press, International Reading Association, Center for Applied Linguistics, and Teachers of English to Speakers of Other Languages.

Halliday, M. A. K. 1993. "Toward a Language-Based Theory of Education." *Linguistics and Education* 5 (2): 93–116.

Halliday, M. A. K., and J. R. Martin. 1993. *Writing Science: Literacy and Discursive Power.* London, UK: Falmer Press.

Halliday, M. A. K., and C. M. I. M. Matthiessen. 1999. *Construing Experience Through Meaning: A Language-based Approach to Cognition.* London, UK: Cassell.

———. 2004. *An Introduction to Functional Grammar.* 3rd ed. London, UK: Arnold.

Hammond, J. 2006. "High Challenge, High Support: Integrating Language and Content Instruction for Diverse Learners in an English Literature Classroom." *Journal of English for Academic Purposes* 5 (4): 269–83.

———. 2008. "Intellectual Challenge and ESL Students: Implications of Quality Teaching Initiatives." *Australian Journal of Language and Literacy* 31 (2): 128–54.

Hammond, J., and P. Gibbons. 2005. "Putting Scaffolding to Work: The Contribution of Scaffolding in Articulating ESL Education." *Prospect Special Issue* 20 (1): 6–30.

Hart, B., and T. R. Risley. 1995. *Meaningful Differences in the Everyday Experiences of Young American Children.* Baltimore, MD: Brookes.

Heath, S. B. 1986. "What No Bedtime Story Means: Narrative Skills at Home and in School." In *Language Socialization Across Cultures,* edited by B. Schieffelin and E. Ochs, 97–124. Cambridge, UK: Cambridge University Press.

Heller, R., and C. L. Greenleaf. 2007. *Literacy Instruction in the Content Areas: Getting to the Core of Middle and High School Improvement.* Washington, DC: Alliance for Excellent Education.

Hess, K. K., D. Carlock, B. Jones, and J. R. Walkup. 2009. "What Exactly Do 'Fewer, Clearer, and Higher Standards' Really Look Like in the Classroom? Using a Cognitive Rigor Matrix to Analyze Curriculum, Plan Lessons, and Implement Assessments." Presentation at Council of Chief State School Officers, Detroit, MI, June 2009. http://www.nciea.org/publications/cognitiverigorpaper_KH12.pdf (accessed October 15, 2013).

Hinkel, E., ed. 2005. *Handbook of Research in Second Language Teaching and Learning.* Mahwah, NJ: Lawrence Erlbaum Associates.

Hyland, K. 2004. *Genre and Second Language Writing.* Ann Arbor, MI: University of Michigan Press.

Kieffer, M., and N. Lesaux. 2008. "The Role of Derivational Morphology in the Reading Comprehension of Spanish-Speaking English Language Learners." *Reading and Writing: An Interdisciplinary Journal* 21 (8): 783–804.

———. 2010. "Morphing into Adolescents: Active Word Learning for English-Language Learners and Their Classmates in Middle School." *Journal of Adolescent and Adult Literacy* 54 (1): 47–56.

Klingner, J. K., S. Vaughn, M. E. Arguelles, M. T. Hughes, and S. A. Leftwich. 2004. "Collaborative Strategic Reading: "Real-World" Lessons from Classroom Teachers." *Remedial and Special Education* 25 (53): 291–302.

Klingner, J. K., S. Vaughn, and J. S. Schumm. 1998. "Collaborative Strategic Reading During Social Studies in Heterogeneous Fourth-Grade Classrooms." *The Elementary School Journal* 99 (1): 1–22.

Kosanovich, M. L., D. K. Reed, and D. H. Miller. 2010. *Bringing Literacy Strategies into Content Instruction: Professional Learning for Secondary Level Teachers.* Portsmouth, NH: RMC Research Corporation, Center on Instruction.

Lesaux, N. K., M. J. Kieffer, S. E. Faller, and J. G. Kelley. 2010. "The Effectiveness and Ease of Implementation of an Academic Vocabulary Intervention for Linguistically Diverse Students in Urban Middle Schools." *Reading Research Quarterly* 45 (2): 196–228.

Mariani, L. 1997. "Teacher Support and Teacher Challenge in Promoting Learner Autonomy." *Perspectives* XXIII (2).

McCutchen, D., and B. Logan. 2011. "Inside Incidental Word Learning: Children's Strategic Use of Morphological Information to Infer Word Meanings." *Reading Research Quarterly* 46 (4): 334–49.

Merino, B., and R. Scarcella. 2005. "Teaching Science to English Language Learners." *UCLMRI (University of California Linguistic Minority Research Institute) Newsletter* 14 (4).

Moje, E. B. 2010. "Comprehending in the Content Areas: The Challenges of Comprehension, Grades 7–12, and What to Do About Them." In *A Comprehensive Look at Reading Comprehension, K–12,* edited by K. Ganske and D. Fisher, 46–72. New York: Guilford.

Nagy, W., and D. Townsend. 2012. "Words as Tools: Learning Academic Vocabulary as Language Acquisition." *Reading Research Quarterly* 47 (1): 91–108.

National Standards in Foreign Language Education Project. 2006. *Standards for Foreign Language Learning in the 21st Century.* 3rd ed. Lawrence, KS: Allen Press, Inc.

O'Dowd, R. 2010. "Online Foreign Language Interaction: Moving from the Periphery to the Core of Foreign Language Education." *Language Teaching* 44 (3): 368–80.

Painter, C. 1999. "Preparing for School: Developing a Semantic Style for Educational Knowledge." In *Pedagogy and the Shaping of Consciousness: Linguistic and Social Processes,* edited by F. Christie. London, UK: Continuum.

Palincsar, A. S., and A. L. Brown. 1984. "Reciprocal Teaching of Comprehension-Fostering and Comprehension-Monitoring Activities." *Cognition and Instruction* 1 (2): 117–75.

Pearson, P. D. 2011. "Toward the Next Generation of Comprehension Instruction: A Coda." In *Comprehension Going Forward,* edited by H. Daniels, 243–53. Portsmouth, NH: Heinemann.

Quinn, H., O. Lee, and G. Valdes. 2012. "Language Demands and Opportunities in Relation to Next Generation Science Standards for English Language Learners: What Teachers Need to Know." Stanford, CA: Stanford University School of Education. http://ell.stanford.edu/sites/default/files/pdf/academic-papers/03-Quinn%20Lee%20Valdes%20Language%20and%20Opportunities%20in%20Science%20FINAL.pdf (accessed October 14, 2013).

Reppen, R. 1994. "A Genre-Based Approach to Content Writing Instruction." *TESOL Journal* 4 (2): 32–35.

Roessingh, H., and S. Elgie. 2009. "Early Language and Literacy Development Among Young English Language Learners: Preliminary Insights from a Longitudinal Study." *TESL Canada Journal* 26 (2): 24–45.

Rose, D., and C. Acevedo. 2006. "Closing the Gap and Accelerating Learning in the Middle Years of Schooling." *Literacy Learning: The Middle Years* 14 (2): 32–45.

Sato, E., R. Lagunoff, and P. Worth. 2008. *Language for Achievement: A Framework for Academic English Language.* San Francisco: WestEd.

Sato, E., R. Lagunoff, and P. Yeagley. Forthcoming. *Academic Language and the Common Core State Standards: Implications for State and District Implementation and Supporting the Achievement of English Language Learners.* San Francisco: WestEd.

Scarcella, R. 2003. *Academic English: A Conceptual Framework.* The University of California Linguistic Minority Research Institute Technical Report 2003-1. http://lmri.ucsb.edu/resdiss/2/pdf_files/scarcella_finalreport.pdf (accessed August 28, 2003).

Schieffelin, B. B., and E. Ochs. 1986. "Language Socialization." *Annual Review of Anthropology* 15:163–91.

Schleppegrell, M. J. 2004. *The Language of Schooling: A Functional Linguistics Perspective.* Mahwah, NJ: Lawrence Erlbaum Associates.

———. 2009. "Language in Academic Subject Areas and Classroom Instruction: What Is Academic Language and How Can We Teach It?" Paper prepared for the Workshop on the Role of Language in School Learning: Implications for Closing the Achievement Gap, October 15–16, Hewlett Foundation, Menlo Park, CA.

_____. 2010. "Functional Grammar in the Classroom." In *Symposium 2009. Genrer och funktionellt språk i teori och praktik,* edited by M. Olofsson, 79–95. Stockholm, Sweden: Stockholm University Publishing.

_____. 2012. "Academic Language in Teaching and Learning: Introduction to the Special Issue." *The Elementary School Journal* 112 (3): 409–18.

Schleppegrell, M. J., M. Achugar, and T. Oteíza. 2004. "The Grammar of History: Enhancing Content-Based Instruction Through a Functional Focus on Language." *TESOL Quarterly* 38 (1): 67–93.

Schleppegrell, M. J., and L. D. de Oliveira. 2006. "An Integrated Language and Content Approach for History Teachers." *Journal of English for Academic Purposes* 5:254–68.

Shanahan, T., and C. Shanahan. 2008. "Teaching Disciplinary Literacy to Adolescents: Rethinking Content-Area Literacy." *Harvard Educational Review* 78 (1): 40–59.

Short, D., J. Echevarría, and C. Richards-Tutor. 2011. "Research on Academic Literacy Development in Sheltered Classrooms." *Language Teaching Research* 15 (3): 363–80.

Short, D., and S. Fitzsimmons. 2007. *Double the Work: Challenges and Solutions to Acquiring Language and Academic Literacy for Adolescent English Language Learners.* Washington, DC: Alliance for Excellent Education.

Silverman, R. D. 2007. "Vocabulary Development of English-Language and English-Only Learners in Kindergarten." *Elementary School Journal* 107 (4): 365–83.

Snow, C. E., J. Lawrence, and C. White. 2009. "Generating Knowledge of Academic Language Among Urban Middle School Students." *Journal of Research on Educational Effectiveness* 2 (4): 325–44.

Snow, C. E., and P. Uccelli. 2009. "The Challenge of Academic Language." In The *Cambridge Handbook of Literacy,* edited by D. R. Olson and N. Torrance, 112–33. New York: Cambridge University Press.

Spycher, P. 2007. "Academic Writing of Adolescent English Learners: Learning to Use 'Although'." *Journal of Second Language Writing* 16 (4): 238–54.

_____. 2009. "Learning Academic Language Through Science in Two Linguistically Diverse Kindergarten Classes." The *Elementary School Journal* 109 (4): 359–79.

Townsend, D., and P. Collins. 2009. "Academic Vocabulary and Middle School English Learners: An Intervention Study." *Reading and Writing* 22 (9): 993–1019.

Tyler, A. 2010. "Usage-Based Approaches to Language and Their Applications to Second Language Learning." *Annual Review of Applied Linguistics* 30:270–91.

Vaughn, S., J. K. Klingner, E. A. Swanson, A. G. Boardman, G. Roberts, S. S. Mohammed, and S. J. Stillman-Spisak. 2011. "Efficacy of Collaborative Strategic Reading with Middle School Students." *American Educational Research Journal* 48 (4): 938–64.

Veel, R. 1999. "Language, Knowledge and Authority in School Mathematics." In *Pedagogy and the Shaping of Consciousness: Linguistic and Social Processes,* edited by F. Christie. London, UK: Continuum.

Veel, R., and C. Coffin. 1996. "Learning to Think Like an Historian: The Language of Secondary School History." In *Literacy in Society,* edited by R. Hasan and G. Williams, 191–231. Harlow, Essex, UK: Addison Wesley Longman.

Vygotsky, L. 1978. *Mind in Society: The Development of Higher Psychological Processes.* Cambridge, UK: Cambridge University Press.

Walquí, A., and L. van Lier. 2010. *Scaffolding the Academic Success of Adolescent English Language Learners: A Pedagogy of Promise.* San Francisco: WestEd.

Wells, G. 1999. *Dialogic Inquiry: Towards a Sociocultural Practice and Theory of Education.* New York: Cambridge University Press.

Wong Fillmore, L., and C. J. Fillmore. 2012. "What Does Text Complexity Mean for English Learners and Language Minority Students?" Stanford, CA: Stanford University School of Education. http://ell.stanford.edu/sites/default/files/pdf/academic-papers/06-LWF%20CJF%20Text%20Complexity%20FINAL_0.pdf (accessed August 27, 2013).

Chapter 5

Many California teachers have observed that their students who are English learners (ELs) develop everyday English quite rapidly and can communicate effectively in informal social situations, but these students sometimes struggle with tasks involving *academic English,* such as writing a logical argument, comprehending their science and history textbooks, or participating in an academic debate (Cummins 2008, 71–83). For K–12 settings, *academic English* broadly refers to the language used in school to help students develop content knowledge, skills, and abilities; it is the language students are expected to use to convey their understanding and mastery of such knowledge, skills, and abilities.

Academic English is different from everyday, or informal, English. Some features of academic English span the disciplines, such as general academic vocabulary (e.g., *evaluate, infer, imply*), but there is also variation depending upon the discipline—in domain-specific vocabulary, for example. However, academic English encompasses much more than vocabulary. It also includes ways of structuring clauses, sentences, and entire texts that convey precision, show relationships between ideas, and present thinking in coherent and cohesive ways in order to achieve specific purposes (e.g., persuading, explaining, entertaining, and describing) with different audiences in discipline-specific ways. Research has shown that not all children come to school equally prepared to engage with academic English.[1] However, research has also demonstrated that ELs can learn academic English, use it to achieve success in academic tasks across the disciplines, and build upon it to prepare for college and careers.

Part II, "Learning About How English Works," offers K–12 teachers a new perspective on how to help EL students develop understanding of and proficiency in using academic English. The goal of Part II is to guide teachers to support EL students in ways that are appropriate to grade level and English language proficiency level so that ELs can (a) unpack meaning in texts they encounter across the disciplines to better comprehend them; and (b) make informed choices about how to use language appropriately—based on discipline, topic, purpose, audience, and task—when producing written texts and oral presentations.

Part II offers something that has been largely absent in prior ELD standards: attention to how the English language resources available to students are, and can be, used to make meaning and achieve particular communicative purposes. Such visibility is intended to support teachers' efforts to make transparent for their students the linguistic features of English in ways that support disciplinary literacy. This new perspective emphasizes the interrelated roles of *content knowledge, communicative purposes* for using English (e.g., recounting a family event, explaining a scientific phenomenon, describing a historical event, arguing for a position), and the *linguistic resources* writers or speakers can choose depending upon the content, purpose, and audience. Part II focuses on the social actions that accompany deep knowledge about language:

- Representing our experiences and expressing our ideas effectively

- Interacting with a variety of audiences

- Structuring our messages in intentional and purposeful ways

---

1. The CA ELD Standards were designed with the view that the languages students bring to school—both the native language and different varieties of English—are considered resources. The English that students use with peers or families is not "improper English"; it is appropriate for particular contexts. Being sensitive to the language resources students bring to school and discussing different ways of using English that are suited to different contexts can help build students' awareness of language while validating and leveraging their knowledge and experiences.

Although the development of everyday English is important for comprehensive English language development, Part II focuses primarily on academic registers[2] of English because of their prominence in the CA CCSS for ELA/Literacy and their importance for college and career readiness.

It is critical to understand that, although Part II is presented separately in order to draw educators' attention to it, the focus in Part II on understanding how English works is integral to and *inseparable from* EL students' development of meaning-making and purposeful interaction as delineated in Part I, "Interacting in Meaningful Ways." This approach parallels that of the CA CCSS for ELA/Literacy themselves, which identify a strand for language standards. However, as Appendix A[3] of the version of the *Common Core State Standards for English Language Arts and Literacy in History/Social Studies, Science, and Technical Subjects* produced by the National Governors Association (NGA) Center for Best Practices and the Council of Chief State School Officers (CCSSO) (hereafter referred to as Appendix A) notes, "The inclusion of Language standards in their own strand should not be taken as an indication that skills related to conventions, effective language use, and vocabulary are unimportant to reading, writing, speaking, and listening; indeed, they are inseparable from such contexts" (NGA Center for Best Practices and CCSSO 2010, 28).

The following sections identify and discuss some of the language demands from the CA CCSS for ELA/Literacy; present key differences between everyday and academic English registers, along with an explanation of how teaching students about language can support their development of academic English; and explain how Part II is organized, how it corresponds to the CA CCSS for ELA/Literacy, and how it works in tandem with Part I in the CA ELD Standards.

Correspondence of the Language Demands in the CA CCSS for ELA/Literacy to the CA ELD Standards

The CA CCSS for ELA/Literacy set high expectations for all students to participate in academic discourse across the disciplines. Among other things, students are called on to sustain dialogue on a range of topics and in a variety of content areas, interpret the meaning of informational and literary texts, explain their thinking and build on others' ideas, construct arguments and justify their positions persuasively with sound evidence, and effectively produce written and oral texts in a variety of disciplines for a variety of audiences and purposes. The CA ELD Standards respond to these demands by conceptualizing language as a complex, dynamic, and social meaning-making resource. Part I in the CA ELD Standards focuses primarily on how EL students interact in meaningful ways to develop academic registers of English while engaged in intellectually challenging, interactive, and dialogue-rich contexts.

In addition, the CA CCSS for ELA/Literacy set expectations for all students to develop an understanding of how the English language works and apply this understanding to reading, listening, viewing and writing, speaking, and creating oral and written texts. Reading complex texts is one area in which developing an understanding of how English works can help students. Appendix A emphasizes the importance of text complexity in reading achievement. Complex informational texts, in particular, are characterized by *discipline-specific content knowledge and the related language used to convey this content meaning,* including ambiguous or abstract meanings, potentially unfamiliar grammatical structures (e.g., complex sentences with long noun phrases), and general academic and domain-specific vocabulary.[4]

---

2. *Registers* refer to the ways in which grammatical and lexical resources are combined to meet the expectations of the context (e.g., the content area, topic, audience, and mode in which the message is conveyed). Informal registers include chatting with a friend or texting a message to a family member about a familiar topic. Formal registers include participating in a structured debate on climate change, writing an essay about a novel, or engaging in a collaborative discussion about solving a math problem using mathematical terms.

3. See http://www.corestandards.org/assets/Appendix_A.pdf (accessed July 23, 2014).

---

4. Note that complex narrative texts (e.g., those that present complex ideas with relatively familiar words and simple sentences) may still present challenges for readers.

Appendix A also emphasizes the importance of grammar and vocabulary instruction to reading comprehension, writing, and speaking and listening. General academic and domain-specific vocabulary play a key role in both the CA CCSS for ELA/Literacy and the CA ELD Standards since research has repeatedly identified vocabulary knowledge as essential for language and literacy proficiency, particularly disciplinary literacy, for EL students (Carlo et al. 2004; Lesaux et al. 2010; Nagy and Townsend 2012; Silverman and Crandell 2010; Spycher 2009).

Regarding grammar, Appendix A noted that grammar and usage development rarely follows a linear path and that former errors may reappear as students synthesize new grammatical and usage knowledge with their current knowledge. As with the CA CCSS for ELA/Literacy, the CA ELD Standards acknowledge the recursive nature of grammatical knowledge development, through a spiraling of specific knowledge about English language resources that should be taught with increasing levels of sophistication through the grades and across English proficiency levels. This knowledge includes developing an awareness of differences between everyday and disciplinary English and between different varieties of English, including the grammatical structures and usage; understanding the purposes for using certain grammatical features in particular disciplines and text types; and knowing how to use knowledge of grammar to comprehend complex academic texts.

Part II in the CA ELD Standards draws from current research demonstrating that teaching about the grammatical patterns of academic English in intellectually engaging ways that are contextualized in disciplinary knowledge promotes EL students' reading comprehension and writing development (Achugar, Schleppegrell, and Oteíza 2007; Aguirre-Muñoz et al. 2008; Gebhard and Martin 2010; de Oliveira and Dodds 2010).

Because of the importance of vocabulary and grammar in the development of academic English, and especially the way they interact with discourse and meaning-making in the disciplines, they are prominently featured in both the CA CCSS for ELA/Literacy and the CA ELD Standards. Appendix A underscored this prominence in referring to how students should be taught about language:

[I]f they are taught simply to vary their grammar and language to keep their writing "interesting," they may actually become more confused about how to make effective language choices . . . As students learn more about the patterns of English grammar in different communicative contexts throughout their K–12 academic careers, they can develop more complex understandings of English grammar and usage. Students can use this understanding to make more purposeful and effective choices in their writing and speaking and more accurate and rich interpretations in their reading and listening. (NGA Center for Best Practices and CCSSO 2010, 29)

The following examples are a small sample of where specific language demands related to text complexity and grammatical and vocabulary knowledge appear in the CA CCSS for ELA/Literacy at various grade levels and across domains:

Reading

RL.1.5: Explain major differences between books that tell stories and books that give information, drawing on a wide reading of a range of text types.[5]

RI.3.8: Describe the logical connection between particular sentences and paragraphs in a text (e.g., comparison, cause/effect, first/second/third in a sequence).

The first example (RL.1.5) sets expectations for first-graders to distinguish text types and explain the differences between them. This necessitates, at a minimum, an understanding of how informational texts, such as science explanations, are structured differently from narrative texts, such as stories. The second example (RI.3.8) sets expectations for third-graders to develop

---

5. The order of the coding system of the CA CCSS for ELA/Literacy is domain, grade level, number of the standard. For example, RL.1.5 is Reading Standards for Literature, grade 1, standard number 5.

an understanding of how language is used throughout a text to create cohesion.[6] The following example sets expectations for fourth-graders to understand how to shift between informal and formal registers to meet the expectations of particular contexts:[7]

Speaking & Listening

SL.4.6: Differentiate between contexts that call for formal English (e.g., presenting ideas) and situations where informal discourse is appropriate (e.g., small-group discussion); use formal English when appropriate to task and situation.

This shift between registers requires, among other things, an understanding of which vocabulary and grammatical structures to use to convey comprehension of the subject matter and topic in question, how to interact with the audience, how to organize the information, and what kind of communicative method to use (e.g., text message, formal presentation, a side conversation). From this perspective, grammatical and lexical choices can be said to be highly dependent upon context.

As students progress through the grades and into secondary schooling, they are expected to draw upon their knowledge of how to use particular linguistic resources (e.g., vocabulary, clause combinations, expanded noun phrases) in increasingly sophisticated ways to achieve specific academic purposes (e.g., arguing for a position), as the following examples demonstrate:

---

6. *Cohesion* refers to how information unfolds, or flows, in a text. A cohesive text is created through a variety of cohesive devices, such as referring to people, ideas, or things with pronouns or synonyms throughout a text so as to avoid repetition (e.g., replace "the first settlers" with "they") or linking clauses, sentences, and larger chunks of text with conjunctions, such as transition words (e.g., *in contrast, consequently, next*).

7. *Context* refers to the environment in which language is used, including disciplinary area, topic, audience, text type, and mode of communication. Context determines language choices, and the language choices used by writers and speakers help to establish context.

Writing

W.8.1: Write arguments to support claims with clear reasons and relevant evidence.

a. Introduce claim(s), acknowledge and distinguish the claim(s) from alternate or opposing claims, and organize the reasons and evidence logically.

b. Support claim(s) with logical reasoning and relevant evidence, using accurate, credible sources and demonstrating an understanding of the topic or text.

c. Use words, phrases, and clauses to create cohesion and clarify the relationships among claim(s), counterclaims, reasons, and evidence.

d. Establish and maintain a formal style.

e. Provide a concluding statement or section that follows from and supports the argument presented.

Language

L.11–12.3: Apply knowledge of language to understand how language functions in different contexts, to make effective choices for meaning or style, and to comprehend more fully when reading or listening.

a. Vary syntax for effect, consulting references (e.g., Tufte's *Artful Sentences*) for guidance as needed; apply an understanding of syntax to the study of complex texts when reading.

As these examples illustrate, the CA CCSS for ELA/Literacy set high expectations for students to use English in advanced ways across disciplines. These expectations represent significant shifts from previous standards, and they necessitate key shifts in the CA ELD Standards. Some of these shifts are shown in table 5.1.

Table 5.1 Comparison of the 1999 CA ELD Standards and the 2012 CA ELD Standards

1999 CA ELD Standards	2012 CA ELD Standards
Prior focus on:	*New emphasis on understanding:*
English as a set of rules →	English as a meaning-making resource with different language choices based on discipline, topic, audience, task, and purpose
Grammar as syntax, separate from meaning, with discrete skills at the center →	An expanded notion of grammar as encompassing discourse, text structure, syntax, and vocabulary and as inseparable from meaning
Language acquisition as a linear, individual process →	Language acquisition as a nonlinear, spiraling, dynamic, and complex social process in which meaningful interaction with others is essential
Language development focused on accuracy and grammatical correctness →	Language development focused on interaction, collaboration, comprehension, and communication, with strategic scaffolding to guide appropriate linguistic choices
Simplified texts and activities, often separate from content knowledge, as necessary for learning English →	Complex texts and intellectually challenging activities focused on building content knowledge as essential to learning academic English

A key goal of the CA ELD Standards is to support EL students to develop advanced proficiency with academic English as they also develop content knowledge across the disciplines. The following section discusses some of the ways teachers can support their EL students in developing proficiency.

Supporting English Learners to Develop Academic English

Part II in the CA ELD Standards is necessarily contextualized in the type of instruction called for in Part I, which focuses on content knowledge and purposeful language development and use. As ELs progress through the grades, they will be expected to move increasingly from everyday English to academic English. This shift from more everyday to more academic registers requires an understanding of how English works on a variety of levels, including the text, sentence, clause, phrase, and word levels.

Understanding at the Text Level

As early as kindergarten, ELs can begin to understand the structures of different text types. For example, a story is typically structured in three main stages: orientation, complication, and resolution. In the orientation stage, the author *orients* the reader to the story by providing information on the characters and setting and also by setting up the plot. In the complication stage, the author introduces some kind of plot twist that complicates the situation and that must be resolved in some way. In the resolution stage, the author ties up everything neatly by *resolving* the complication and sometimes by offering a moral to the story or a lesson to be learned. This is not the only way a story can be structured, but this organization illustrates the basic features of many stories students encounter in school, especially in the elementary grades. When students are aware of the text structure of stories, they are in a better position to (a) comprehend stories that are read to them or that they read independently; they can also (b) write their own stories, meeting the expectations of story structure.

As students progress through the grades and into secondary schooling, the academic texts they are expected to comprehend and produce become more varied and complex. The academic texts students encounter in middle and high school are dense with meaning, authoritatively presented, and highly structured (Schleppegrell 2004). These characteristics are part of what distinguishes academic English from more informal, everyday ways of using English. One academic text type that is prominently featured in the CA CCSS for ELA/Literacy and in the CA ELD Standards is argument.[8] Arguments are written to persuade others to think or act in a certain way, to discuss different viewpoints on an issue, or to assess or evaluate ideas, texts, events, and so forth. Particularly in secondary settings, ELs need to understand how various types of successful arguments are structured so that they can better understand the arguments they read and produce arguments that meet the expectations of the CA CCSS for ELA/Literacy, the CA ELD Standards, and other content standards.

Working with students to understand argument text structure is necessarily contextualized in intellectually challenging content. In order to take a stand and argue for or against something, students must build knowledge of the content and topic, have opportunities to talk about their ideas, and develop the linguistic resources they will need to convey their thinking.

Some ways to foster these practices are illustrated in a unit that a middle school English teacher taught on the benefits and costs of conventional and organic farming, which culminated with students writing arguments. Over the course of the unit, the class read multiple primary sources and viewed several documentaries on the history of farming and recent developments in sustainable and organic agriculture. The students engaged in collaborative discussions where they debated the content in the texts, analyzed and evaluated the meaning and validity of written arguments on the topic, learned domain-specific and general academic vocabulary they would need to present their ideas, as well as other ways of using language to present their ideas persuasively, and delivered oral presentations on particular aspects of the topic, such as the use of pesticides in farming.

Another important activity was one in which the teacher repeatedly guided students to analyze the text structure of arguments, including the stages that are typically found in written arguments (e.g., provide a position statement, state the issue, make several points supported by evidence, reiterate the position). The teacher also highlighted the particular language features that made the text more cohesive or made it "hang together" (e.g., connecting or transition words). As the unit progressed, students built up the points and evidence supporting their arguments, and the culminating activity was for each student to take a position and pull their arguments together in the form of an editorial for the school newspaper. Figure 5.2 shows an example of the type of argument a teacher might guide students to analyze in order to make explicit the text structure of arguments while also maintaining a clear focus on content knowledge and meaning.

---

8. In the K–5 CA CCSS for ELA/Literacy and the CA ELD Standards, "argument" is referred to as "opinion."

Table 5.2 Example of Argument Text Structure—Middle School

	Argument Text Structure
Stages	**Middle school newspaper editorial**: *Our School Should Serve Organic Foods*
Position Statement *Issue Appeal*	All students who come to Rosa Parks Middle School deserve to be served safe, healthy, and delicious food. Organic foods are more nutritious and safer to eat than non-organic foods, which are treated with pesticides. Our school should serve only organic foods because it's our basic right to know that we're being taken care of by the adults in our school. Organic foods might be more expensive than non-organic foods, but I think we can all work together to make sure we eat only the healthiest foods, and that means organic.
Arguments *Point A Elaboration*	Eating organic foods is safer for you because the crops aren't treated with chemical pesticides like non-organic crops are. According to a recent study by Stanford University, 38 percent of non-organic produce had pesticides on them, compared with only 7 percent of organic produce. Some scientists say that exposure to pesticides in food is related to neurobehavioral problems in children, such as attention-deficit/hyperactivity disorder (ADHD). Other studies show that even low levels of pesticide exposure can hurt us. I definitely don't want to take the risk of poisoning myself every time I eat lunch.
Point B Elaboration	Organic food is more nutritious and healthier for your body. The Stanford University study also reported that organic milk and chicken contain more omega-3 fatty acids than non-organic milk and chicken. Omega-3 fatty acids are important for brain health and also might help reduce heart disease, so we should be eating foods that contain them. According to Michael Pollan and other experts, fruits and vegetables grown in organic soils have more nutrients in them. They also say that eating the fruits and vegetables close to the time they were picked preserves more nutrients. This is a good reason to get our school's food from local organic farms. Eating local organic foods helps keep us healthier, and it also supports the local economy. We might even be able to get organic crops more cheaply if we work with more local farms.
Point C Elaboration	Organic foods are better for the environment and for the people who grow the food. Farmers who grow organic produce don't use chemicals to fertilize the soil or pesticides to keep away insects or weeds. Instead, they use other methods like beneficial insects and crop rotation. This means that chemicals won't run off the farm and into streams and our water supply. This helps to protect the environment and our health. In addition, on organic farms, the farmworkers who pick the food aren't exposed to dangerous chemicals that could damage their health. This isn't just good for our school; it's something good we should do for ourselves, other human beings, and the planet.
Reiteration of Appeal	To put it simply, organic foods are more nutritious, safer for our bodies, and better for the environment. But there's another reason we should switch to organic food: It tastes better. Non-organic food can sometimes taste like cardboard, but organic food is always delicious. When I bite into an apple or a strawberry, I want it to taste good, and I don't want a mouthful of pesticides. Some people might say that organic is too expensive. I say that we can't afford to risk the health of students at this school by not serving organic foods. Therefore, we must find a way to make organic foods part of our school lunches.

Note: Figure used with permission from WestEd's English Language and Literacy Acceleration (ELLA) project.

Clearly, this type of writing requires time for students to develop. Students need time to learn and interpret the content, time to analyze and evaluate the content of arguments, time to discuss and debate their ideas, and time to build the language resources necessary to write arguments. By the same token, students who understand how an argument is structured—through classroom activities such as analyzing and evaluating models of arguments, jointly constructing arguments as a class or with peers, and producing multiple drafts of arguments with opportunities to revise and edit based on useful feedback—are in a better position to comprehend the arguments they read in school and to produce arguments that meet their teachers' expectations.

Students also need to understand how writers and speakers make their texts cohesive. Cohesion refers to how information unfolds, or flows, throughout a text and how the text "hangs together." A cohesive text is created through the selection of a variety of language resources, such as referring back or forward in the text to people, ideas, or things using pronouns or synonyms (e.g., replacing *farmers* with the pronoun *they* or *people* with *human beings*) or linking chunks of text with text connectives (e.g., *instead, in addition, to put it simply*) in order to signal shifts in meaning in the text, among other language resources supporting cohesion.

One focus that teachers need to consistently maintain when teaching students to better understand text structure and cohesion is *meaning*. The central purpose of writing an argument is to persuade others to think or do something, and a successful argument involves more than structure. It also involves a range of language resources that are useful for conveying meaning. In the case of argument, language resources that are especially effective are those that are associated with persuasion, including an appeal to people's humanity (*our* basic right to be taken care of; that farmworkers are not exposed to dangerous chemicals), building a sense of community (*our school;* the use of the pronoun *we*), and the use of modality to establish authority and temper statements (*we should* do this, organic food *might be* more expensive, *we must, definitely*). Teachers who are aware of text structure, cohesive language resources, and

language that makes arguments more persuasive are in a better position to support their students to write convincing arguments that are well supported by good reasons and evidence.

Understanding at the Sentence Level and Clause Level

In addition to understanding text structure and cohesion, students need to learn how sentences are constructed in particular ways to convey meaning effectively in different contexts. For example, a student might tell her friend, "Polluting the air is wrong, and I think people should really stop polluting," which is a perfectly appropriate way to express this idea to a peer in an informal interaction. However, this idea will likely be presented in a different way in a textbook or journal article and may be articulated as "Although many countries are addressing pollution, environmental degradation continues to create devastating human health problems each year." This shift from more "spoken" or commonsense ways of expressing ideas or phenomena to more "written" or specialized ways requires students to develop content knowledge (in this case, knowledge about the consequences of various types of pollution and which countries around the world allow pollution) along with the language needed for humans to express (or comprehend) this understanding. This is one reason developing full proficiency in English cannot occur in isolation from content learning.

Academic English includes a variety of linguistic resources that are different from those used in informal, everyday interactions in English. The particular linguistic resources used in academic texts in the different disciplines vary, but in general, academic texts tend to include a higher proportion of general academic and domain-specific vocabulary, complex sentences that connect ideas with subordinating conjunctions (e.g., *although, rather than, in order to*), expanded noun phrases, and longer stretches of discourse that are tightly organized depending upon the text type and academic discipline area. Teachers can draw students' attention to these linguistic resources in order to make the resources more transparent and understandable. Table 5.3 illustrates some of the ways in which everyday English registers differ from academic English registers.

Although both sentences are grammatically correct and could be used as the thesis statement in an argument, the sentence in the "Academic English Registers" column better meets the expectations established in the CA CCSS for ELA/Literacy for writing an argument in secondary settings. In addition, this example illustrates how *academic English is not just everyday English translated into an academic register.* Rather, it requires both content and linguistic knowledge, which is one reason it has been widely argued that content and language are inextricably linked. Content knowledge is embedded in language, and language conveys content in particular ways. Correspondingly, Part II of the CA ELD Standards should not be applied—whether in instruction or in assessment—in ways that isolate language use from the purposeful meaning-making and interaction presented in Part I.

The CA ELD Standards allow teachers to focus on critical linguistic features of academic English so that teachers can make those features transparent to students. The following example illustrates how one of these linguistic features of academic English (connecting ideas in logical ways to show relationships through clause combining) appears in the CA ELD Standards:

ELD Standard, Grade 7, Part II, C.6 (Bridging)

Combine clauses in a wide variety of ways (e.g., creating compound, complex, and compound–complex sentences) to make connections between and join ideas, for example, to show the relationship between multiple events or ideas (e.g., *After eating lunch, the students worked in groups while their teacher walked around the room*) or to evaluate an argument (e.g., *The author claims X, although there is a lack of evidence to support this claim*).

The examples in this standard illustrate a specific way of using language (combining clauses) in purposeful ways (e.g., to make connections between and join ideas) in order to convey understanding of content meaning. This understanding of how language works is particularly important as students move into secondary schooling and encounter the densely packed language of science and history. In order to support their students' ability to combine clauses in a variety of ways (in writing and/or speaking), teachers might first

show them how to be more analytical as they read by deconstructing complex sentences. Deconstructing sentences serves dual purposes: analyzing the structure (linguistic features) and deriving meaning (comprehension). Teachers may also work with students to help them revise their writing and adopt some of these same ways of making connections between ideas through clause combining. For example, using the sentence in the "Academic English Registers" column of table 5.3, which is part of a longer selection that students have previously read, a teacher might guide students to deconstruct, or unpack, the sentence, first by focusing on what it means (in order to support comprehension) and then by focusing on the structure (in order to support both comprehension and subsequent writing by students).

Table 5.3 Differences Between Everyday and Academic English Registers

Everyday English Registers	Academic English Registers
"Polluting the air is wrong, and I think people should really stop polluting."	"Although many countries are addressing pollution, environmental degradation continues to create devastating human health problems each year."
Register: More typical of spoken (informal) English	*Register:* More typical of written (formal) English
Background knowledge: More typical of everyday interactions about common-sense things in the world	*Background knowledge:* Specialized or content-rich knowledge about topics, particularly developed through school experiences and wide reading
Vocabulary: Fewer general academic and domain-specific words (pollute, pollution)	*Vocabulary:* More general academic words (address, although, devastating) and domain-specific words/phrases (environmental degradation, pollution)
Sentence structure: Compound sentence	*Sentence structure:* Complex sentence
Clauses: Two independent clauses connected with a coordinating conjunction (and)	*Clauses:* One independent clause and one dependent clause connected with a subordinating conjunction (although) to show concession

To focus on meaning, the teacher might lead a discussion with students on unpacking the meaning in the densely packed text, resulting in the following summary:

Sentence to Unpack

"Although many countries are addressing pollution, environmental degradation continues to create devastating human health problems each year."

Meaning

- Pollution is a big problem around the world.

- A lot of countries are doing something about pollution.

- Pollution destroys the environment.

- The ruined environment leads to health problems in people.

- The health problems are still happening every year.

- The health problems are really, really bad.

- Even though the countries are doing something about pollution, there are still problems.

This focus on meaning is essential because the goal of close reading is to derive meaning. However, a strategic instructional focus on sentence and clause structures from time to time serves to help students read more closely and analytically in order to derive meaning from densely packed texts. Table 5.4 shows one way a teacher might begin to show students how to deconstruct the sentence, with a focus on both structure and meaning.

Table 5.4 Sentence Deconstruction Focusing on Structure and Meaning

Structure: *Type of Clause and How to Know*	Text: *Broken into Clauses*	Meaning: *What It Means*
Dependent It starts with *although*, so it can't stand on its own. It "depends" on the other clause.	Although many countries are addressing pollution,	The clause gives credit to a lot of countries for doing something about pollution. Use of the word *although* tells me that the rest of the sentence will show the efforts are not enough.
Independent It can stand on its own, even if the other clause is removed.	environmental degradation continues to create devastating human health problems each year.	This type of clause has the most important information. Pollution keeps hurting a lot of people every year all over the world.

These examples show that by helping their EL students to become more analytical about how sentences and clauses are constructed, teachers can support their EL students to better understand the densely packed texts they encounter in school. The techniques can be used in a variety of flexible ways. For example, in high school, ELD teachers and teachers of academic subjects may work together to collaboratively identify densely packed sentences in academic subject-matter texts—sentences that could make it difficult for students to understand the knowledge being presented. During ELD instruction, the ELD teacher may support EL students to manage these language challenges and better comprehend texts by guiding the students to unpack these densely packed sentences, focusing on both structure and meaning. When appropriate, content teachers in secondary settings may also show their students strategies to unpack sentences in the texts being used. Elementary teachers, who typically teach both core content and ELD, can choose when it would be most appropriate to teach their EL students how to unpack sentences—during designated ELD instruction, during content instruction, or both. In each of these scenarios, when students are provided with opportunities to learn about and discuss how sentences and clauses are structured to make meaning, they develop a more analytical stance when reading their academic texts. These practices allow teachers to have engaging conversations with their students about both the meaning and the form of language, in ways that move beyond simply identifying parts of speech or types of sentences.

Understanding at the Phrase Level

Similarly, teachers can show students how to unpack expanded noun phrases, which consist of a head noun with pre- and post-modifiers (words that come before and after the head noun). In the following example, the head noun is in boldface, and the modifiers are added incrementally to expand the noun phrase:

frog → That frog → That green frog → That fat green frog → That very fat green frog → That very fat green frog on the rock → That very fat green frog on the rock with a fly in its mouth . . .

Teachers often ask their students to "add more detail" or to make their writing more interesting. Expanding noun phrases is one way to add detail and also to create precision in writing. Long noun phrases are common in academic texts, particularly in science texts, where a great deal of content is densely packed into the noun phrase. In the following example, the expanded noun phrases are in boldface, and the head nouns are italicized:

Non-native *plants* are *species* introduced to California after European contact and as a direct or indirect result of human activity (NGA and CCSSO 2010).

It can be challenging for students to unpack the meaning of these types of long noun phrases while reading. Teachers of all disciplines can help their students by showing them how to deconstruct the noun phrases to derive meaning. In secondary settings, ELD teachers may work closely with content teachers to identify long noun phrases that are critical for comprehension but that may pose challenges for EL students. During ELD instruction, the ELD teachers may show students how to identify the head noun ("plants" in the first noun phrase shown earlier and "species" in the second), then the pre-modifiers (e.g., articles, adjectives) and, finally, the post-modifiers, which are often in the form of prepositional phrases or embedded clauses. The following example shows how a teacher might represent this deconstruction (adapted from Fang 2010):

Pre-modifiers	Head noun	Post-modifiers
Non-native	*plants*	
	species	introduced to California after European contact . . .

Students will notice that the first expanded noun phrase ("non-native plants") is relatively easy to identify and replicate. However, the second noun phrase is quite a bit longer and more challenging to unpack. This is the challenge EL students face in comprehending text; showing them how to unpack the meaning through a focus on the structure of the noun phrase can aid comprehension. This type of deconstructive activity can be extended by identifying types of pre- and post-modifiers (e.g., adjectives, embedded clauses, prepositional phrases). Teachers may also create activities for students to expand noun phrases in meaningful ways and discuss how the use of certain modifiers creates different meanings. These practices of deconstructing and then constructing long noun phrases in purposeful ways, all the while keeping a sharp focus on meaning, can be implemented in strategic ways by both content and ELD teachers in secondary settings and by elementary teachers who teach both core content and ELD in self-contained classroom settings; at the elementary school setting, grade-level teams could work collaboratively to address content and ELD.

Understanding at the Word Level

In addition to learning the meanings of and using general academic and domain-specific vocabulary[9] in context, students will encounter a special kind of language resource called *nominalization* as they progress into secondary schooling. One of the prominent features of academic texts is that they are densely packed with meaning. Nominalization is one linguistic resource that helps to achieve this density and makes texts more cohesive. A simple type of nominalization that is relatively straightforward is when a verb is transformed into a noun or noun phrase (e.g., They *destroyed* the rain forest → The *destruction* of the rain forest _____). Sometimes, adjectives are nominalized as well (e.g., *strong* → *strength; different* → *difference*). Additional examples of how verbs may be transformed into nouns are as follows:

Verb		Noun
develop	→	development
grow	→	growth
interact	→	interaction

Sometimes nominalization collapses an entire clause or even multiple clauses into nouns or noun phrases. For example, in conversational language, a student might say, "The ranchers came to the rain forest, and they cut down a lot of trees. The next year, the river flooded everything." Nominalization allows writers or speakers to densely pack these three clauses into one, achieving a more academic register: "The *destruction* of the rain forest led to *widespread flooding*." Also note how the nominalized subject of the example sentence ("destruction") hides the agents involved in the act, which is characteristic of history texts and a common reason for using nominalization in history texts.

At the text level, this collapsing of entire clauses through nominalization helps to create cohesion in texts and also contributes to the lexical density (i.e., percentage of content words to total words) of academic texts by condensing larger chunks of information into single words or phrases, often through summarizing nouns (e.g., *this event, the problem*). By turning actions into things, nominalization allows writers or speakers to create abstractions, condensing entire events, theories, and concepts into nouns and noun phrases (e.g., *democracy, photosynthesis, the symbolic presence of children in the scene, the disappearance of native languages*). This allows writers and speakers to create relationships between the abstractions, develop arguments with them, and evaluate them.

Secondary ELD teachers can support content teachers in raising students' awareness of how nominalization works in academic texts to achieve particular purposes. They can develop opportunities during ELD instruction for students to identify nominalization in the texts they read in their content classes, discuss how nominalization conveys meaning (and how it is different from everyday language), and practice using their growing understanding of nominalization when writing texts such as arguments or explanations for their content classes. In this way, students can learn to be more analytical when reading and also develop new ways of conveying ideas and structuring texts in more academic ways. Secondary content teachers and elementary teachers who teach the intermediate grades can also use their understanding of nominalization to build their EL students' awareness of and proficiency in using nominalization.

Part II in the CA ELD Standards provides a framework for teachers to design these types of activities and talk with their students about how English works. Part II supports teachers' efforts to ensure that all EL students can:

a. comprehend the disciplinary texts they read, view, or listen to by thinking about how the language in the texts is used to convey meaning;

b. meet academic discourse demands within disciplines when writing, speaking, and creating texts by making conscious and informed choices about the linguistic resources they use.

---

9. Domain-specific vocabulary and general academic vocabulary are explicitly addressed in Parts I and II of the CA ELD Standards.

Organization of Part II

Part II in the CA ELD Standards, "Learning About How English Works," identifies key language demands in the CA CCSS for ELA/Literacy, as well as those in academic English texts, that may present particular challenges to EL students as they develop academic English across the disciplines. Research has demonstrated that identifying these linguistic challenges and attending to them in meaningful ways through instruction can help ELs develop proficiency with academic English (NGA and CCSSO 2010).

The language demands that are featured prominently and repeatedly in the CA CCSS for ELA/Literacy are grouped together and represented by key language processes: structuring cohesive texts, expanding and enriching ideas, and connecting and condensing ideas. These language processes are further unpacked into numbered strands as follows:

A. Structuring Cohesive Texts

　　1. Understanding text structure

　　2. Understanding cohesion

B. Expanding and Enriching Ideas

　　3. Using verbs and verb phrases

　　4. Using nouns and noun phrases

　　5. Modifying to add details

C. Connecting and Condensing Ideas

　　6. Connecting ideas

　　7. Condensing ideas

Part II in the CA ELD Standards provides guidance to teachers on intentionally, strategically, and judiciously addressing the language demands in the CA CCSS for ELA/Literacy and in the texts used in instruction. Table 5.5 provides an example of how multiple CA CCSS for ELA/Literacy across the domains correspond with the CA ELD Standards in Part II, "Learning About How English Works." California additions to the CA CCSS for ELA/Literacy appear in boldface and are designated with "CA."

Table 5.5 Correspondence of Grade 5 CA CCSS for ELA/Literacy and CA ELD Standards

Grade 5 CA CCSS for ELA/Literacy	Grade 5 CA ELD Standards Part II: Learning About How English Works Structuring Cohesive Texts, Strands 1 and 2		
	→ Emerging →	→ Expanding →	→ Bridging →
RL.5.5 Explain how a series of chapters, scenes, or stanzas fits together to provide the overall structure of a particular story, drama, or poem. RI.5.5 Compare and contrast the overall structure (e.g., chronology, comparison, cause/effect, problem/solution) of events, ideas, concepts, or information in two or more texts. W.5.1 Write opinion pieces on topics or texts, supporting a point of view with reasons and information. a. Introduce a topic or text clearly, state an opinion, and create an organizational structure in which ideas are logically grouped to support the writer's purpose. b. Provide logically ordered reasons that are supported by facts and details. c. Link opinion and reasons using words, phrases, and clauses (e.g., *consequently, specifically*). d. Provide a concluding statement or section related to the opinion presented. (See similar cohesion expectations in W.5.2 and W.5.3.) W.5.4 Produce clear and coherent writing **(including multiple-paragraph texts)** in which the development and organization are appropriate to task, purpose, and audience. **CA** W.5.5 With guidance and support from peers and adults, develop and strengthen writing as needed by planning, revising, editing, rewriting, or trying a new approach. SL.5.4 Report on a topic or text or present an opinion, sequencing ideas logically and using appropriate facts and relevant, descriptive details to support main ideas or themes; speak clearly at an understandable pace. **a. Plan and deliver an opinion speech that: states an opinion, logically sequences evidence to support the speaker's position, uses transition words to effectively link opinions and evidence (e.g., *consequently* and *therefore*), and provides a concluding statement related to the speaker's position. CA** L.5.1 Demonstrate command of the conventions of standard English grammar and usage when writing or speaking. L.5.3 Use knowledge of language and its conventions when writing, speaking, reading, or listening.	*1. Understanding text structure* Apply basic understanding of how different text types are organized to express ideas (e.g., how a story is organized sequentially with predictable stages versus how opinions/arguments are organized around ideas) to comprehending texts and writing basic texts. *2. Understanding cohesion* a. Apply basic understanding of language resources for referring the reader to the text (e.g., how pronouns refer to nouns in text) to comprehend texts and write basic texts. b. Apply basic understanding of how ideas, events, or reasons are linked throughout a text using a select set of everyday connecting words or phrases (e.g., *first/next, at the beginning*) to comprehending texts and writing basic texts.	*1. Understanding text structure* Apply growing understanding of how different text types are organized to express ideas (e.g., how a story is organized sequentially with predictable stages versus how opinions/arguments are structured logically around reasons and evidence) to comprehending texts and writing texts with increasing cohesion. *2. Understanding cohesion* a. Apply growing understanding of language resources that refer the reader to text (e.g., how pronouns or synonyms refer to nouns in text) to comprehend texts and write texts with increasing cohesion. b. Apply growing understanding of how ideas, events, or reasons are linked throughout a text using a variety of connecting words or phrases (e.g., *for example, in the first place, as a result*) to comprehending texts and writing texts with increasing cohesion.	*1. Understanding text structure* Apply increasing understanding of how different text types are organized to express ideas (e.g., how a historical account is organized chronologically versus how opinions/arguments are structured logically around reasons and evidence) to comprehending texts and writing cohesive texts. *2. Understanding cohesion* a. Apply increasing understanding of language resources that refer the reader to text (e.g., how pronouns, synonyms, or nominalizations refer to nouns in text) to comprehend texts and write cohesive texts. b. Apply increasing understanding of how ideas, events, or reasons are linked throughout a text using an increasing variety of academic connecting and transitional words or phrases (e.g., *consequently, specifically, however*) to comprehending texts and writing cohesive texts.

By design, multiple CA CCSS for ELA/Literacy across several domains correlate with a single CA ELD Standard strand, and multiple CA ELD Standard strands correspond to the same CA CCSS for ELA/Literacy. This "many-to-many" correspondence is explicitly shown on each page of a grade level's CA ELD Standards, as seen in the following example from grade 5.

Section 2: Elaboration on Critical Principles for Developing Language and Cognition in Academic Contexts
Part II: Learning About How English Works

Texts and Discourse in Context		ELD Proficiency Level Continuum		
		→ Emerging →	→ Expanding →	→ Bridging →
Part II, strands 1–2, corresponding to the CA CCSS for ELA/Literacy 1. RL.5.5; RI.5.5; W.5.1–5; SL.5.4 2. RL.5.5; RI.5.5; W.5.1–4; SL.5.4; L.5.1, 3 **Purposes for using language include but are not limited to:** Describing, entertaining, informing, interpreting, analyzing, recounting, explaining, persuading, negotiating, justifying, evaluating, and so on. **Informational text types include but are not limited to:** Description (e.g., science log entry), procedure (e.g., how to solve a mathematics problem), recount (e.g., autobiography, science experiment results), information report (e.g., science or history report), explanation (e.g., how or why something happened), exposition (e.g., opinion), response (e.g., literary analysis), and so on. **Literary text types include but are not limited to:** Stories (e.g., fantasy, legends, fables), drama (e.g., readers' theater), poetry, retelling a story, and so on. **Audiences include but are not limited to:** Peers (one to one) Small group (one to a group) Whole group (one to many)	**A. Structuring Cohesive Texts**	***1. Understanding text structure*** Apply basic understanding of how different text types are organized to express ideas (e.g., how a narrative is organized sequentially with predictable stages versus how opinions/arguments are organized around ideas) to comprehending texts and writing basic texts. ***2. Understanding cohesion*** a. Apply basic understanding of language resources for referring the reader back or forward in text (e.g., how pronouns refer back to nouns in text) to comprehending texts and writing basic texts. b. Apply basic understanding of how ideas, events, or reasons are linked throughout a text using a select set of everyday connecting words or phrases (e.g., *first/next, at the beginning*) to comprehending texts and writing basic texts.	***1. Understanding text structure*** Apply growing understanding of how different text types are organized to express ideas (e.g., how a narrative is organized sequentially with predictable stages versus how opinions/arguments are structured logically around reasons and evidence) to comprehending texts and writing texts with increasing cohesion. ***2. Understanding cohesion*** a. Apply growing understanding of language resources for referring the reader back or forward in text (e.g., how pronouns or synonyms refer back to nouns in text) to comprehending texts and writing texts with increasing cohesion. b. Apply growing understanding of how ideas, events, or reasons are linked throughout a text using a variety of connecting words or phrases (e.g., *for example, in the first place, as a result*) to comprehending texts and writing texts with increasing cohesion.	***1. Understanding text structure*** Apply increasing understanding of how different text types are organized to express ideas (e.g., how a historical account is organized chronologically versus how opinions/arguments are structured logically around reasons and evidence) to comprehending texts and writing cohesive texts. ***2. Understanding cohesion*** a. Apply increasing understanding of language resources for referring the reader back or forward in text (e.g., how pronouns, synonyms, or nominalizations refer back to nouns in text) to comprehending texts and writing cohesive texts. b. Apply increasing understanding of how ideas, events, or reasons are linked throughout a text using an increasing variety of academic connecting and transitional words or phrases (e.g., *consequently, specifically, however*) to comprehending texts and writing cohesive texts.

Use of the CA ELD Standards

As emphasized previously, the CA ELD Standards are not intended to be used as a stand-alone document. Rather, they are designed to be used with the CA CCSS for ELA/Literacy, as well as other California content standards, to provide a robust and comprehensive instructional program for ELs. The examples provided in previous sections illustrate how designated ELD instruction in elementary and secondary settings can support the language practices found in core content curriculum. ELD instruction should not be provided in a manner that is disconnected or isolated from core content instruction. The focus of instruction determines the standards' role. For example, the CA ELD Standards serve as the focal standards in settings specifically designed for English language development—such as designated ELD instruction in secondary school or designated block of time for ELD in elementary school where ELs are grouped by English proficiency level. Additionally, the CA ELD Standards are designed and intended to be used *in tandem with* other academic content standards to support ELs in mainstream academic content classrooms. Parts I, II, and III of the CA ELD Standards should be consulted and used strategically during content instruction (e.g., English language arts, science, history, mathematics) that is focused on the CA CCSS for ELA/Literacy and other content standards that have been approved by the California State Board of Education. Applied in this way, the CA ELD Standards foster more comprehensive instruction for ELs by helping content-area teachers recognize the opportunities for language development in content instruction and foster the language needed to engage in discipline-specific practices and to express content knowledge.

When used as part of a coordinated application of standards, the CA ELD Standards will help California educators to support ELs to:

- read, analyze, interpret, and create a variety of literary and informational text types;

- develop an understanding of how language is a complex, dynamic, and social resource for making meaning;

- develop an understanding of how content is organized in different text types across disciplines using text structure, language features, and vocabulary, depending upon purpose and audience;

- become aware that different languages and varieties of English exist;

- recognize their home languages and cultures as resources to value and draw upon in building English proficiency;

- contribute actively to class and group discussions by asking questions, responding appropriately, and providing useful feedback;

- demonstrate knowledge of content through oral presentations, writing, collaborative conversations, and multimedia;

- develop proficiency in shifting registers based on context.

This complex undertaking requires deep commitment, collaboration among groups of educators, support for teachers to develop and refine instructional practices, and, most importantly, a sustained focus on the strengths and needs of individual ELs and a persistent belief that all ELs can achieve the highest levels of academic and linguistic excellence. Fostering the academic and linguistic development of ELs is best done in professional communities of practice, in which teams of teachers work together to recognize and identify language challenges in core content, develop strategies to address these challenges, regularly discuss student work, and reflect on the effectiveness of their instruction for student learning. This collaborative approach among teachers requires districts to adopt an appropriate paradigm of support—one in which teachers have adequate time to collaborate to develop lessons; participate in relevant, sustained professional learning and refine their practice; and are held accountable for implementing the practices (Elmore 2002). In such a collaborative and supportive environment, teachers are better prepared to meet the needs of their EL students, and EL students have ongoing opportunities to meet the expectations of the CA CCSS for ELA/Literacy and the CA ELD Standards.

References

Achugar, M., M. Schleppegrell, and T. Oteíza. 2007. "Engaging Teachers in Language Analysis: A Functional Linguistics Approach to Reflective Literacy." *English Teaching: Practice and Critique* 6 (2): 8–24.

Aguirre-Munoz, Z., J. Park, A. Amabisca, and C. Boscardin. 2008. "Developing Teacher Capacity for Serving ELLs' Writing Instructional Needs: A Case for Systemic Functional Linguistics." *Bilingual Research Journal* 31 (1/2): 295–323.

Carlo, M. S., D. August, B. McLaughlin, C. E. Snow, C. E. Dressler, D. N. Lippman, T. J. Lively, and C. E. White. 2004. "Closing the Gap: Addressing the Vocabulary Needs of English-Language Learners in Bilingual and Mainstream Classrooms." *Reading Research Quarterly* 39:188–215.

Cummins, J. 2008. "BICS and CALP: Empirical and Theoretical Status of the Distinction." In *Encyclopedia of Language and Education,* 2nd ed., vol. 2 (Literacy). New York: Springer Science and Business Media LLC.

de Oliveira, L. C., and K. N. Dodds. 2010. "Beyond General Strategies for English Language Learners: Language Dissection in Science." *Electronic Journal of Literacy Through Science* 9 (1):1–14.

Elmore, R. F. 2002. *Bridging the Gap Between Standards and Achievement: The Imperative for Professional Development in Education.* Washington, DC: Albert Shanker Institute.

Fang, Z. 2010. *Language and Literacy in Inquiry-Based Science.* Thousand Oaks, CA: Corwin Press and National Science Teachers Association.

Gebhard, M., and J. Martin. 2010. "Grammar and Literacy Learning." In *Handbook of Research on Teaching the English Language Arts,* edited by D. Fisher and D. Lapp. Mahwah, NJ: Erlbaum/Taylor & Francis.

Lesaux, N. K., M. J. Kieffer, S. E. Faller, and J. G. Kelley. 2010. "The Effectiveness and Ease of Implementation of an Academic Vocabulary Intervention for Linguistically Diverse Students in Urban Middle Schools." *Reading Research Quarterly* 45 (2): 196–228.

Nagy, W., and D. Townsend. 2012. "Words as Tools: Learning Academic Vocabulary as Language Acquisition." *Reading Research Quarterly* 47 (1): 91–108.

National Governors Association (NGA) Center for Best Practices and Council of Chief State School Officers (CCSSO). 2010. "Appendix A: Research Supporting Key Elements of the Standards." In *Common Core State Standards for English Language Arts and Literacy in History/Social Studies, Science, and Technical Subjects.* Washington, DC: NGA Center for Best Practices and CCSSO.

Schleppegrell, M. J. 2004. *The Language of Schooling: A Functional Linguistics Perspective.* Mahwah, NJ: Lawrence Erlbaum Associates.

Schleppegrell, M., M. Achugar, and T. Oteíza. 2004. "The Grammar of History: Enhancing Content-Based Instruction Through a Functional Focus on Language." *TESOL Quarterly* 38 (1): 67–93.

Schleppegrell, M., and L. de Oliveira. 2006. "An Integrated Language and Content Approach for History Teachers." *Journal of English for Academic Purposes* 5 (4): 254–68.

Silverman, R., and J. D. Crandell. 2010. "Vocabulary Practices in Prekindergarten and Kindergarten Classrooms." *Reading Research Quarterly* 45 (3): 318–40.

Spycher, P. 2009. "Learning Academic Language Through Science in Two Linguistically Diverse Kindergarten Classes." *Elementary School Journal* 109 (4): 359–79.

Chapter 6

Foundational Literacy Skills for English Learners

Foundational literacy skills—which primarily address print concepts, phono-logical awareness, phonics and word recognition, and fluency, as described in the Reading Standards for Foundational Skills K–5 (RF Standards) section of the California Common Core State Standards for English Language Arts and Literacy (CA CCSS for ELA/Literacy)—are critical for English learners (ELs) at all ages who need to learn basic literacy (August and Shanahan 2006; Riches and Genesee 2006). ELs face an additional challenge in developing literacy in English since they must develop oral proficiency in English—including depth and breadth of vocabulary—at the same time that they are learning to read and write (Roessingh and Elgie 2009; Short and Fitzsimmons 2007; Torgesen et al. 2007). While more research on English learner literacy is needed (IRA and NICHD 2007), the research results available so far show that ELs can transfer native language literacy skills to English literacy learning (August and Shanahan 2006; Riches and Genesee 2006); thus, literacy instruction for ELs will need to be adapted based on each student's previous literacy experiences in his or her native language, as well as on his or her age and level of schooling. Adapted instruction for ELs needs to consider additional individual student charac-teristics—the student's level of oral proficiency in the native language and in English, how closely the student's native language is related to English,[1] and, for students with native language literacy, the type of writing system used.[2]

Research Summary and Implications for English Learners

Below is a summary of key findings from the research cited above, with implica-tions for foundational literacy skills instruction for ELs.

● English learners benefit from Reading Foundational Skills instruction.

> **Research Findings:** Instruction in the components of reading founda-tional skills—such as phonemic awareness, phonics, fluency, vocabu-lary, and text comprehension (NICHD 2000)—benefits ELs.

> **Implications:** Instruction in foundational literacy skills is essential for ELs. However, the instruction should be adjusted based on students' spoken English proficiency (they may or may not be familiar with the English sound system) and native language or English literacy profi-ciency (they may or may not be familiar with any type of writing system or with the Latin alphabet writing system in particular). Note that some ELs at any age may not be literate in any language when they arrive in the U.S. school system; their native language may not have a written form, or they may not have had opportunities to develop literacy in their native language or in a local language of wider communication.[3]

● Oral English language proficiency is crucial for English literacy learning.

> **Research Findings:** Oral proficiency in English (including oral vo-cabulary, grammar, and listening comprehension) is critical for ELs to develop proficiency in text-level English reading comprehension. Word-identification skills are necessary, but not sufficient.

---

1. For information on which languages are related to each other, visit http://www.ethnologue.com/ (accessed October 30, 2013).

2. For information on writing systems for the world's languages, visit http://www.omniglot.com/ (accessed October 30, 2013).

---

3. Students who have learning disabilities (as diagnosed separately from their EL designation)—or whose literacy skills in either their native language or English remain below grade level after intensive and extensive instruction—may need specialized literacy intervention services.

Implications: Instruction for ELs in oral language knowledge, skills, and abilities must be explicit, intensive, and extensive. In order to be successful in reading English, ELs must develop proficiency in listening and speaking skills in English—depth and breadth of vocabulary, as well as grammatical structures—at the same time that they are developing foundational skills in reading and writing English.

- Native language literacy skills facilitate English literacy learning.

    Research Findings: ELs' native language literacy skills can help them learn English foundational literacy skills.

    Implications: Instruction for ELs will need to vary based on variations among ELs' native language writing systems, as well as ELs' experiences with literacy in their native language. For example, students who are literate in a language that uses the Latin alphabet (such as Spanish) will be able to transfer decoding and writing skills more easily than a student who is literate in a language with a non-Latin alphabet (such as Arabic, Korean, or Russian) or a language with a symbol-based writing system (such as Chinese). Similarly, students who are literate in a language related to English (such as Spanish) will be able to use knowledge of cognates (words with similar meaning and spelling in both languages), whereas students who are literate in unrelated languages (such as Arabic, Chinese, or Korean) will not.

Alignment Charts for Foundational Literacy Skills in English Language Development and the CA CCSS for ELA/Literacy — the Reading Standards for Foundational Skills

The charts presented in this chapter outline general guidance for providing instruction to ELs on foundational literacy skills that are aligned with the RF Standards. This guidance is intended to provide a general overview; it does not address the full set of potential individual characteristics of ELs that need to be taken into consideration in foundational literacy skills instruction (e.g., students who have changed schools or programs frequently, or who have interrupted schooling in either their native language or English). While the focus of this chapter is on foundational literacy skills, instruction in these skills should be integrated with instruction in reading comprehension and in content across all disciplines, as emphasized in the CA ELD Standards. The organization and content of the charts is described below.

First Column: Student Language and Literacy Characteristics

- This column outlines some general characteristics of ELs' previous experience with language and literacy—in both their native language and in English—that need to be considered when teachers determine which foundational literacy skills a student may need to develop. These characteristics are:

    Oral Skills: Spoken English proficiency

    Print Skills: Native language literacy; reading and writing skills in a language with a non-alphabetic, non-Latin alphabetic, or Latin alphabetic writing system

Second Column: Considerations for Foundational Literacy Skills Instruction

- This column describes considerations for foundational literacy skills instruction when the characteristics in the first column are known. Considerations include the foundational literacy skills that a student with particular language or literacy characteristics may need to learn, and the native language literacy skills the student may be able to transfer to facilitate developing English literacy.

Third Column: California Common Core State Standards for ELA/Literacy, the Reading Standards for Foundational Skills

- This column shows the set of RF Standards for each elementary-grade level and all secondary-grade levels that a student requiring instruction in English foundational literacy skills will need to achieve in order to reach proficiency in English literacy, *along with intensive and extensive oral English vocabulary learning.*

The RF Standards are identified as follows: strand (RF), grade level (K–5), standard number. Thus, RF.K.1 stands for Reading Standards for Foundational Skills, kindergarten, standard 1, and RF.5.3 stands for Reading Standards for Foundational Skills, grade 5, standard 3. California additions to the CA CCSS for ELA/Literacy appear in bold-face and are designated with "CA."

- ELs who enter school after kindergarten and need specific instruction in foundational English literacy skills based on the RF Standards (as described in the first two columns) will require *accelerated learning* of those skills.

- Since the RF Standards address expectations for students in kindergarten through grade 5 who start at kindergarten and continue to develop these skills as they progress through the grade levels, it will be necessary to *adapt the RF Standards* for ELs who need foundational English literacy skills after kindergarten, based on the students' age, cognitive abilities, and life and school experiences, including their level of oral language and literacy proficiency in their native language.

Table 6.1 Kindergarten

	Student Language and Literacy Characteristics	Considerations for Foundational Literacy Skills Instruction	CA CCSS for ELA/Literacy Reading Standards for Foundational Skills
Oral Skills	No or little spoken English proficiency	Students will need instruction in recognizing and distinguishing the sounds of English as compared or contrasted with sounds in their native language (e.g., vowels, consonants, consonant blends, syllable structures).	**Phonological Awareness** 2. Demonstrate understanding of spoken words, syllables, and sounds (phonemes). • RF.K.2
Oral Skills	Spoken English proficiency	Students will need instruction in applying their knowledge of the English sound system to foundational literacy learning.	
Print Skills	No or little native language literacy	Students will need instruction in print concepts.	**Print Concepts** 1. Demonstrate understanding of the organization and basic features of print. • RF.K.1 **Phonics and Word Recognition** 3. Know and apply grade-level phonics and word analysis skills in decoding words **both in isolation and in text. CA** • RF.K.3 **Fluency** 4. Read emergent-reader texts with purpose and understanding. • RF.K.4
Print Skills	Some foundational literacy proficiency in a language not using the Latin alphabet (e.g., Arabic, Chinese, Korean, Russian)	Students will be familiar with print concepts and will need instruction in learning the Latin alphabet for English, as compared or contrasted with their native language writing system (e.g., direction of print, symbols representing whole words, syllables or phonemes).	
Print Skills	Some foundational literacy proficiency in a language using the Latin alphabet (e.g., Spanish)	Students will need instruction in applying their knowledge of print concepts, phonics, and word recognition to the English writing system, as compared or contrasted with their native language alphabet (e.g., letters that are the same or different, or represent the same or different sounds) and native language vocabulary (e.g., cognates) and sentence structure (e.g., subject-verb-object versus subject-object-verb word order).	

Elementary Level: Grades 1–5

As noted at the beginning of this chapter, foundational literacy skills are the same for all students who need to learn basic literacy skills, including students who begin learning literacy skills after kindergarten. However, the way the skills are taught and how quickly the students can be expected to acquire the basic skills and move on to higher-level reading and writing depend on their age, cognitive level, and previous oral and written literacy experiences in their native language and in English. Since the RF Standards are intended to guide instruction for students in kindergarten through grade 5, these standards need to be adapted—using appropriate instructional strategies and materials—to meet the particular pedagogical and literacy needs of ELs who begin learning literacy skills after kindergarten and addressing the need to teach foundational literacy skills in an accelerated time frame.[4] In particular, the curriculum will need to be flexible so that it can address the different profiles of upper-elementary students needing foundational literacy skills instruction. Considerations contributing to the variety of student profiles include:

- **Oral proficiency** (e.g., extent of vocabulary and knowledge of varied grammatical structures) in English. Oral proficiency is the basis for written literacy proficiency; literacy learning for students with higher levels of oral language proficiency can be accelerated.

- **Native language literacy,** both oral and written: When effectively leveraged, oral and written literacy knowledge and abilities can transfer to the acquisition of English literacy, accelerating the learning time.

- **Similarity of native language to English.** The more closely the student's native language and English are related, the more students can apply knowledge of similarities in vocabulary and grammar in the two languages to learning foundational literacy skills in English, such as spelling of familiar words or determination of where a sentence starts and ends.

- **Native language writing system** (for students with written literacy knowledge in their native language). The more closely the student's native language writing system and English are related, the more students can apply knowledge of similarities of print or alphabetic features in the two languages to learning to read and write with the English alphabet, such as sound–letter correspondences or direction of print.

- Previous experiences with school or school programs. Students' previous schooling experiences in both the native language and English may affect their proficiency and progress related to all of the above. The extent of time and consistency of school attendance, as well as of instructional setting and services (e.g., structured English immersion with or without native language support; 90/10 or 50/50 dual language immersion; early- or late-exit transitional bilingual instruction; ELD pull-out) may affect a student's experiences with literacy learning and their needs for particular literacy instruction.

---

4. The forthcoming California ELA/ELD Framework will address in more detail the development and application of a foundational literacy skills curriculum for elementary-level ELs who begin literacy instruction after kindergarten.

Grade 1

Note: The Reading Standards for Foundational Skills from kindergarten need to be adapted to the student's age, cognitive level, and educational experience.

	Student Language and Literacy Characteristics	Considerations for Foundational Literacy Skills Instruction	CA CCSS for ELA/Literacy Reading Standards for Foundational Skills
Oral Skills	No or little spoken English proficiency	Students will need instruction in recognizing and distinguishing the sounds of English as compared or contrasted with sounds in their native language (e.g., vowels, consonants, consonant blends, syllable structures).	**Phonological Awareness** 2. Demonstrate understanding of spoken words, syllables, and sounds (phonemes). • RF.K.2 • RF.1.2
	Spoken English proficiency	Students will need instruction in applying their knowledge of the English sound system to foundational literacy learning.	
Print Skills	No or little native language literacy	Students will need instruction in print concepts.	**Print Concepts** 1. Demonstrate understanding of the organization and basic features of print. • RF.K.1 • RF.1.1 **Phonics and Word Recognition** 3. Know and apply grade-level phonics and word analysis skills in decoding words both in isolation and in text. CA • RF.K.3 • RF.1.3 **Fluency** 4. Read with sufficient accuracy and fluency to support comprehension. • RF.1.4
	Some foundational literacy proficiency in a language not using the Latin alphabet (e.g., Arabic, Chinese, Korean, Russian)	Students will be familiar with print concepts and will need instruction in learning the Latin alphabet for English, as compared or contrasted with their native language writing system (e.g., direction of print, symbols representing whole words, syllables or phonemes).	
	Some foundational literacy proficiency in a language using the Latin alphabet (e.g., Spanish)	Students will need instruction in applying their knowledge of print concepts, phonics, and word recognition to the English writing system, as compared or contrasted with their native language alphabet (e.g., letters that are the same or different, or represent the same or different sounds) and native language vocabulary (e.g., cognates) and sentence structure (e.g., subject-verb-object versus subject-object-verb word order).	

Grade 2

Note: **The Reading Standards for Foundational Skills from kindergarten and grade 1 need to be adapted to the student's age, cognitive level, and educational experience.**

	Student Language and Literacy Characteristics	Considerations for Foundational Literacy Skills Instruction	CA CCSS for ELA/Literacy Reading Standards for Foundational Skills
Oral Skills	No or little spoken English proficiency	Students will need instruction in recognizing and distinguishing the sounds of English as compared or contrasted with sounds in their native language (e.g., vowels, consonants, consonant blends, syllable structures).	**Phonological Awareness** 2. Demonstrate understanding of spoken words, syllables, and sounds (phonemes). ● RF.K.2 ● RF.1.2
	Spoken English proficiency	Students will need instruction in applying their knowledge of the English sound system to foundational literacy learning.	Review of **Phonological Awareness** skills as needed.
Print Skills	No or little native language literacy	Students will need instruction in print concepts.	**Print Concepts** 1. Demonstrate understanding of the organization and basic features of print. ● RF.K.1 ● RF.1.1 **Phonics and Word Recognition** 3. Know and apply grade-level phonics and word analysis skills in decoding words **both in isolation and in text. CA** ● RF.K.3 ● RF.1.3 ● RF.2.3 **Fluency** 4. Read with sufficient accuracy and fluency to support comprehension. ● RF.2.4
	Foundational literacy proficiency in a language not using the Latin alphabet (e.g., Arabic, Chinese, Korean, Russian)	Students will be familiar with print concepts and will need instruction in learning the Latin alphabet for English, as compared or contrasted with their native language writing system (e.g., direction of print, symbols representing whole words, syllables or phonemes) and native language vocabulary (e.g., cognates) and sentence structure (e.g., subject-verb-object versus subject-object-verb word order).	
	Foundational literacy proficiency in a language using the Latin alphabet (e.g., Spanish)	Students will need instruction in applying their knowledge of print concepts and phonics and word recognition to the English writing system, as compared or contrasted with their native language alphabet (e.g., letters that are the same or different or represent the same or different sounds) and native language vocabulary (e.g., cognates) and sentence structure (e.g., subject-verb-object versus subject-object-verb word order).	**Phonics and Word Recognition** 3. Know and apply grade-level phonics and word analysis skills in decoding words **both in isolation and in text. CA** ● RF.K.3 ● RF.1.3 ● RF.2.3 **Fluency** 4. Read with sufficient accuracy and fluency to support comprehension. ● RF.2.4

Grade 3

Note: The Reading Standards for Foundational Skills from kindergarten through grade 2 need to be adapted to the student's age, cognitive level, and educational experience.

	Student Language and Literacy Characteristics	Considerations for Foundational Literacy Skills Instruction	CA CCSS for ELA/Literacy Reading Standards for Foundational Skills
Oral Skills	No or little spoken English proficiency	Students will need instruction in recognizing and distinguishing the sounds of English as compared or contrasted with sounds in their native language (e.g., vowels, consonants, consonant blends, syllable structures).	**Phonological Awareness** 2. Demonstrate understanding of spoken words, syllables, and sounds (phonemes). • RF.K.2 • RF.1.2
	Spoken English proficiency	Students will need instruction in applying their knowledge of the English sound system to foundational literacy learning.	Review of **Phonological Awareness** skills as needed.
Print Skills	No or little native language literacy	Students will need instruction in print concepts.	**Print Concepts** 1. Demonstrate understanding of the organization and basic features of print. • RF.K.1 • RF.1.1 **Phonics and Word Recognition** 3. Know and apply grade-level phonics and word analysis skills in decoding words **both in isolation and in text. CA** • RF.K.3 • RF.1.3 • RF.2.3 • RF.3.3 **Fluency** 4. Read with sufficient accuracy and fluency to support comprehension. • RF.3.4
	Foundational literacy proficiency in a language not using the Latin alphabet (e.g., Arabic, Chinese, Korean, Russian)	Students will be familiar with print concepts and will need instruction in learning the Latin alphabet for English, as compared or contrasted with their native language writing system (e.g., direction of print, symbols representing whole words, syllables or phonemes) and native language vocabulary (e.g., cognates) and sentence structure (e.g., subject-verb-object versus subject-object-verb word order).	
	Foundational literacy proficiency in a language using the Latin alphabet (e.g., Spanish)	Students will need instruction in applying their knowledge of print concepts, phonics and word recognition to the English writing system, as compared or contrasted with their native language alphabet (e.g., letters that are the same or different or represent the same or different sounds) and native language vocabulary (e.g., cognates) and sentence structure (e.g., subject-verb-object versus subject-object-verb word order).	**Phonics and Word Recognition** 3. Know and apply grade-level phonics and word analysis skills in decoding words **both in isolation and in text. CA** • RF.K.3 • RF.1.3 • RF.2.3 • RF.3.3 **Fluency** 4. Read with sufficient accuracy and fluency to support comprehension. • RF.3.4

Grade 4

Note: The Reading Standards for Foundational Skills from kindergarten through grade 3 need to be adapted to the student's age, cognitive level, and educational experience.

	Student Language and Literacy Characteristics	Considerations for Foundational Literacy Skills Instruction	CA CCSS for ELA/Literacy Reading Standards for Foundational Skills
Oral Skills	No or little spoken English proficiency	Students will need instruction in recognizing and distinguishing the sounds of English as compared or contrasted with sounds in their native language (e.g., vowels, consonants, consonant blends, syllable structures).	**Phonological Awareness** 2. Demonstrate understanding of spoken words, syllables, and sounds (phonemes). • RF.K.2 • RF.1.2
	Spoken English proficiency	Students will need instruction in applying their knowledge of the English sound system to literacy foundational learning.	Review of **Phonological Awareness** skills as needed.
Print Skills	No or little native language literacy	Students will need instruction in print concepts.	**Print Concepts** 1. Demonstrate understanding of the organization and basic features of print. • RF.K.1 • RF.1.1
	Foundational literacy proficiency in a language not using the Latin alphabet (e.g., Arabic, Chinese, Korean, Russian)	Students will be familiar with print concepts and will need instruction in learning the Latin alphabet for English, as compared or contrasted with their native language writing system (e.g., direction of print, symbols representing whole words, syllables or phonemes) and native language vocabulary (e.g., cognates) and sentence structure (e.g., subject-verb-object versus subject-object-verb word order).	**Phonics and Word Recognition** 3. Know and apply grade-level phonics and word analysis skills in decoding words **both in isolation and in text. CA** • RF.K.3 • RF.1.3 • RF.2.3 • RF.3.3 3. Know and apply grade-level phonics and word analysis skills in decoding words. • RF.4.3 **Fluency** 4. Read with sufficient accuracy and fluency to support comprehension. • RF.4.4
	Foundational literacy proficiency in a language using the Latin alphabet (e.g., Spanish)	Students will need instruction in applying their knowledge of print concepts, phonics, and word recognition to the English writing system, as compared or contrasted with their native language alphabet (e.g., letters that are the same or different or represent the same or different sounds) and native language vocabulary (e.g., cognates) and sentence structure (e.g., subject-verb-object versus subject-object-verb word order).	**Phonics and Word Recognition** 3. Know and apply grade-level phonics and word analysis skills in decoding words **both in isolation and in text. CA** • RF.K.3 • RF.1.3 • RF.2.3 • RF.3.3 3. Know and apply grade-level phonics and word analysis skills in decoding words. • RF.4.3 **Fluency** 4. Read with sufficient accuracy and fluency to support comprehension. • RF.4.4

Grade 5

Note: The Reading Standards for Foundational Skills from kindergarten through grade 4 need to be adapted to the student's age, cognitive level, and educational experience.

	Student Language and Literacy Characteristics	Considerations for Foundational Literacy Skills Instruction	CA CCSS for ELA/Literacy Reading Standards for Foundational Skills
Oral Skills	No or little spoken English proficiency	Students will need instruction in recognizing and distinguishing the sounds of English as compared or contrasted with sounds in their native language (e.g., vowels, consonants, consonant blends, syllable structures).	**Phonological Awareness** 2. Demonstrate understanding of spoken words, syllables, and sounds (phonemes). • RF.K.2 • RF.1.2
	Spoken English proficiency	Students will need instruction in applying their knowledge of the English sound system to literacy foundational learning.	Review of **Phonological Awareness** skills as needed.
Print Skills	No or little native language literacy	Students will need instruction in print concepts.	**Print Concepts** 1. Demonstrate understanding of the organization and basic features of print. • RF.K.1 • RF.1.1
	Foundational literacy proficiency in a language not using the Latin alphabet (e.g., Arabic, Chinese, Korean, Russian)	Students will be familiar with print concepts and will need instruction in learning the Latin alphabet for English, as compared or contrasted with their native language writing system (e.g., direction of print, symbols representing whole words, syllables or phonemes) and native language vocabulary (e.g., cognates) and sentence structure (e.g., subject-verb-object versus subject-object-verb word order).	**Phonics and Word Recognition** 3. Know and apply grade-level phonics and word analysis skills in decoding words **both in isolation and in text. CA** • RF.K.3 • RF.1.3 • RF.2.3 • RF.3.3 3. Know and apply grade-level phonics and word analysis skills in decoding words. • RF.4.3 • RF.5.3 **Fluency** 4. Read with sufficient accuracy and fluency to support comprehension. • RF.5.4
	Foundational literacy proficiency in a language using the Latin alphabet (e.g., Spanish)	Students will need instruction in applying their knowledge of print concepts, phonics, and word recognition to the English writing system, as compared or contrasted with their native language alphabet (e.g., letters that are the same or different or represent the same or different sounds) and native language vocabulary (e.g., cognates) and sentence structure (e.g., subject-verb-object versus subject-object-verb word order).	**Phonics and Word Recognition** 3. Know and apply grade-level phonics and word analysis skills in decoding words **both in isolation and in text. CA** • RF.K.3 • RF.1.3 • RF.2.3 • RF.3.3 3. Know and apply grade-level phonics and word analysis skills in decoding words. • RF.4.3 • RF.5.3 **Fluency** 4. Read with sufficient accuracy and fluency to support comprehension. • RF.5.4

Secondary Level: Grades 6–12

As noted in the beginning of this chapter, foundational literacy skills are the same for all students who need to learn basic literacy skills, including secondary students. However, the way the skills are taught and how quickly the students can be expected to acquire the basic skills and move on to higher-level reading and writing depend on their age, cognitive level, and previous oral and written literacy experiences in their native language and in English. Since the RF Standards are intended to guide instruction for students in kindergarten through grade 5, *these standards need to be adapted—using appropriate instructional strategies and materials—to meet the particular pedagogical and literacy needs of ELs at the secondary level and in an accelerated time frame.*[5] In particular, the curriculum will need to be flexible so that it can address the different profiles of secondary students needing foundational literacy skills instruction. Considerations contributing to the variety of student profiles include:

- **Oral proficiency** (e.g., extent of vocabulary and knowledge of varied grammatical structures) in English. Oral proficiency is the basis for written literacy proficiency; literacy learning for students with higher levels of oral language proficiency can be accelerated.

- **Native language literacy,** both oral and written. When effectively leveraged, oral and written literacy knowledge and abilities can transfer to the acquisition of English literacy, accelerating the learning time.

- **Similarity of native language to English.** The more closely the student's native language and English are related, the more students can apply knowledge of similarities in vocabulary and grammar in the two languages to learning foundational literacy skills in English, such as spelling of familiar words or determination of where a sentence starts and ends.

- **Native language writing system** (for students with written literacy knowledge in their native language). The more closely the student's native language writing system and English are related, the more students can apply knowledge of similarities of print or alphabetic features in the two languages to learning to read and write with the English alphabet, such as sound–letter correspondences or direction of print.

- **Previous experiences with school or school programs.** Students' previous schooling experiences in both the native language and English may affect their proficiency and progress related to all of the above. The extent of time and consistency of school attendance, as well as of instructional setting and services (e.g., structured English immersion with or without native language support; 90/10 or 50/50 dual language immersion; early- or late-exit transitional bilingual instruction ELD pull-out) may affect a student's experiences with literacy learning and their needs for particular literacy instruction.

---

5. The forthcoming California ELA/ELD Framework will address in more detail the development and application of a foundational literacy skills curriculum for secondary-level ELs.

Note: The Reading Standards for Foundational Skills from kindergarten through grade 5 need to be adapted to the student's age, cognitive level, and educational experience.

	Student Language and Literacy Characteristics	Considerations for Foundational Literacy Skills Instruction	CA CCSS for ELA/Literacy Reading Standards for Foundational Skills

Oral Skills	No or little spoken English proficiency	Students will need instruction in recognizing and distinguishing the sounds of English as compared or contrasted with sounds in their native language (e.g., vowels, consonants, consonant blends, syllable structures).	**Phonological Awareness**
			2. Demonstrate understanding of spoken words, syllables, and sounds (phonemes).
			  • RF.K.2
			  • RF.1.2

	Spoken English proficiency	Students will need instruction in applying their knowledge of the English sound system to literacy foundational learning.	Review of **Phonological Awareness** skills as needed.

Print Skills	No or little native language literacy	Students will need instruction in print concepts.	**Print Concepts**
			1. Demonstrate understanding of the organization and basic features of print.
			  • RF.K.1
			  • RF.1.1
			
			Phonics and Word Recognition
			3. Know and apply grade-level phonics and word analysis skills in decoding words **both in isolation and in text. CA**
			  • RF.K.3
			  • RF.1.3
			  • RF.2.3
			  • RF.3.3
			
			3. Know and apply grade-level phonics and word analysis skills in decoding words.
			  • RF.4.3
			  • RF.5.3
			
			Fluency
			4. Read with sufficient accuracy and fluency to support comprehension.
			    • RF.5.4 (at the 6–12 grade level)

	Foundational literacy proficiency in a language not using the Latin alphabet (e.g., Arabic, Chinese, Korean, Russian)	Students will be familiar with print concepts and will need instruction in learning the Latin alphabet for English, as compared or contrasted with their native language writing system (e.g., direction of print, symbols representing whole words, syllables or phonemes) and native language vocabulary (e.g., cognates) and sentence structure (e.g., subject-verb-object versus subject-object-verb word order).	
	Foundational literacy proficiency in a language using the Latin alphabet (e.g., Spanish)	Students will need instruction in applying their knowledge of print concepts, phonics, and word recognition to the English writing system, as compared or contrasted with their native language alphabet (e.g., letters that are the same or different or represent the same or different sounds) and native language vocabulary (e.g., cognates) and sentence structure (e.g., subject-verb-object versus subject-object-verb word order).	Review of **Phonics and Word Recognition** skills as needed.

References

August, D., and T. Shanahan. 2006. *Developing Literacy in Second-Language Learners: Report of the National Literacy Panel on Language-Minority Children and Youth.* Mahwah, NJ: Lawrence Erlbaum Associates.

International Reading Association (IRA) and National Institute of Child Health and Human Development (NICHD). 2007. *Key Issues and Questions in English Language Learners Literacy Research.* http://www.ncela.gwu.edu/files/rcd/BE023800/Key_Issues_and_Questions.pdf (accessed October 30, 2013).

National Institute of Child Health and Human Development (NICHD). 2000. *Teaching Children to Read: An Evidence-Based Assessment of the Scientific Research Literature on Reading and Its Implications for Reading Instruction* (Report of the National Reading Panel, NIH Publication No. 00-4769). Washington, DC: U.S. Government Printing Office.

Riches, C., and F. Genesee. 2006. "Literacy: Crosslinguistic and Crossmodal Issues." In *Educating English Language Learners: A Synthesis of Research Evidence,* edited by F. Genesee, K. Lindholm Leary, W. Saunders, and D. Christian, 64–108. New York: Cambridge University Press.

Roessingh, H., and S. Elgie. 2009. "Early Language and Literacy Development Among Young English Language Learners: Preliminary Insights from a Longitudinal Study." *TESL Canada Journal* 26 (2): 24–45.

Short, D., and S. Fitzsimmons. 2007. *Double the Work: Challenges and Solutions to Acquiring Language and Academic Literacy for Adolescent English Language Learners.* Washington, DC: Alliance for Excellent Education.

Torgesen, J. K., D. D. Houston, L. M. Rissman, S. M. Decker, G. Roberts, S. Vaughn, J. Wexler, D. J. Francis, M. O. Rivera, and N. Lesaux. 2007. *Academic Literacy Instruction for Adolescents: A Guidance Document from the Center on Instruction.* Portsmouth, NH: RMC Research Corporation, Center on Instruction.

Glossary of Key Terms

This glossary provides definitions of key terms used in the California English Language Development Standards (CA ELD Standards) and in related chapters. Many of these terms derive from traditional grammar and from linguistics, and some have evolved in their meaning or have different meanings that vary by linguistic tradition. The definitions provided here are intended to be teacher-friendly and are specific to use within the CA ELD Standards and related chapters.

adjectives and adjective phrases. Adjectives provide details about (or modify) nouns or pronouns. For example, adjectives such as *appalling, obnoxious, desperate, alluring,* and *pleasant* allow speakers and writers to add nuance and precision to a description of a person or thing. An adjective can be made even more precise by adding pre- or post-modifiers, as shown in the following table:

Adjective phrase

	Pre-modifier	Head adjective	Post-modifier
She was	quite	distraught.	
	even more	distraught	than yesterday.
	so	distraught	that she couldn't eat.

Note: In addition to the terminology found in the glossary, the terms listed below were referenced where relevant in the CA ELD Standards, but are not summarized here. Appendix A (NGA Center for Best Practices and CCSSO 2010, referenced in chapter 5) provides extensive and detailed explanations and elaboration of these terms: *text complexity, Reading Foundational Skills, text types: argument (informational/explanatory writing and narrative writing), oral language development, conventions and knowledge of language,* and *acquiring vocabulary.*

adverbs. Adverbs add detail to (or modify) verbs, adjectives, and other adverbs about when, where, why, or the conditions under which something happens or happened. Examples are shown below (the adverb is in boldface, and the word that it modifies is italicized).

Sentence with adverb	Word modified
He *ate* his dinner **slowly**.	Verb
It was a **very** *graceful* gesture.	Adjective
She moved **extremely** *quickly* across the room.	Adverb

clause. A clause is a unit of meaning that expresses a message. A clause always contains a verb (e.g., *go*) and is usually accompanied by a subject noun or noun phrase (e.g., *She* went). A clause may be independent or dependent.

- ***independent clause* (also known as the *main clause*).** A clause that contains a complete idea and can stand alone (independently) as a complete sentence. For example:

  The bees swarmed in the attic.

  I couldn't hear anything.

Two independent clauses can be combined to form a compound sentence by using a **coordinating conjunction** (*and, but, for, nor, or, so, yet*). For example:

  The bees swarmed in the attic, but I couldn't hear anything.

- **dependent clause (also known as a *subordinate clause*).** A clause that is dependent on the independent (or main) clause for its meaning and therefore cannot stand alone as a complete sentence. Dependent clauses are formed in several different ways. Two examples are provided below.

  Use of a subordinating conjunction. A subordinating conjunction (e.g., *because, although, if*) introduces a dependent (or subordinate) clause. Different kinds of subordinating conjunctions create different types of relationships between the clauses. In the first example below, the relationship is one of cause. In the second example, the relationship is one of concession. The dependent clauses are italicized, and the subordinating conjunctions are in boldface.

  Because *they were hungry,* the horses ate all the hay.

  Although *she loves to swim,* she decided not to go to the pool today.

  Use of a relative pronoun. A relative pronoun (e.g., *that, who, whom, which, whose*) introduces a relative clause (a type of embedded clause also called an adjective clause). Sometimes, the relative pronoun is omitted. In the following examples, the dependent clause is *italicized,* and the relative pronoun is in **boldface**. Words that can be omitted are in brackets.

  Butterflies are winged insects **that** *undergo complete metamorphosis.*

  He's the teacher **who** *changed my life.*

  Serotonin is a natural neurotransmitter *[***that** *is] produced in the human body.*

cohesion. Cohesion refers to how information is connected and flows in a text. A cohesive text is created through a variety of cohesive devices that facilitate understanding across the text or discourse. One device is to refer back to people, ideas, or things with pronouns or synonyms throughout a text so as not to be repetitive (e.g., replacing *the first settlers* with *they*). Another is to link clauses, sentences, and larger chunks of text with conjunctions, such as transition words (e.g., *in contrast, consequently, next*).

connecting words and phrases. Connecting words and phrases signal how different parts of a text are linked. In narratives and other text types organized by time or sequences of events, temporal connectives (e.g., *first, next, after awhile, the next day*) are often used. In text types organized around ideas, such as arguments and explanations, connectives may be used in various ways to show relationships between ideas (e.g., *on the contrary, for example*); to organize events or sequence ideas (e.g., *previously, until that time, first of all, to conclude*); or to add information (e.g., *in addition, furthermore*).

context. *Context* refers to the environment in which language is used, including content area, topic, audience, text type, and mode of communication.

modality. Modality refers to the degree of ability, necessity, obligation, prohibition, certainty, or possibility of an action or situation. Understanding of modality allows speakers and writers to temper statements, give information about the degree of obligation or certainty of a situation or idea, or express the degree to which we are willing to entertain other possibilities may be considered.

  modal adverb. High-modality adverbs include *definitely, absolutely,* and *certainly.* Medium-modality adverbs include *probably* and *apparently.* Low-modality adverbs include *possibly, perhaps,* and *maybe.*

  modal auxiliary. High-modality auxiliaries include *must* and *will.* Medium-modality auxiliaries include *should* and *need to.* Low-modality auxiliaries include *could* and *might.*

mood. There are a variety of ways to structure messages into statements, questions, commands, and so on, depending on the relationship between the speakers and listeners or the writers and readers. Examples of some of the main sentence types identified by mood follow.

- Declarative (statements):
  Bats are mammals.
  Once upon a time, there was a little girl who loved books.
  You're impossible to live with.

- Interrogative (questions):

  How do you solve this problem?

  What's your name?

  Why are you here?

- Imperative (commands):

  Don't you ever do that again!

  Put that over there, please.

- Subjunctive (expressing wishes, desires, or suggestions):

  I wish I were younger.

  If I were you, I wouldn't boast so loudly.

  It is necessary that I be allowed to participate in this event.

nominalization. Nominalization is the process of creating a noun or noun phrase from another part of speech or condensing large amounts of information (e.g., an event or concept) into a noun or noun phrase. Often, a verb or verb phrase is nominalized (e.g., They *destroyed* the rain forest. → The *destruction* of the rain forest), though adjectives are nominalized as well (e.g., strong → strength; different → difference). Nominalization can also collapse a clause or even multiple clauses at once. For example, in conversational language, a student might say, "The ranchers came to the rain forest, and they cut down all the trees. The next year, the rain flooded many areas of the rain forest." With nominalization, these three clauses can be collapsed into one clause: "The *arrival* of the ranchers and the *clearing* of the rainforest led to *widespread flooding.*"

nouns and noun phrases. Nouns and noun phrases represent people, places, things, or ideas. A noun phrase includes a noun (e.g., *ball*) plus its modifiers, including articles (e.g., **the** *ball*) and adjectives (e.g., *the* **blue** *ball*).

> *expanding noun phrases.* More detail can be added to nouns by expanding the noun phrase with pre- and post-modifiers (words that come before and after the head noun). In the following example, the head noun is in boldface, and modifiers are added incrementally:
>
> **frog** → That **frog** → That green **frog** → That fat green **frog** → That very fat green **frog** → That very fat green **frog** on the rock

prepositions and prepositional phrases. A preposition (e.g., *to, of, with, at, in, over, through*) combines with a noun or noun phrase to form a prepositional phrase. Prepositional phrases provide more information or specific details about people, things, ideas, activities, or events in a sentence. Specifically, they enable a writer or speaker to add detail about where things are, why things occur, or how things are in comparison to other things. Prepositional phrases can be used to locate something in space or time (e.g., **under** *the table,* **on** *the moon*); to show reason (e.g., **due to** *the rain*), purpose (e.g., **for** *tomorrow*), or comparison (e.g., **like** *a dog*); or to specify which thing is referenced (e.g., the lady **with** *the blue hat*).

register. Register refers to variation in the vocabulary, grammar, and discourse of a language to meet the expectations of a particular context. A context can be defined by numerous elements, such as audience, task, purpose, setting, social relationship, and mode of communication (written versus spoken). Specific examples of contextual variables are the nature of the communicative activity (e.g., talking with someone about a movie, persuading someone in a debate, or writing a science report); the nature of the relationship between the language users in the activity (e.g., friend-to-friend, expert-to-learner); the subject matter and topic (e.g., photosynthesis in science, the Civil War in history); and the medium through which a message is conveyed (e.g., a text message versus an essay).

scaffolding.* Scaffolding is temporary guidance or assistance provided to a student by a teacher, another adult, or a more capable peer, enabling the student to perform a task he or she otherwise would not be able to do alone, with the goal of fostering the student's capacity to perform the task on his or her own later on. (Though Vygotsky himself does not use the term *scaffolding,* the educational meaning of the term relates closely to his concept of the zone of proximal development. See L. S. Vygotsky [1978]. *Mind in Society: The Development of Higher Psychological Processes.* Cambridge, MA: Harvard University Press.)

---

*This definition, including the parenthetical note, is drawn directly from page 43 of Appendix A (NGA Center for Best Practices and CCSSO [2010], referenced in chapter 5); see http://www.corestandards.org/assets/Appendix_A.pdf (accessed October 23, 2013).

See chapter 4, "Theoretical Foundations and the Research Base of the English Language Development Standards," for further explanation of scaffolding for English learners.

sentences. There are four types of sentences: simple, compound, complex, and compound-complex.

Simple sentences consist of a single independent clause. See the example below (the independent clause is italicized, and the verb is in boldface):

*Earthworms **are** invertebrates.*

*One interesting thing about earthworms **is** their regeneration ability.*

Compound sentences consist of two or more independent clauses connected with coordinating conjunctions (e.g., *and, but, or, so*). An example is shown below (the independent clauses are in italics, and the verbs are in boldface):

*Earthworms **have** no legs, but they **do have** five hearts.*

Complex sentences consist of one independent clause and one or more dependent clauses connected with a subordinating conjunction (e.g., *because, when, although*). An example is shown below (the independent clause is in boldface, and the dependent clauses are italicized):

If you want to graduate, **you need to pass your classes.**

Her first film was a huge success, *although she'd never made a movie before.*

Compound-complex sentences consist of at least two independent clauses and one or more dependent clauses. An example is shown below (the independent clauses are in boldface, and the dependent clause is italicized):

Although I'd love to go to the soccer game, **I haven't finished my homework yet,** *and* **I also need to wash the dishes.**

shades of meaning. Shades of meaning can be created by using various language resources—including vocabulary, figurative language, phrasing, using dependent clauses to begin sentences in order to emphasize something, and so forth. For example, vocabulary can be used to evaluate (e.g., Misty was a *stubborn* horse) or express degree or intensity (e.g., It's *very likely* that _____; It was an *extremely* gloomy room). In addition, phrases and clauses can be used to create nuances or precision and to shape how the message will be interpreted by readers or listeners. This often occurs at the beginning of sentences (e.g., *In my opinion,* _____; *Bizarrely,* she interrupted _____). As English learners progress through the grades, they learn to create shades of meaning in increasingly sophisticated and subtle ways in order to cause a certain reaction in the reader (e.g., to build suspense or characterize a historical figure) or to persuade readers to believe something or to take action.

verbs and verb phrases. Verbs are used to express happenings, doings, and states of being. A verb phrase may consist of a single verb (e.g., *She **ran***) or a number of words (auxiliary verbs and other infinitive or participle constructions) around the verb (e.g., *She **might have been running***).

verb types. There are different types of verbs that create precision in texts. The CA ELD Standards refer to four types of verbs:

- Doing/action verbs (e.g., *go, take, gather, abandon*)
- Saying verbs (e.g., *ask, say, suggest, explain, promise*)
- Being/having verbs (e.g., *am/is/are, seem, appear, symbolize, have, include*)
- Thinking/feeling verbs (e.g., *know, decide, dislike, smell*)

verb tenses. Verb tenses (present, past, future, simple, progressive, and perfect) help to convey time relationships, status of completion, or habitualness of an activity, or state denoted by the verb (e.g., *she **ran** yesterday; she **runs** every day; she **will run** tomorrow; **she has been running** since she was in college*).

vocabulary. The CA ELD Standards and the CA CCSS for ELA/Literacy define three categories of vocabulary.

1. **Domain-specific vocabulary.** Vocabulary that is specific to a particular discipline (field of study, or domain). Domain-specific words and phrases carry content meaning (e.g., *lava, hypotenuse, chromosome, democratic, stanza*).

2. **General academic vocabulary.** Vocabulary that is found across text types, particularly in written texts, that provides more nuanced or sophisticated ways of expressing meaning than everyday language (e.g., *devastation, reluctance, significantly, misfortune, specificity*).

3. **Conversational vocabulary.** The vocabulary of everyday interaction (e.g., *run, table, friend*). This is also referred to as *frequently occurring vocabulary or everyday vocabulary.*

voice (active and passive). In addition to verb types and tenses, sentences can be structured in the active voice (*He told the children to do their best*) or the passive voice (*The children were told to do their best*).

There are a number of reasons to choose the passive voice over the active voice. One reason often seen in academic texts is to suppress the human agents in an event, discovery, and so on, either because the event or discovery is important or because the speaker or writer does not wish to reveal who is responsible for certain acts. For example:

> The discovery that "junk DNA" actually plays critical roles in controlling cell, tissue, and organ behavior was first made last year.
>
> > (Here, the scientists who made the discovery are not as important as the discovery.)

> Mistakes were made.
>
> > (A conscious effort was made to conceal the identities of the people who made the mistakes.)

R17-014 PR17-013 7-18 5,000

OSP 16 144620